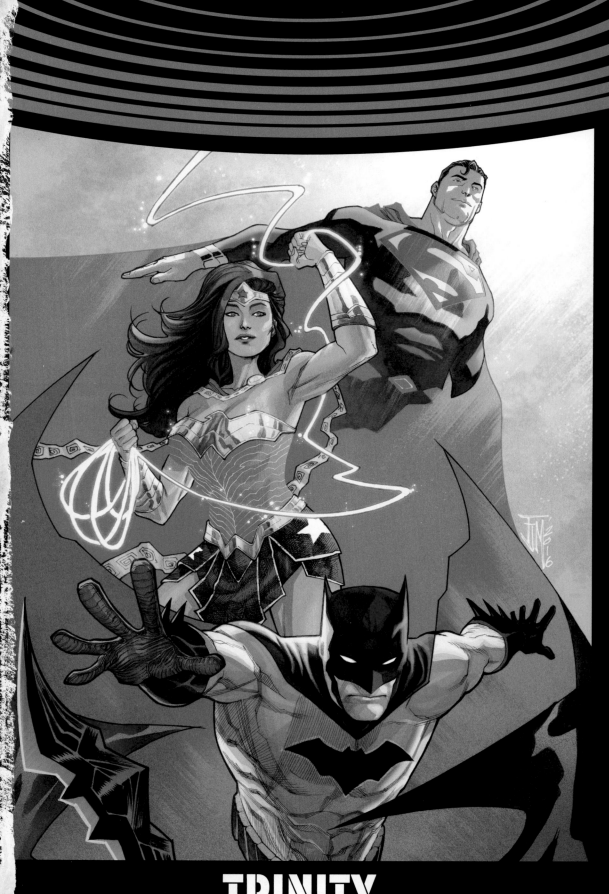

TRINITY

VOL.1 BETTER TOGETHER

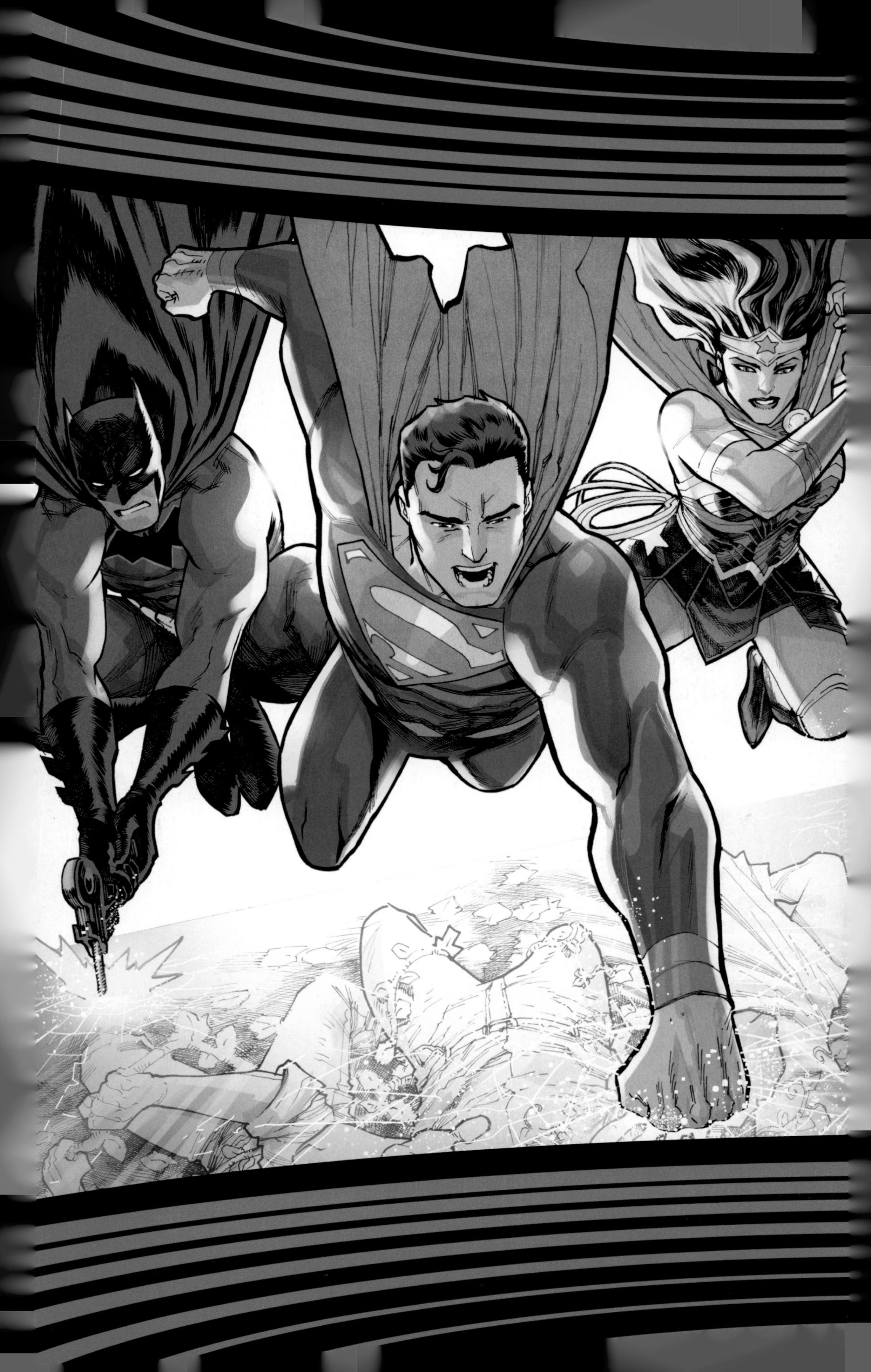

TRINITY
VOL.1 BETTER TOGETHER

FRANCIS MANAPUL
writer

FRANCIS MANAPUL
EMANUELA LUPACCHINO * RAY McCARTHY * MATT SANTORELLI * CLAY MANN * SETH MANN
artists

FRANCIS MANAPUL
BRAD ANDERSON * HI-FI
colorists

STEVE WANDS
letterer

FRANCIS MANAPUL
collection cover artist

SUPERMAN created by **JERRY SIEGEL** and **JOE SHUSTER**.
By special arrangement with the Jerry Siegel family.
BATMAN created by **BOB KANE** with **BILL FINGER**.
WONDER WOMAN created by **WILLIAM MOULTON MARSTON**.

EDDIE BERGANZA Editor - Original Series • **PAUL KAMINSKI** Associate Editor - Original Series • **JEB WOODARD** Group Editor - Collected Editions
PAUL SANTOS Editor - Collected Edition • **STEVE COOK** Design Director - Books • **DAMIAN RYLAND** Publication Design

BOB HARRAS Senior VP - Editor-in-Chief, DC Comics

DIANE NELSON President • **DAN DiDIO** Publisher • **JIM LEE** Publisher • **GEOFF JOHNS** President & Chief Creative Officer
AMIT DESAI Executive VP - Business & Marketing Strategy, Direct to Consumer & Global Franchise Management • **SAM ADES** Senior VP - Direct to Consumer
BOBBIE CHASE VP - Talent Development • **MARK CHIARELLO** Senior VP - Art, Design & Collected Editions
JOHN CUNNINGHAM Senior VP - Sales & Trade Marketing • **ANNE DePIES** Senior VP - Business Strategy, Finance & Administration
DON FALLETTI VP - Manufacturing Operations • **LAWRENCE GANEM** VP - Editorial Administration & Talent Relations
ALISON GILL Senior VP - Manufacturing & Operations • **HANK KANALZ** Senior VP - Editorial Strategy & Administration
JAY KOGAN VP - Legal Affairs • **THOMAS LOFTUS** VP - Business Affairs
JACK MAHAN VP - Business Affairs • **NICK J. NAPOLITANO** VP - Manufacturing Administration
EDDIE SCANNELL VP - Consumer Marketing • **COURTNEY SIMMONS** Senior VP - Publicity & Communications
JIM (SKI) SOKOLOWSKI VP - Comic Book Specialty Sales & Trade Marketing • **NANCY SPEARS** VP - Mass, Book, Digital Sales & Trade Marketing

TRINITY VOL.1 BETTER TOGETHER

DC Comics, 2900 West Alameda Ave., Burbank, CA 91505. Printed by LSC Communications, Salem, VA, USA. 5/5/17.
First Printing. ISBN: 978-1-4012-7076-6

Library of Congress Cataloging-in-Publication Data is available.

PEFC Certified
Printed on paper from sustainably managed forests, controlled sources
PEFC
PEFC/29-31-337
www.pefc.org

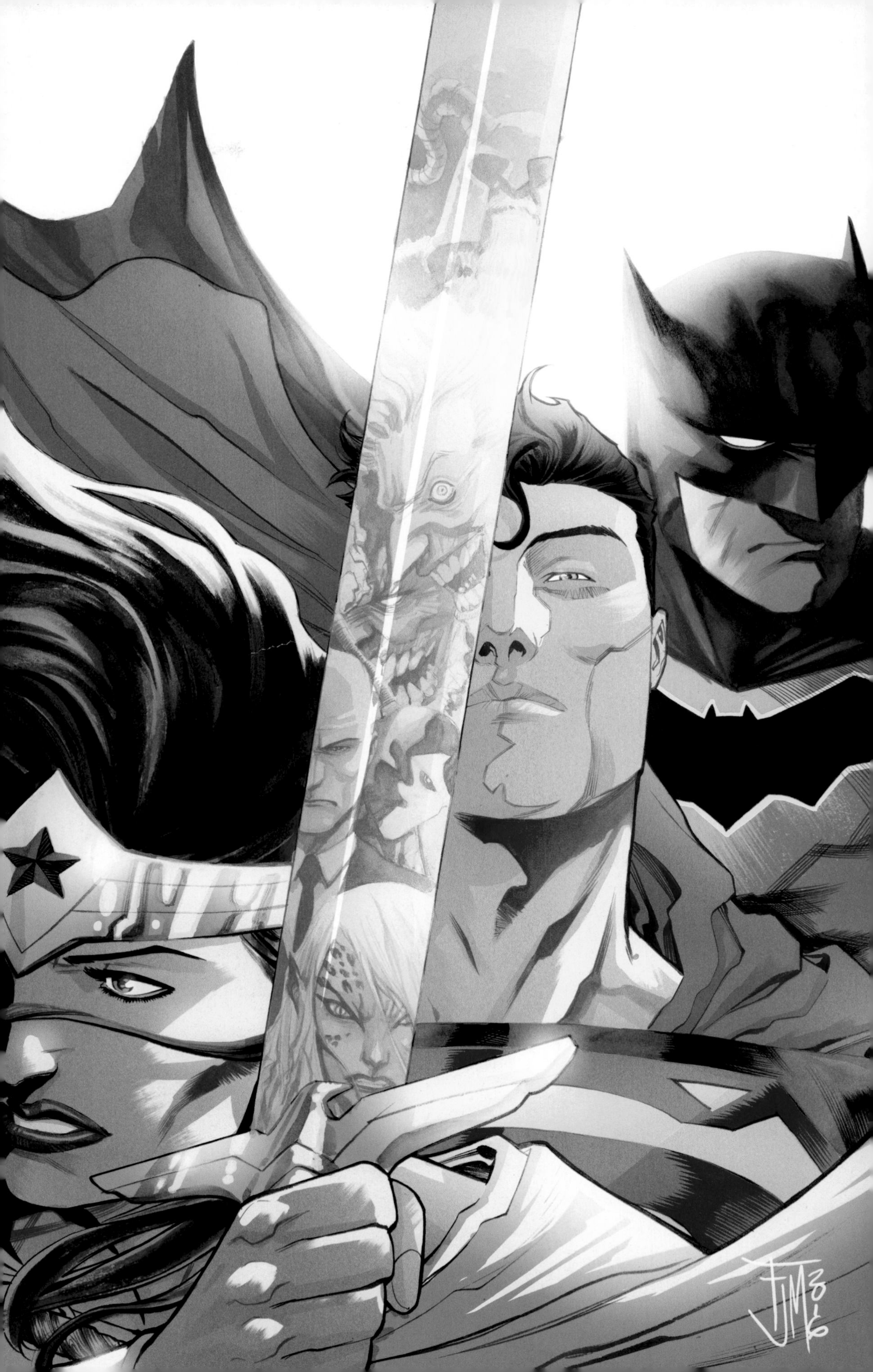

BETTER TOGETHER Part One: FAMILY DINNER
FRANCIS MANAPUL artist

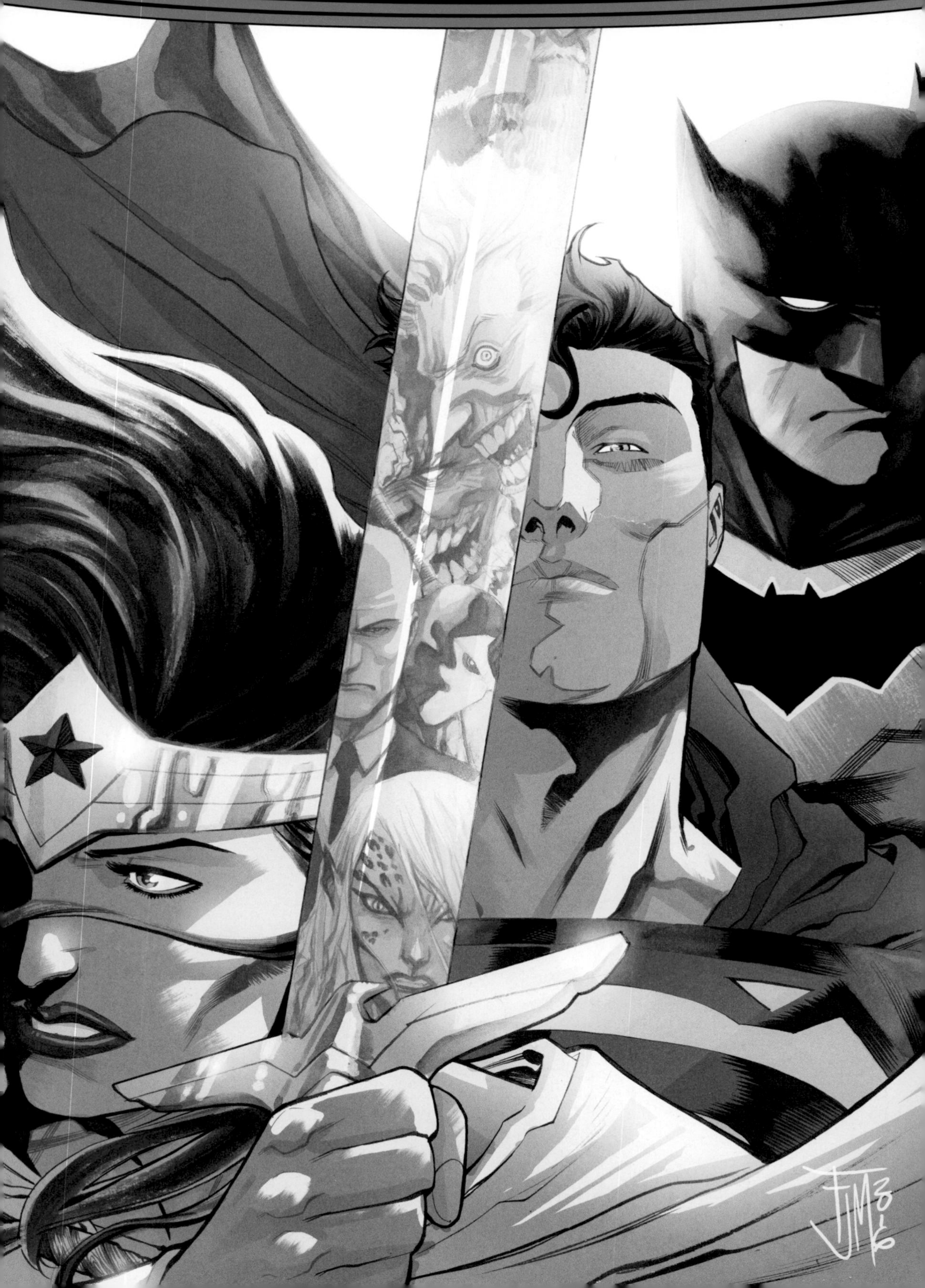

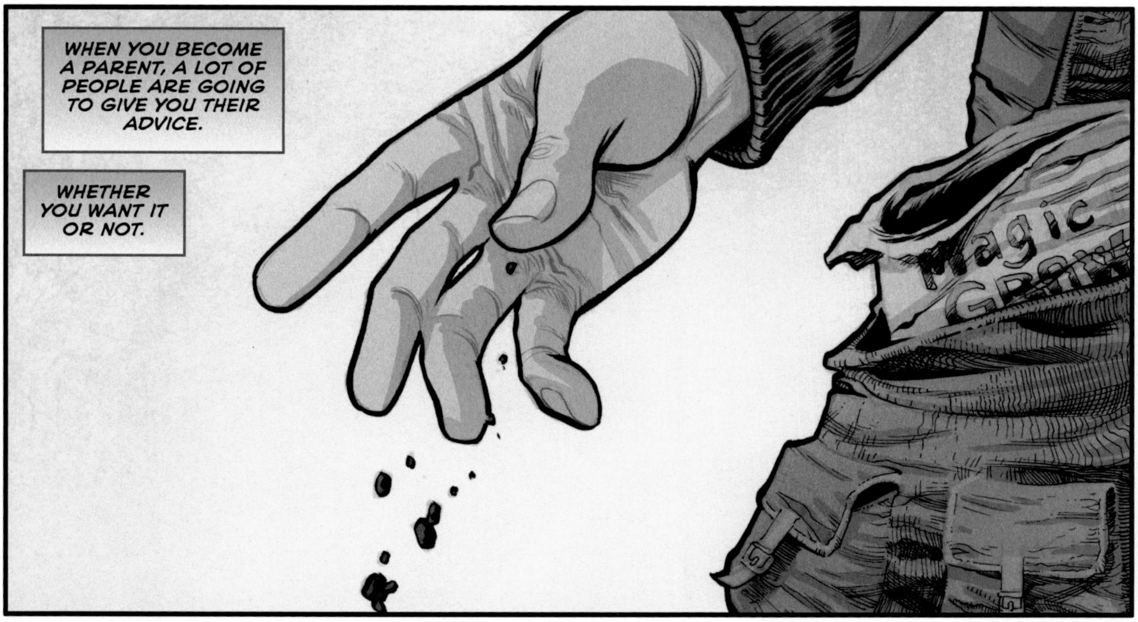
WHEN YOU BECOME A PARENT, A LOT OF PEOPLE ARE GOING TO GIVE YOU THEIR ADVICE.
WHETHER YOU WANT IT OR NOT.

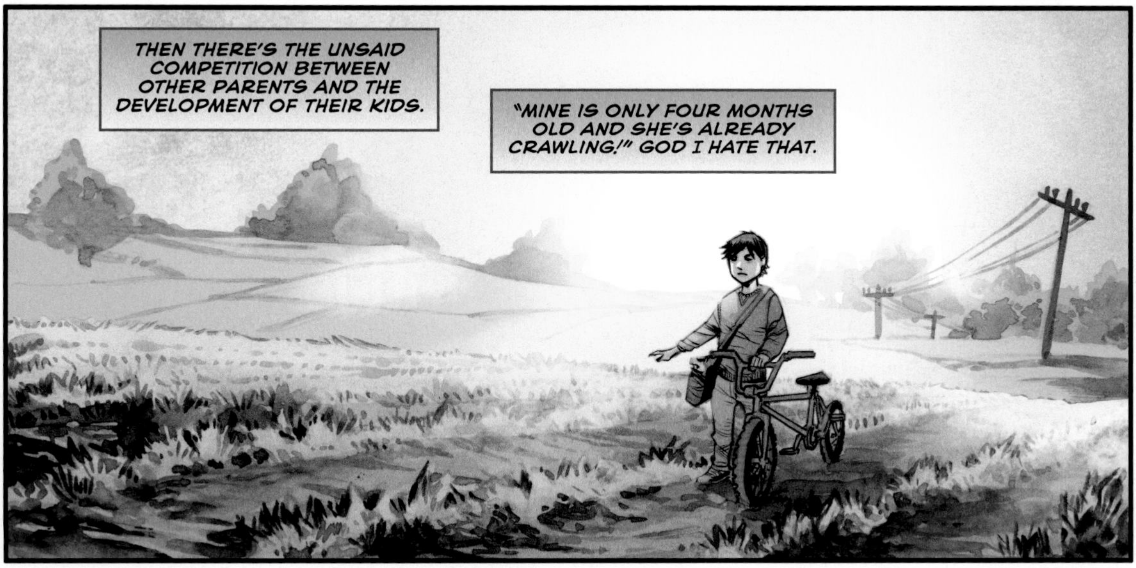
THEN THERE'S THE UNSAID COMPETITION BETWEEN OTHER PARENTS AND THE DEVELOPMENT OF THEIR KIDS.
"MINE IS ONLY FOUR MONTHS OLD AND SHE'S ALREADY CRAWLING!" GOD I HATE THAT.

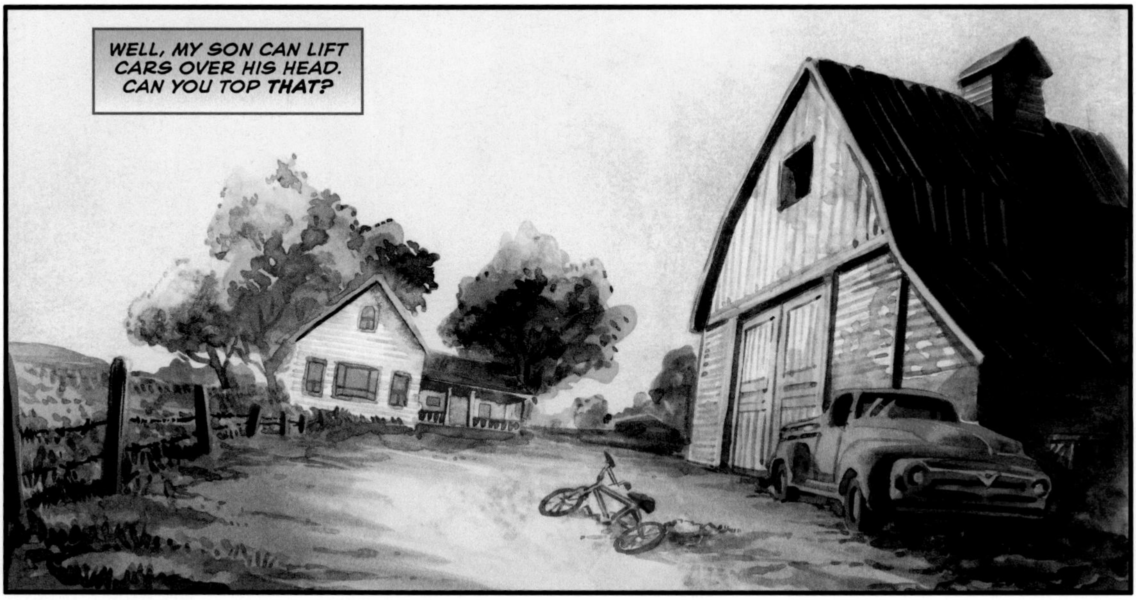
WELL, MY SON CAN LIFT CARS OVER HIS HEAD. CAN YOU TOP THAT?

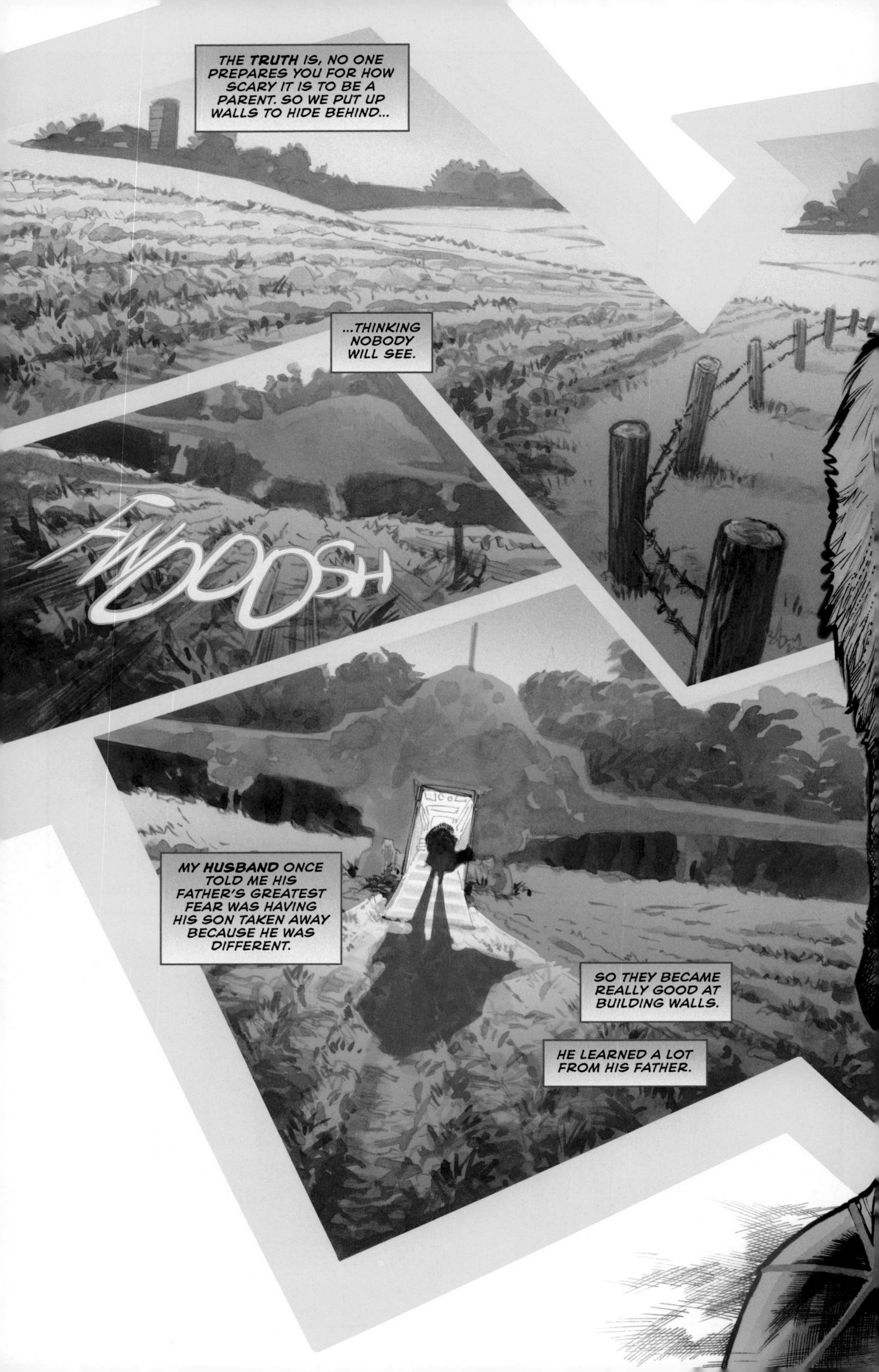
THE TRUTH IS, NO ONE PREPARES YOU FOR HOW SCARY IT IS TO BE A PARENT. SO WE PUT UP WALLS TO HIDE BEHIND...
...THINKING NOBODY WILL SEE.
FWOOOSH
MY HUSBAND ONCE TOLD ME HIS FATHER'S GREATEST FEAR WAS HAVING HIS SON TAKEN AWAY BECAUSE HE WAS DIFFERENT.
SO THEY BECAME REALLY GOOD AT BUILDING WALLS.
HE LEARNED A LOT FROM HIS FATHER.

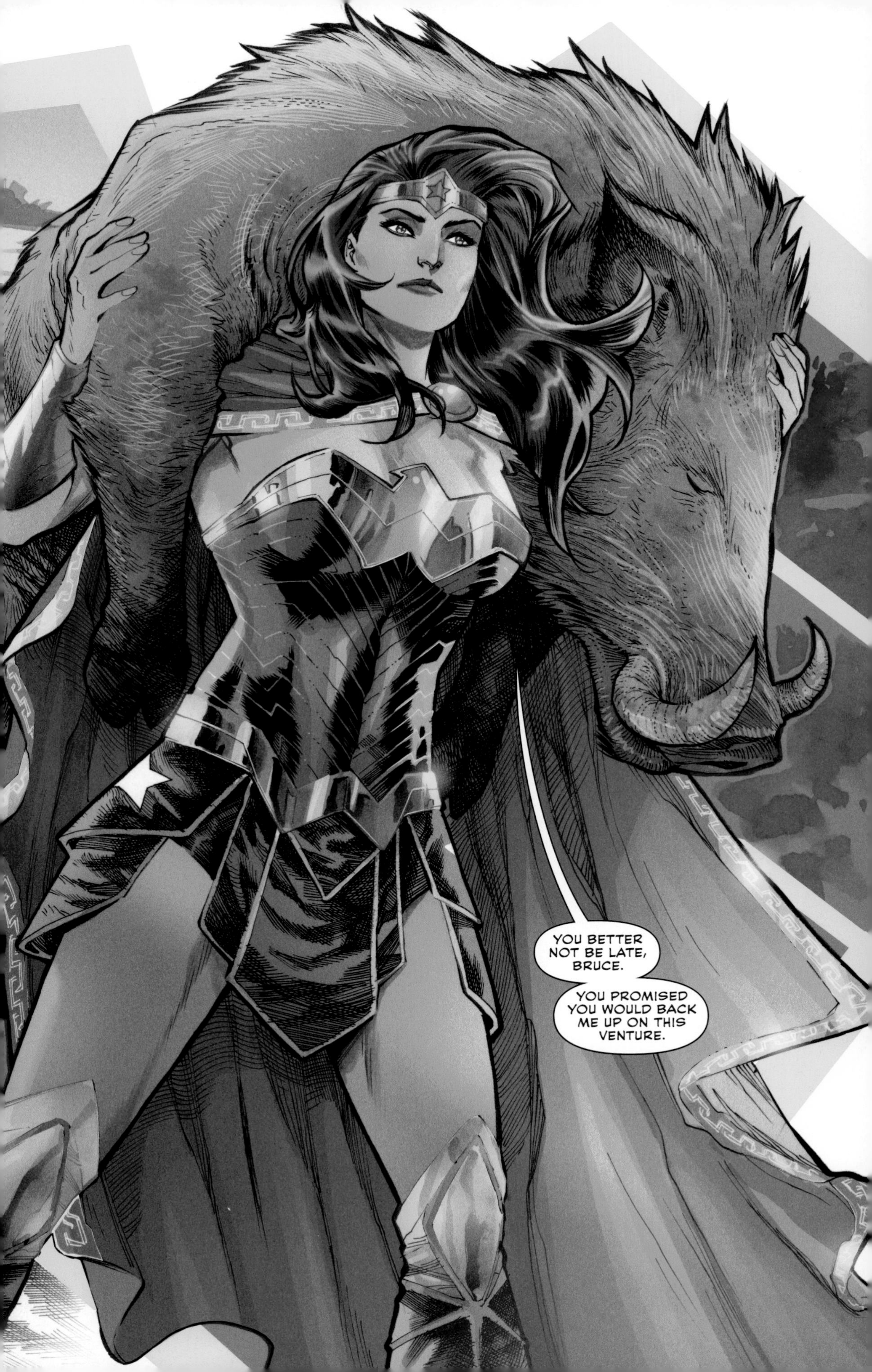
YOU BETTER NOT BE LATE, BRUCE.
YOU PROMISED YOU WOULD BACK ME UP ON THIS VENTURE.

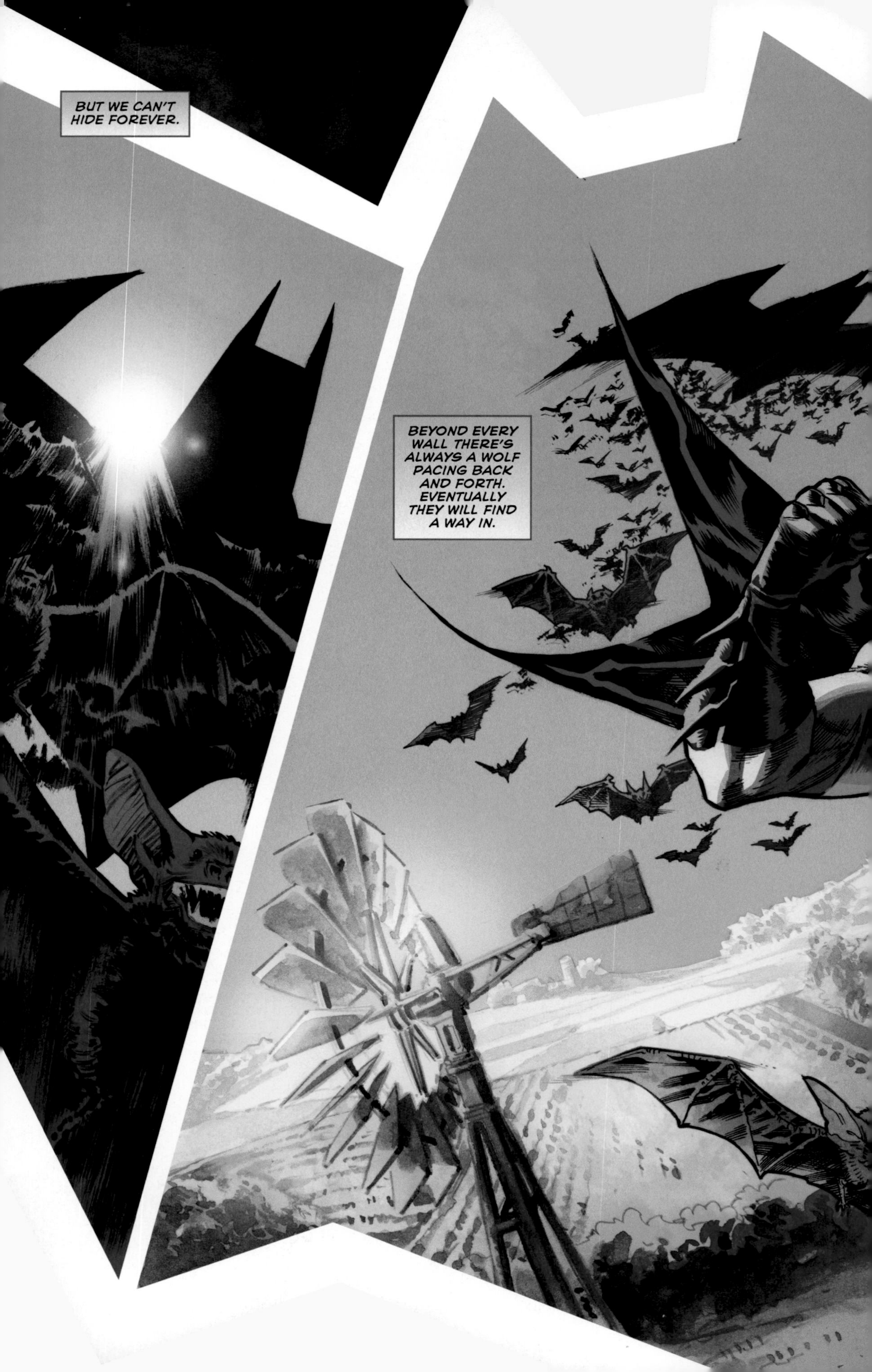
BUT WE CAN'T HIDE FOREVER.
BEYOND EVERY WALL THERE'S ALWAYS A WOLF PACING BACK AND FORTH. EVENTUALLY THEY WILL FIND A WAY IN.

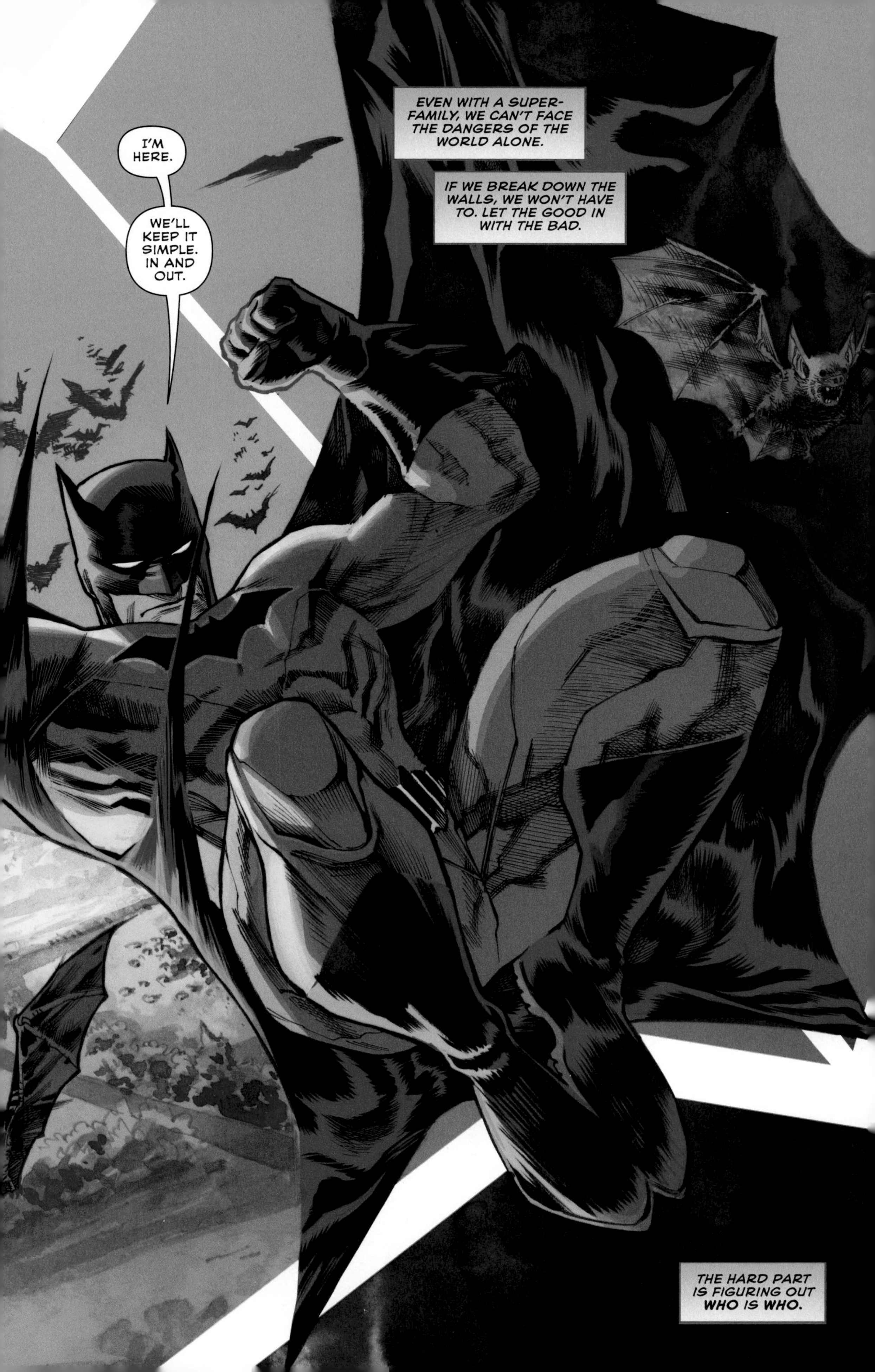

I'M HERE.
WE'LL KEEP IT SIMPLE. IN AND OUT.
EVEN WITH A SUPER-FAMILY, WE CAN'T FACE THE DANGERS OF THE WORLD ALONE.
IF WE BREAK DOWN THE WALLS, WE WON'T HAVE TO. LET THE GOOD IN WITH THE BAD.
THE HARD PART IS FIGURING OUT WHO IS WHO.

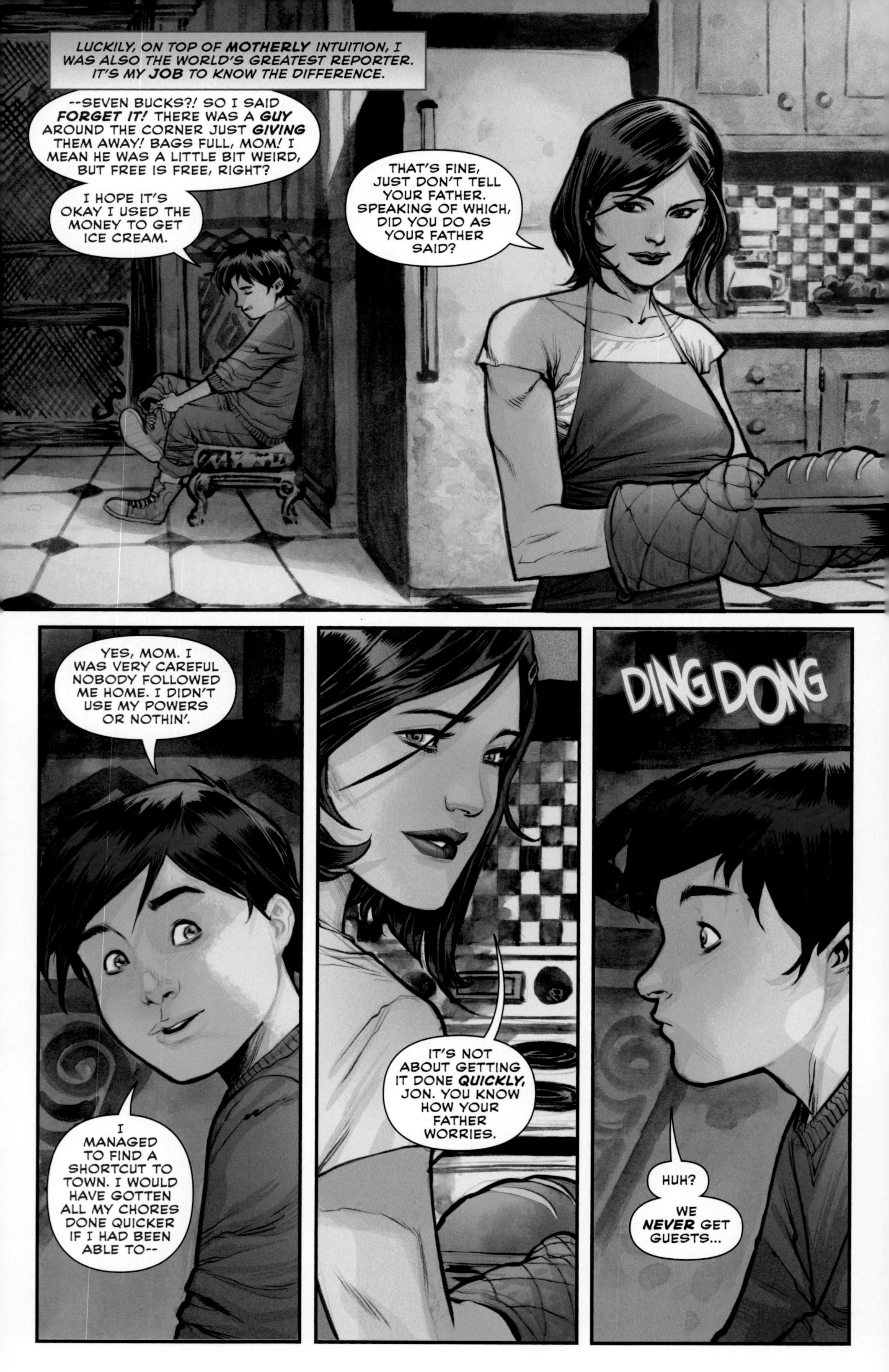
LUCKILY, ON TOP OF MOTHERLY INTUITION, I WAS ALSO THE WORLD'S GREATEST REPORTER. IT'S MY JOB TO KNOW THE DIFFERENCE.
--SEVEN BUCKS?! SO I SAID FORGET IT! THERE WAS A GUY AROUND THE CORNER JUST GIVING THEM AWAY! BAGS FULL, MOM! I MEAN HE WAS A LITTLE BIT WEIRD, BUT FREE IS FREE, RIGHT?
I HOPE IT'S OKAY I USED THE MONEY TO GET ICE CREAM.
THAT'S FINE, JUST DON'T TELL YOUR FATHER. SPEAKING OF WHICH, DID YOU DO AS YOUR FATHER SAID?
YES, MOM. I WAS VERY CAREFUL NOBODY FOLLOWED ME HOME. I DIDN'T USE MY POWERS OR NOTHIN'.
I MANAGED TO FIND A SHORTCUT TO TOWN. I WOULD HAVE GOTTEN ALL MY CHORES DONE QUICKER IF I HAD BEEN ABLE TO--
IT'S NOT ABOUT GETTING IT DONE QUICKLY, JON. YOU KNOW HOW YOUR FATHER WORRIES.
DING DONG
HUH?
WE NEVER GET GUESTS...

I GOT IT!

THIS ISN'T *ME*, DIANA. I DON'T *DO* THIS KIND OF THING.

AND YOU BROUGHT A BOAR?

WILD BOAR.

MY DAD SAID I SHOULD ONLY USE MY POWERS TO KEEP US SAFE. I'M SURE HE'D BE OKAY IF I TOOK A LITTLE PEEK.

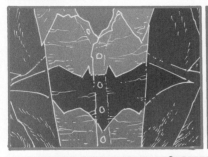
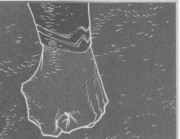

JEEZ!

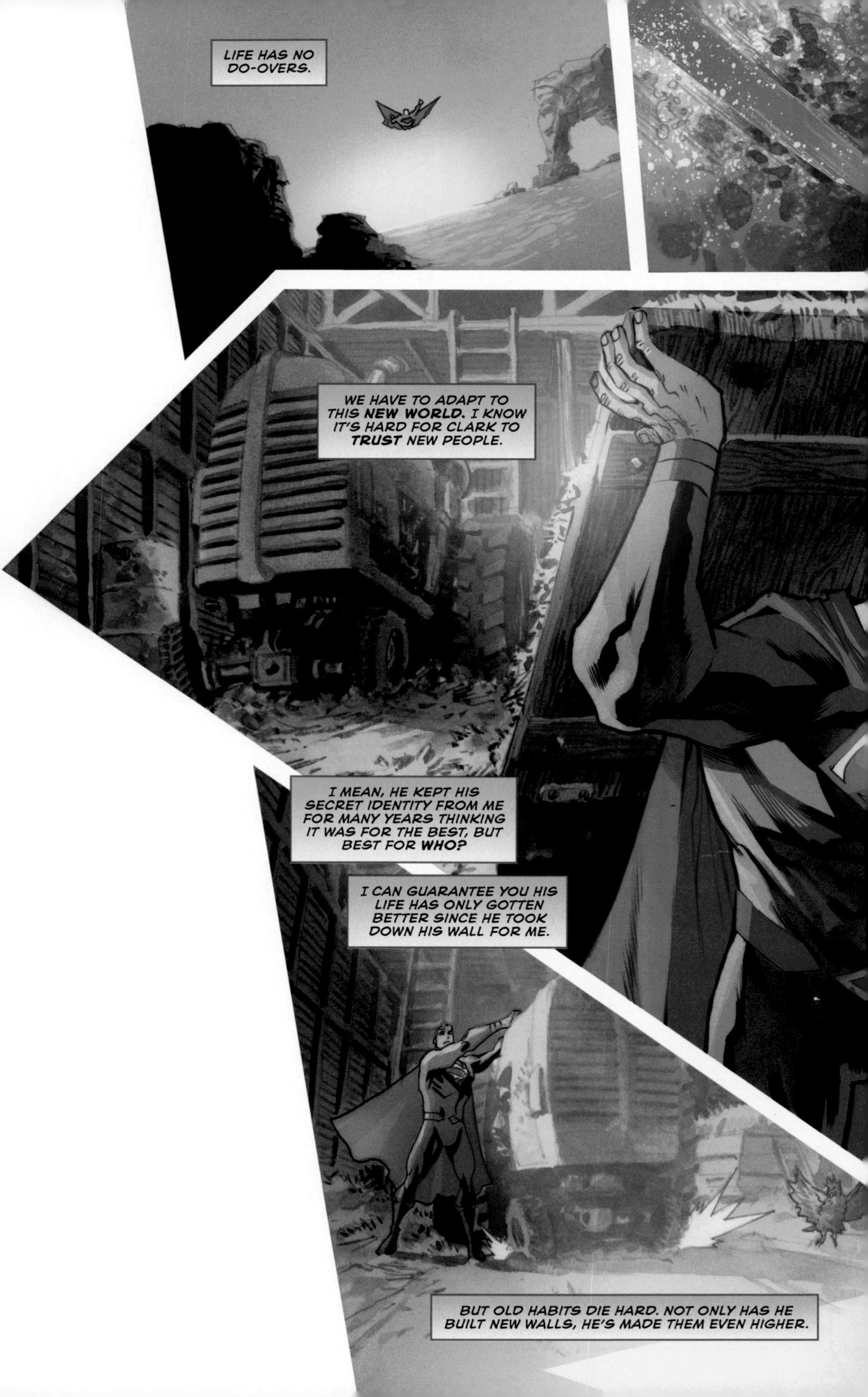
LIFE HAS NO DO-OVERS.
WE HAVE TO ADAPT TO THIS NEW WORLD. I KNOW IT'S HARD FOR CLARK TO TRUST NEW PEOPLE.
I MEAN, HE KEPT HIS SECRET IDENTITY FROM ME FOR MANY YEARS THINKING IT WAS FOR THE BEST, BUT BEST FOR WHO?
I CAN GUARANTEE YOU HIS LIFE HAS ONLY GOTTEN BETTER SINCE HE TOOK DOWN HIS WALL FOR ME.
BUT OLD HABITS DIE HARD. NOT ONLY HAS HE BUILT NEW WALLS, HE'S MADE THEM EVEN HIGHER.

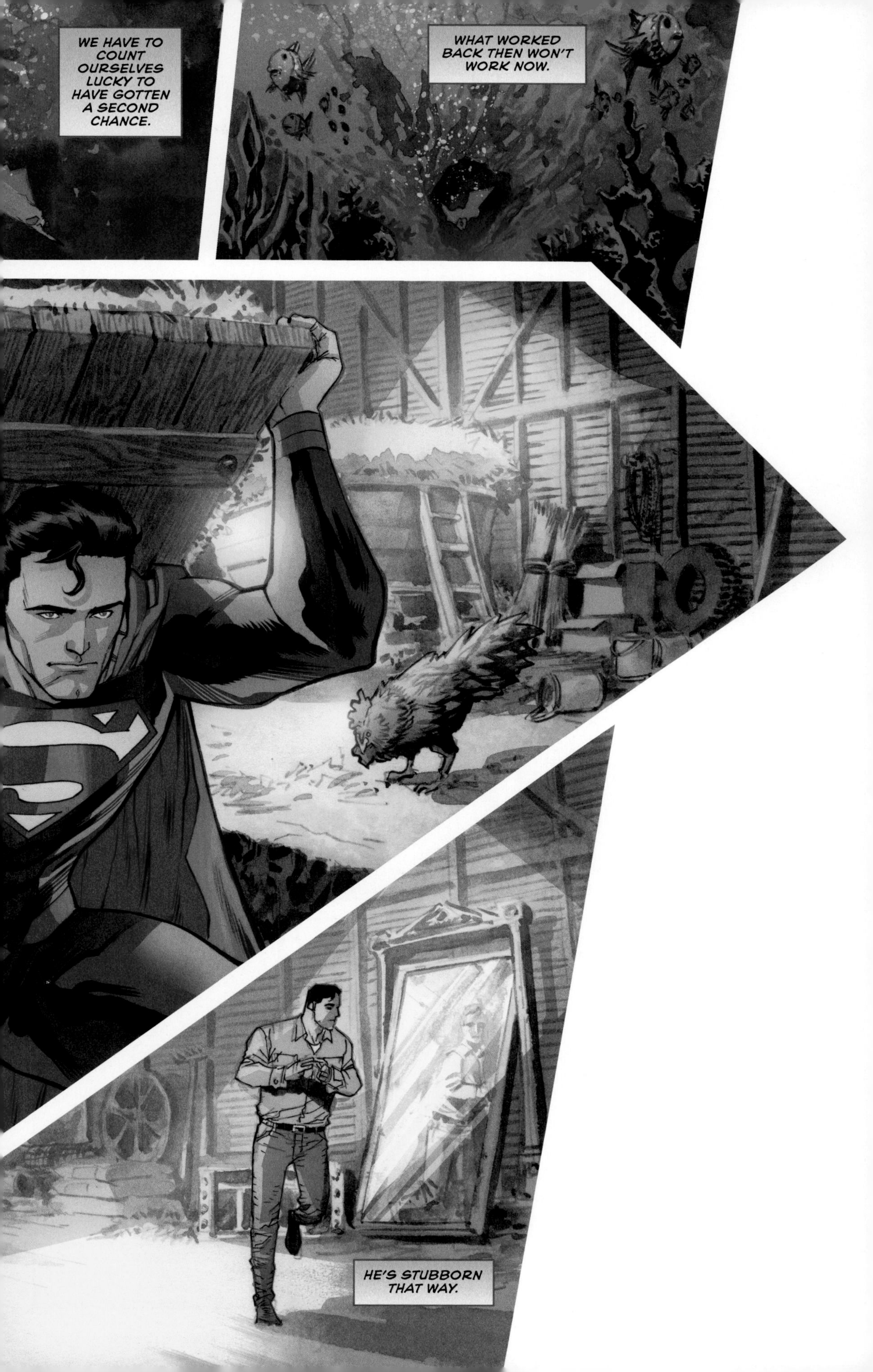
WE HAVE TO COUNT OURSELVES LUCKY TO HAVE GOTTEN A SECOND CHANCE.
WHAT WORKED BACK THEN WON'T WORK NOW.
HE'S STUBBORN THAT WAY.

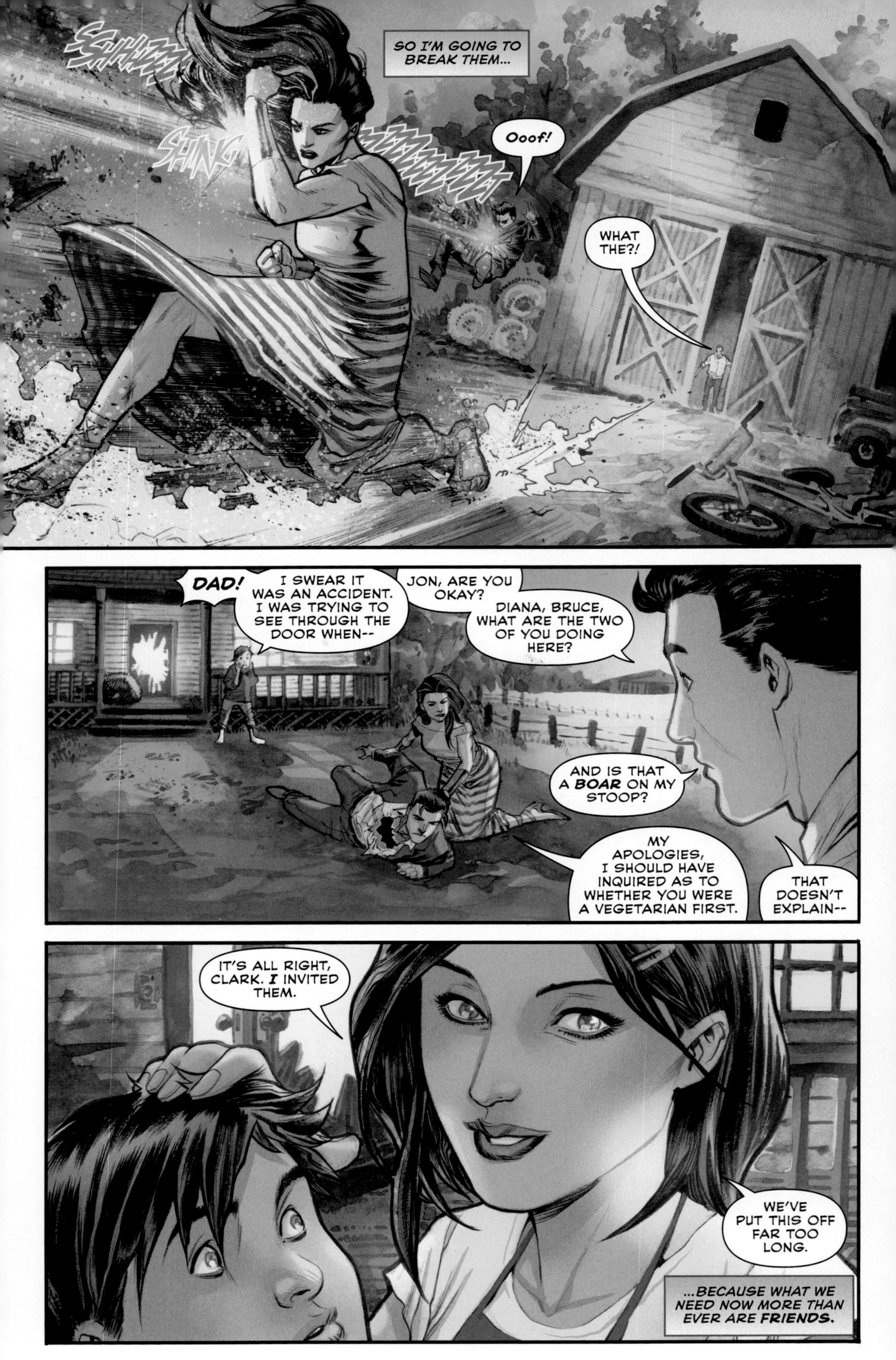
SO I'M GOING TO BREAK THEM...
SCHHHM
SHING
Ooof!
WHAT THE?!
DAD!
I SWEAR IT WAS AN ACCIDENT. I WAS TRYING TO SEE THROUGH THE DOOR WHEN--
JON, ARE YOU OKAY?
DIANA, BRUCE, WHAT ARE THE TWO OF YOU DOING HERE?
AND IS THAT A BOAR ON MY STOOP?
MY APOLOGIES, I SHOULD HAVE INQUIRED AS TO WHETHER YOU WERE A VEGETARIAN FIRST.
THAT DOESN'T EXPLAIN--
IT'S ALL RIGHT, CLARK. I INVITED THEM.
WE'VE PUT THIS OFF FAR TOO LONG.
...BECAUSE WHAT WE NEED NOW MORE THAN EVER ARE FRIENDS.

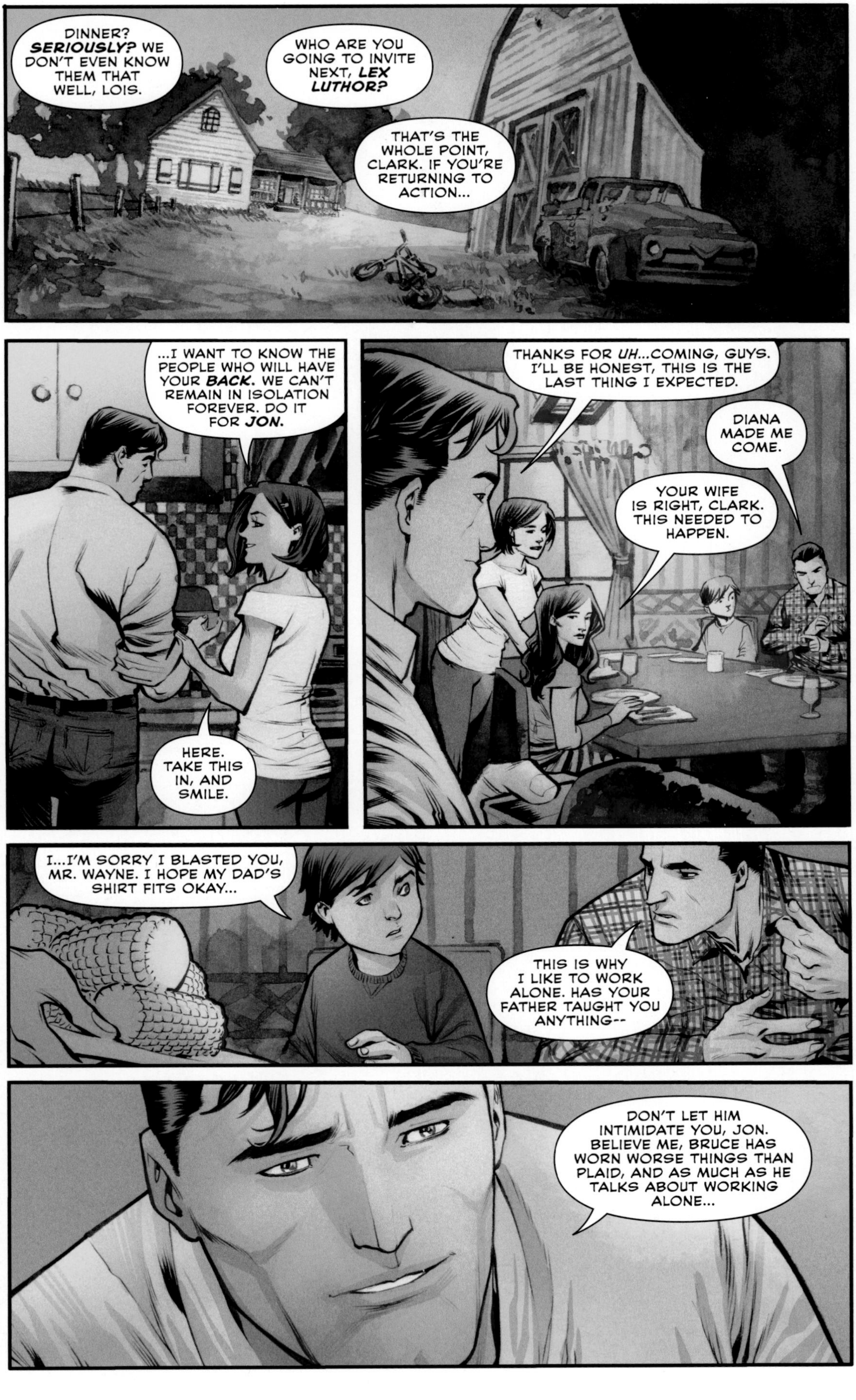

DINNER? SERIOUSLY? WE DON'T EVEN KNOW THEM THAT WELL, LOIS.
WHO ARE YOU GOING TO INVITE NEXT, LEX LUTHOR?
THAT'S THE WHOLE POINT, CLARK. IF YOU'RE RETURNING TO ACTION...
...I WANT TO KNOW THE PEOPLE WHO WILL HAVE YOUR BACK. WE CAN'T REMAIN IN ISOLATION FOREVER. DO IT FOR JON.
HERE. TAKE THIS IN, AND SMILE.
THANKS FOR UH...COMING, GUYS. I'LL BE HONEST, THIS IS THE LAST THING I EXPECTED.
DIANA MADE ME COME.
YOUR WIFE IS RIGHT, CLARK. THIS NEEDED TO HAPPEN.
I...I'M SORRY I BLASTED YOU, MR. WAYNE. I HOPE MY DAD'S SHIRT FITS OKAY...
THIS IS WHY I LIKE TO WORK ALONE. HAS YOUR FATHER TAUGHT YOU ANYTHING--
DON'T LET HIM INTIMIDATE YOU, JON. BELIEVE ME, BRUCE HAS WORN WORSE THINGS THAN PLAID, AND AS MUCH AS HE TALKS ABOUT WORKING ALONE...

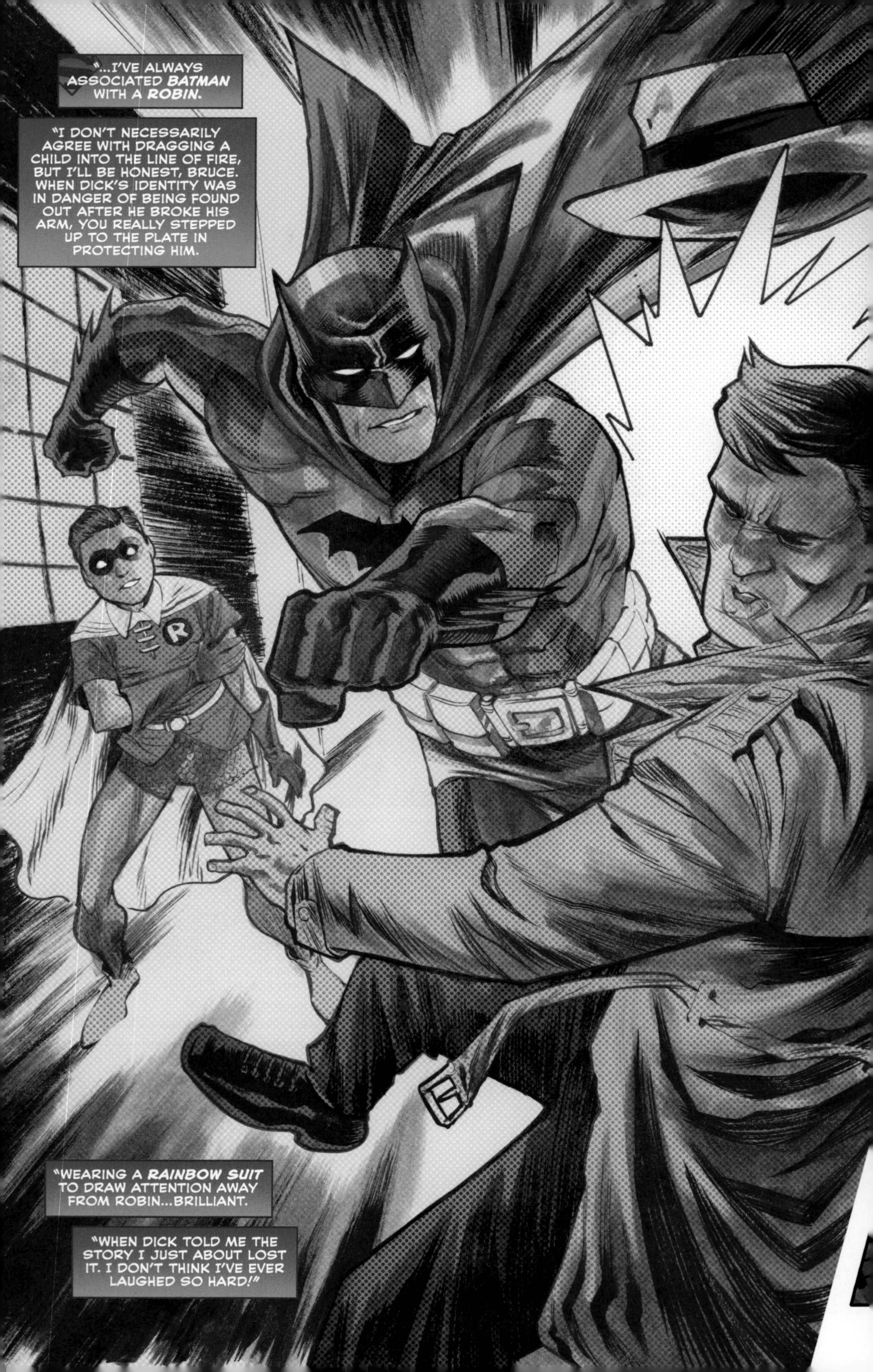
"...I'VE ALWAYS ASSOCIATED BATMAN WITH A ROBIN.
"I DON'T NECESSARILY AGREE WITH DRAGGING A CHILD INTO THE LINE OF FIRE, BUT I'LL BE HONEST, BRUCE. WHEN DICK'S IDENTITY WAS IN DANGER OF BEING FOUND OUT AFTER HE BROKE HIS ARM, YOU REALLY STEPPED UP TO THE PLATE IN PROTECTING HIM.
"WEARING A RAINBOW SUIT TO DRAW ATTENTION AWAY FROM ROBIN...BRILLIANT.
"WHEN DICK TOLD ME THE STORY I JUST ABOUT LOST IT. I DON'T THINK I'VE EVER LAUGHED SO HARD!"

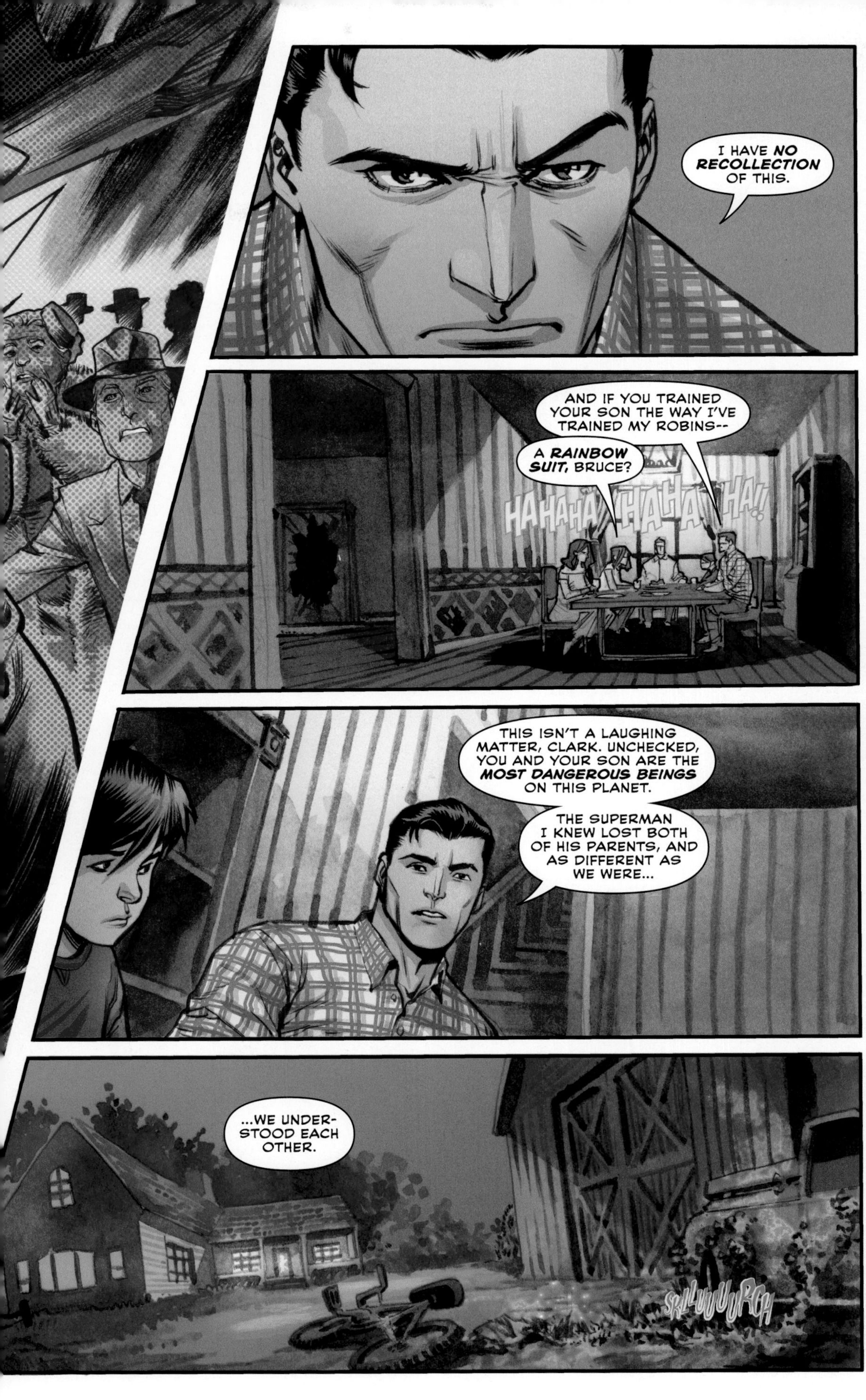
I HAVE **NO RECOLLECTION** OF THIS.
AND IF YOU TRAINED YOUR SON THE WAY I'VE TRAINED MY ROBINS--
A **RAINBOW SUIT,** BRUCE?
HAHAHA HAHA HA HA!!
THIS ISN'T A LAUGHING MATTER, CLARK. UNCHECKED, YOU AND YOUR SON ARE THE **MOST DANGEROUS BEINGS** ON THIS PLANET.
THE SUPERMAN I KNEW LOST BOTH OF HIS PARENTS, AND AS DIFFERENT AS WE WERE...
...WE UNDER-STOOD EACH OTHER.
SKLUUUURCH

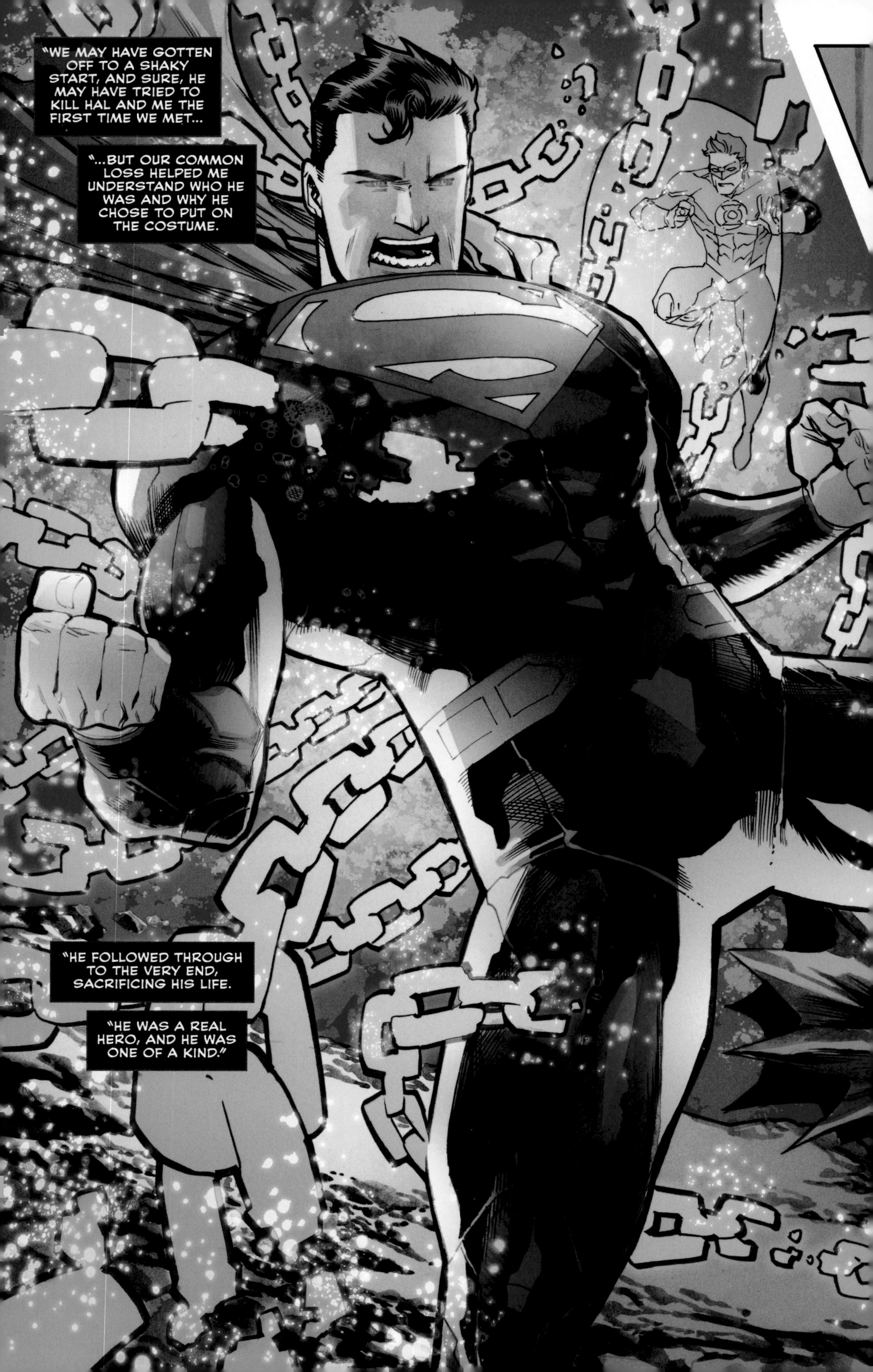
"WE MAY HAVE GOTTEN OFF TO A SHAKY START, AND SURE, HE MAY HAVE TRIED TO KILL HAL AND ME THE FIRST TIME WE MET...
"...BUT OUR COMMON LOSS HELPED ME UNDERSTAND WHO HE WAS AND WHY HE CHOSE TO PUT ON THE COSTUME.
"HE FOLLOWED THROUGH TO THE VERY END, SACRIFICING HIS LIFE.
"HE WAS A REAL HERO, AND HE WAS ONE OF A KIND."

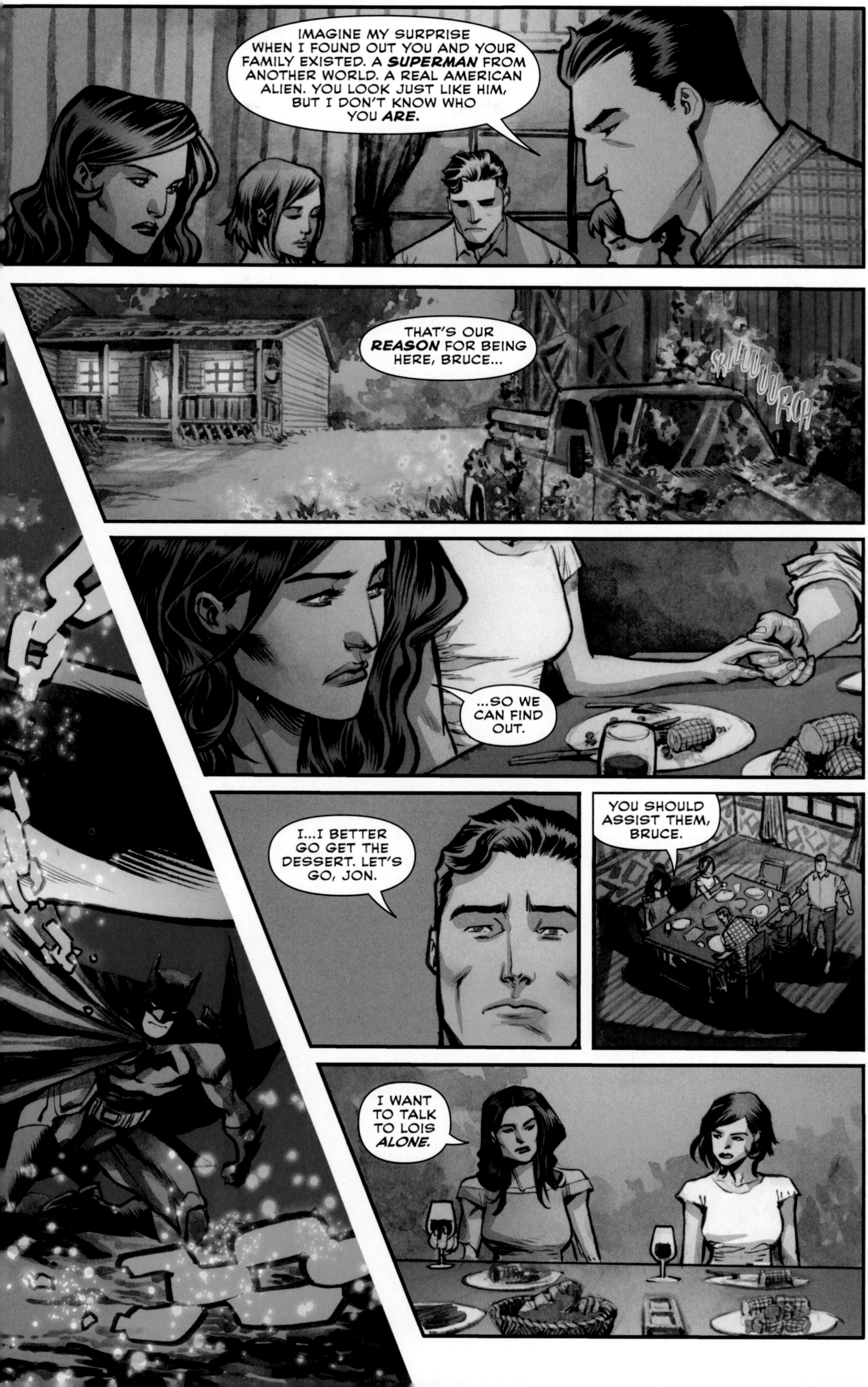
IMAGINE MY SURPRISE WHEN I FOUND OUT YOU AND YOUR FAMILY EXISTED. A *SUPERMAN* FROM ANOTHER WORLD. A REAL AMERICAN ALIEN. YOU LOOK JUST LIKE HIM, BUT I DON'T KNOW WHO YOU *ARE.*
THAT'S OUR *REASON* FOR BEING HERE, BRUCE...
SKLUUUURCH
...SO WE CAN FIND OUT.
I...I BETTER GO GET THE DESSERT. LET'S GO, JON.
YOU SHOULD ASSIST THEM, BRUCE.
I WANT TO TALK TO LOIS *ALONE.*

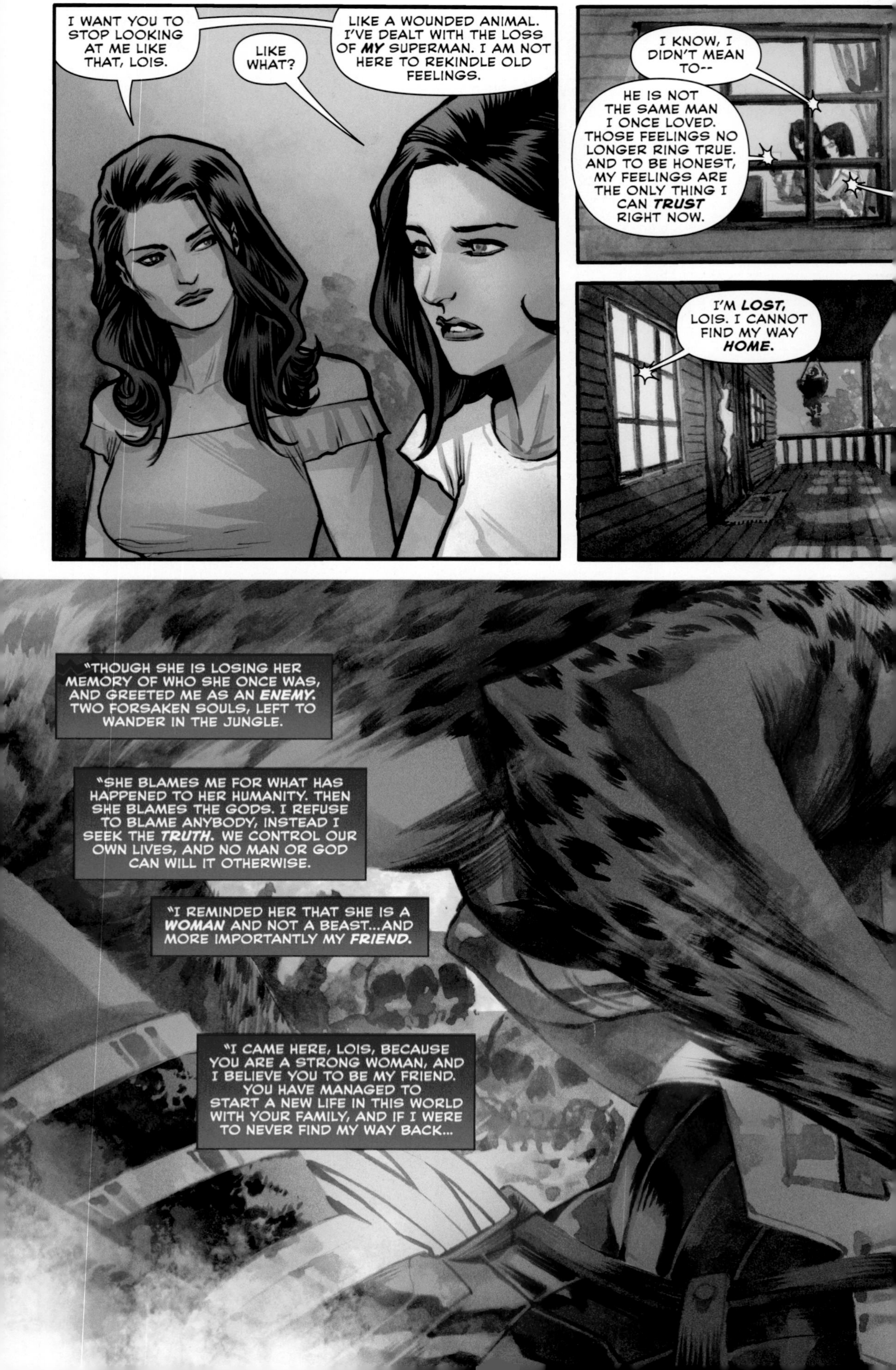
I WANT YOU TO STOP LOOKING AT ME LIKE THAT, LOIS.
LIKE WHAT?
LIKE A WOUNDED ANIMAL. I'VE DEALT WITH THE LOSS OF MY SUPERMAN. I AM NOT HERE TO REKINDLE OLD FEELINGS.
I KNOW, I DIDN'T MEAN TO--
HE IS NOT THE SAME MAN I ONCE LOVED. THOSE FEELINGS NO LONGER RING TRUE. AND TO BE HONEST, MY FEELINGS ARE THE ONLY THING I CAN TRUST RIGHT NOW.
I'M LOST, LOIS. I CANNOT FIND MY WAY HOME.
"THOUGH SHE IS LOSING HER MEMORY OF WHO SHE ONCE WAS, AND GREETED ME AS AN ENEMY. TWO FORSAKEN SOULS, LEFT TO WANDER IN THE JUNGLE.
"SHE BLAMES ME FOR WHAT HAS HAPPENED TO HER HUMANITY. THEN SHE BLAMES THE GODS. I REFUSE TO BLAME ANYBODY, INSTEAD I SEEK THE TRUTH. WE CONTROL OUR OWN LIVES, AND NO MAN OR GOD CAN WILL IT OTHERWISE.
"I REMINDED HER THAT SHE IS A WOMAN AND NOT A BEAST...AND MORE IMPORTANTLY MY FRIEND.
"I CAME HERE, LOIS, BECAUSE YOU ARE A STRONG WOMAN, AND I BELIEVE YOU TO BE MY FRIEND. YOU HAVE MANAGED TO START A NEW LIFE IN THIS WORLD WITH YOUR FAMILY, AND IF I WERE TO NEVER FIND MY WAY BACK...

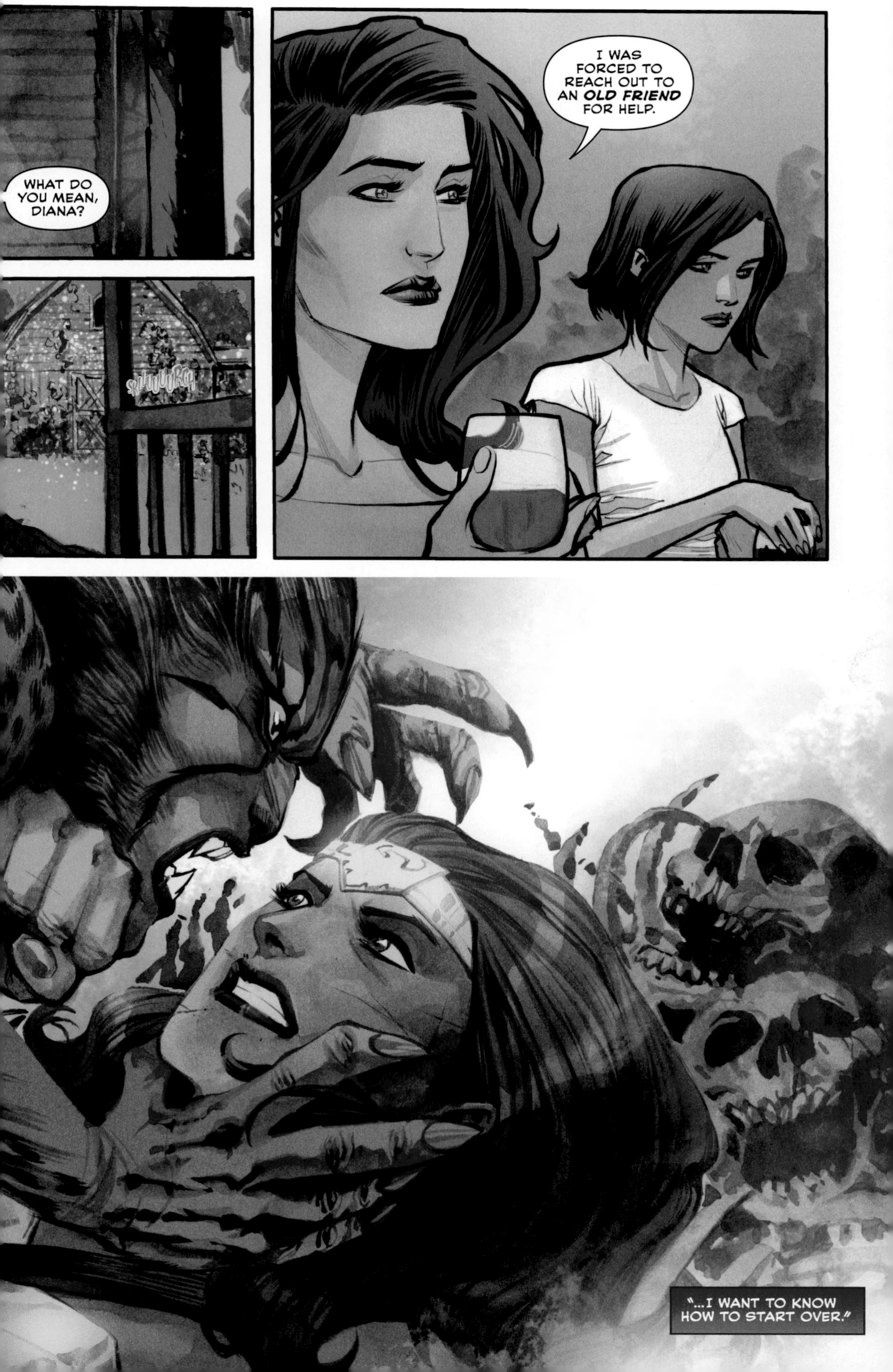

WHAT DO YOU MEAN, DIANA?
I WAS FORCED TO REACH OUT TO AN ***OLD FRIEND*** FOR HELP.
SKLUUUORCH
"...I WANT TO KNOW HOW TO START OVER."

GREAT THINGS START SMALL.

SKLLUUURCH

SKLUUURCH

SONS GROW UP TO BE FATHERS.

GOOD NIGHT, JON.

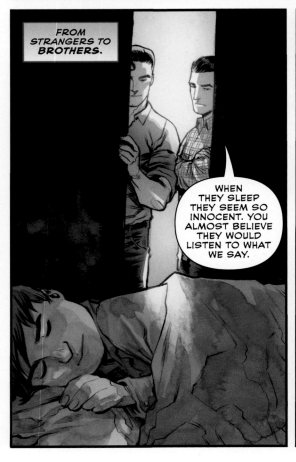

FROM STRANGERS TO BROTHERS.

WHEN THEY SLEEP THEY SEEM SO INNOCENT. YOU ALMOST BELIEVE THEY WOULD LISTEN TO WHAT WE SAY.

YOU'LL ALWAYS HAVE A HOME HERE, DIANA.

AND MOST IMPORTANTLY, A FRIEND.

RIVALS TO SISTERS.

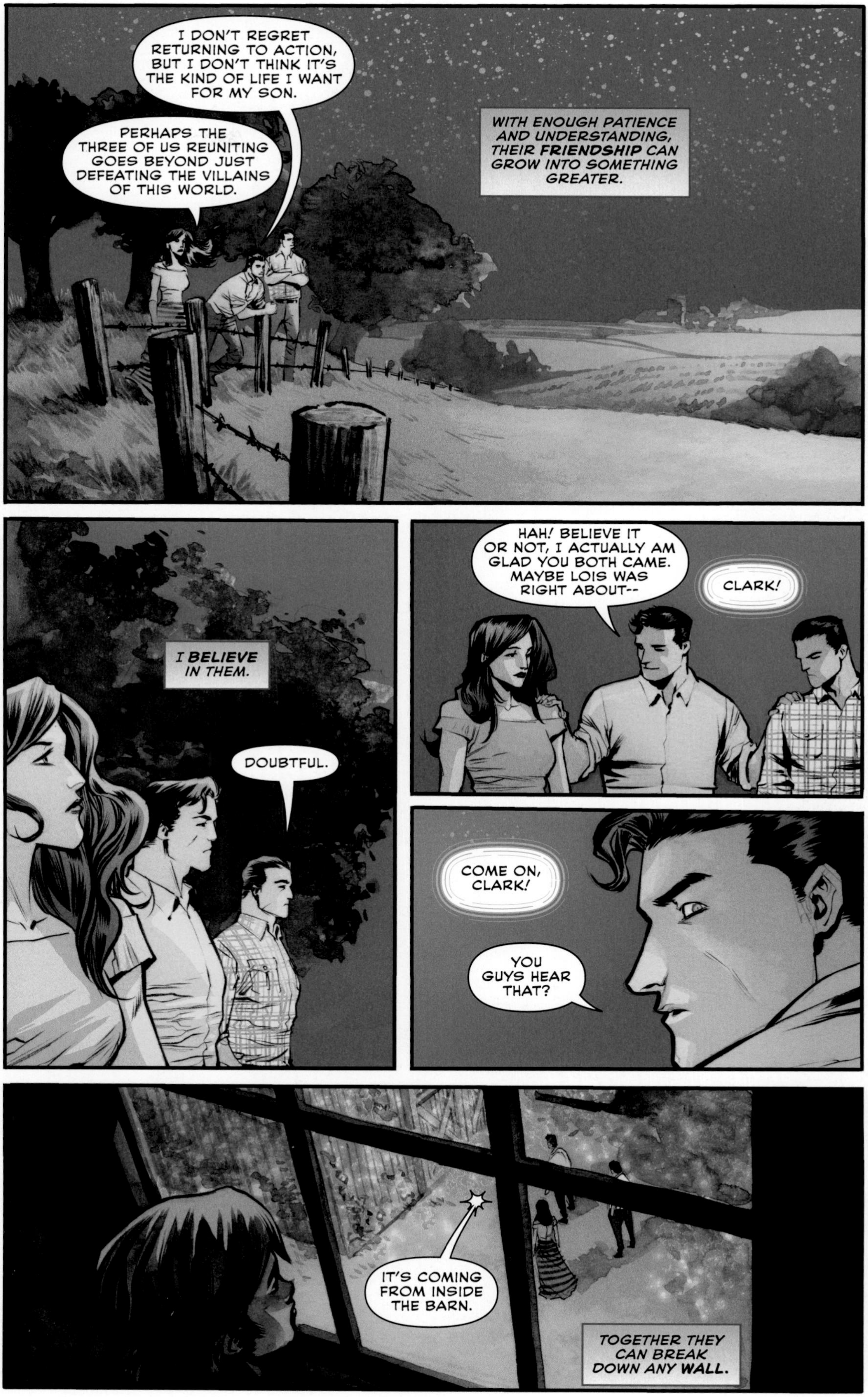
I DON'T REGRET RETURNING TO ACTION, BUT I DON'T THINK IT'S THE KIND OF LIFE I WANT FOR MY SON.
PERHAPS THE THREE OF US REUNITING GOES BEYOND JUST DEFEATING THE VILLAINS OF THIS WORLD.
WITH ENOUGH PATIENCE AND UNDERSTANDING, THEIR FRIENDSHIP CAN GROW INTO SOMETHING GREATER.
I BELIEVE IN THEM.
DOUBTFUL.
HAH! BELIEVE IT OR NOT, I ACTUALLY AM GLAD YOU BOTH CAME. MAYBE LOIS WAS RIGHT ABOUT--
CLARK!
COME ON, CLARK!
YOU GUYS HEAR THAT?
IT'S COMING FROM INSIDE THE BARN.
TOGETHER THEY CAN BREAK DOWN ANY WALL.

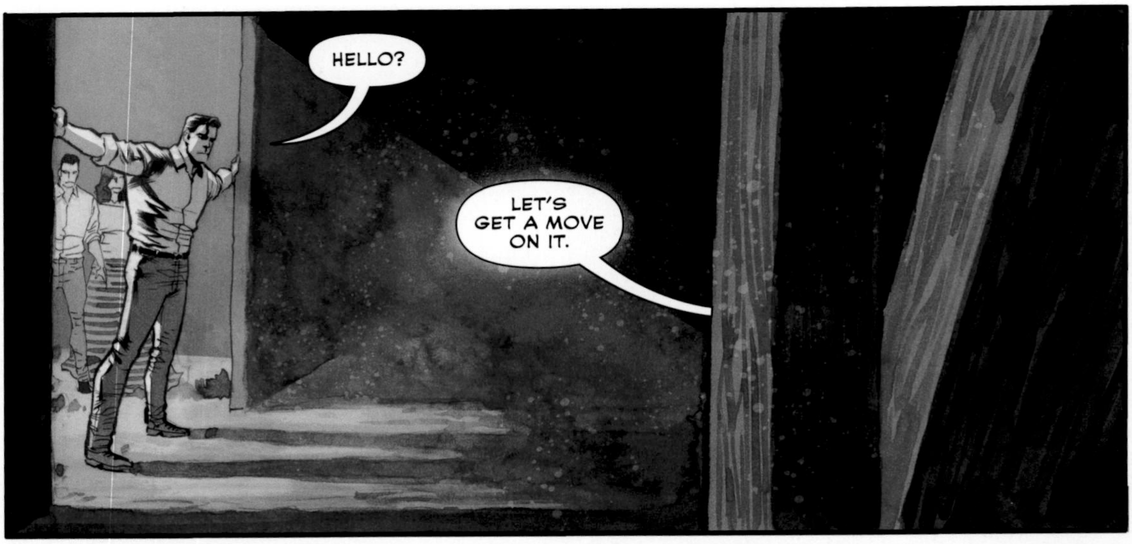
HELLO?
LET'S GET A MOVE ON IT.

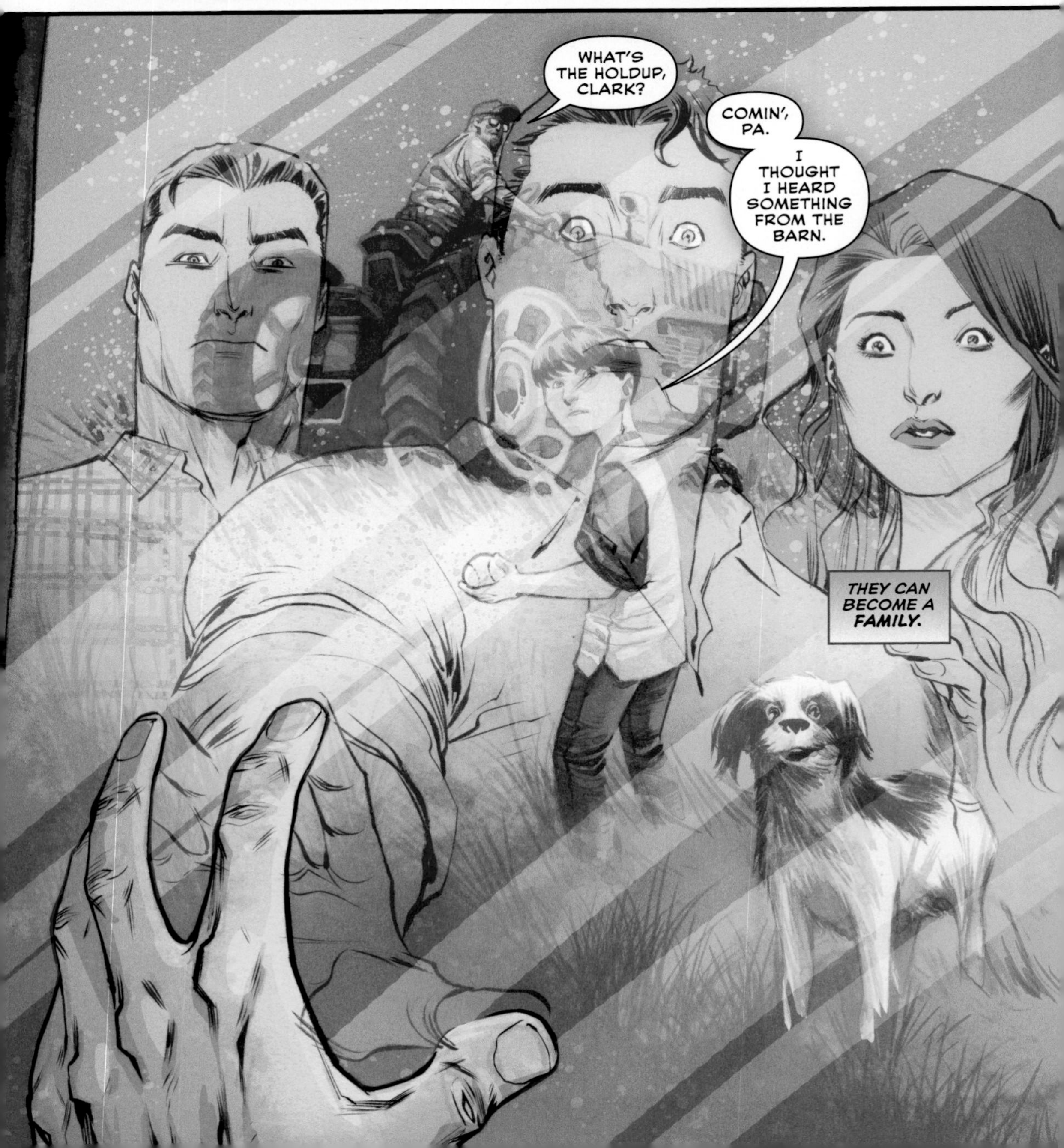
WHAT'S THE HOLDUP, CLARK?
COMIN', PA.
I THOUGHT I HEARD SOMETHING FROM THE BARN.
THEY CAN BECOME A FAMILY.

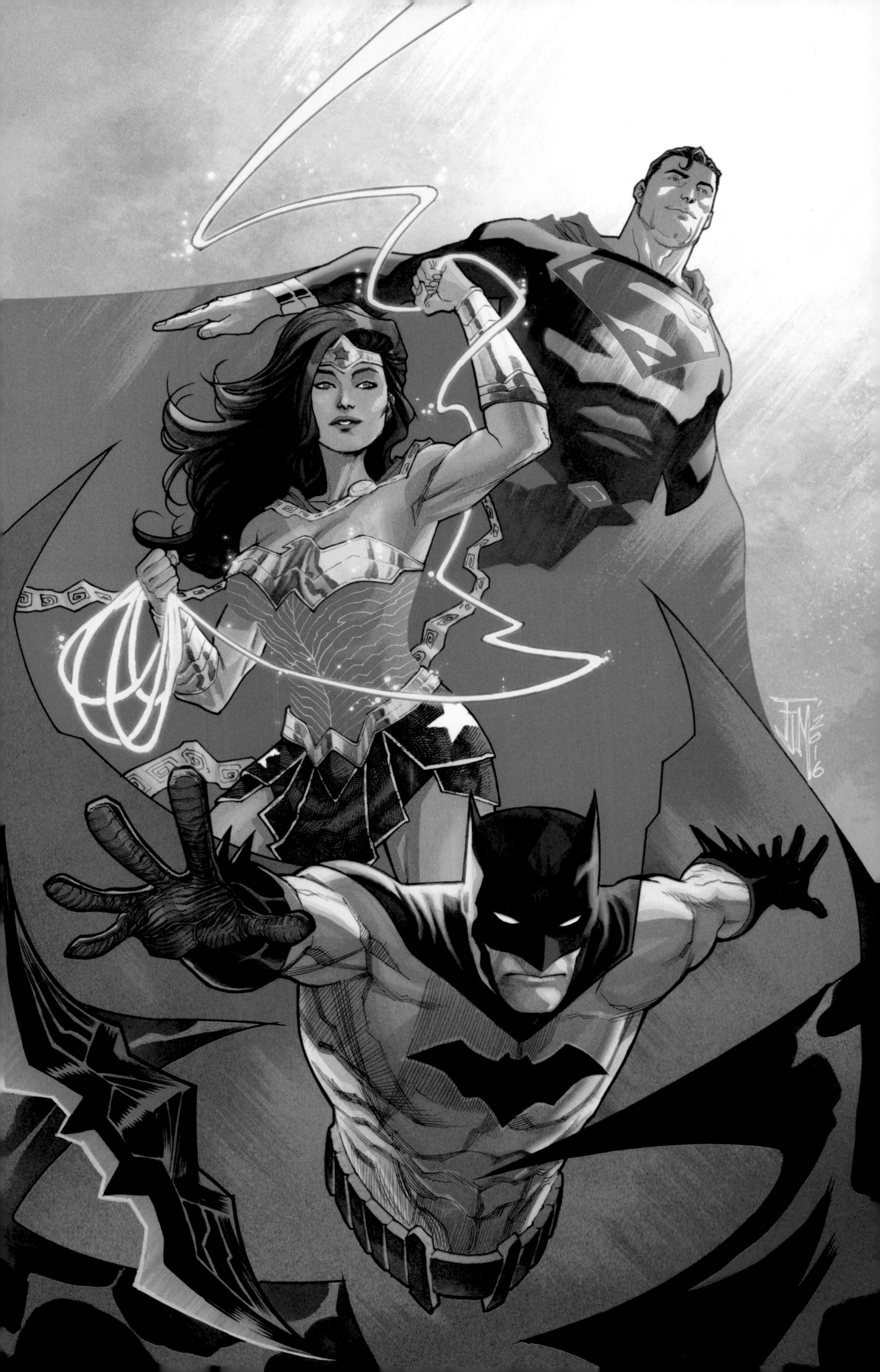

BETTER TOGETHER Part Two: SMALLVILLE
FRANCIS MANAPUL artist

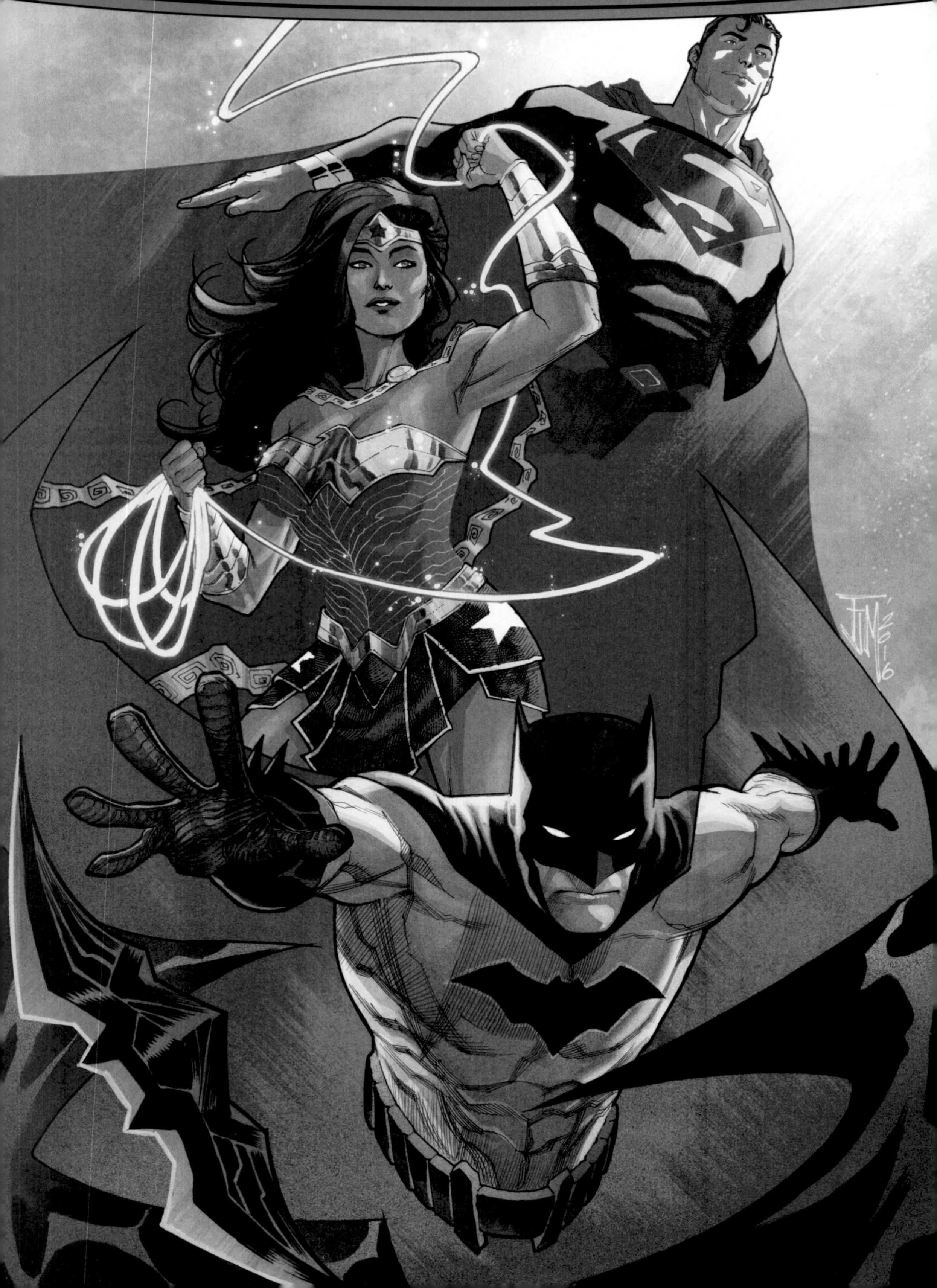

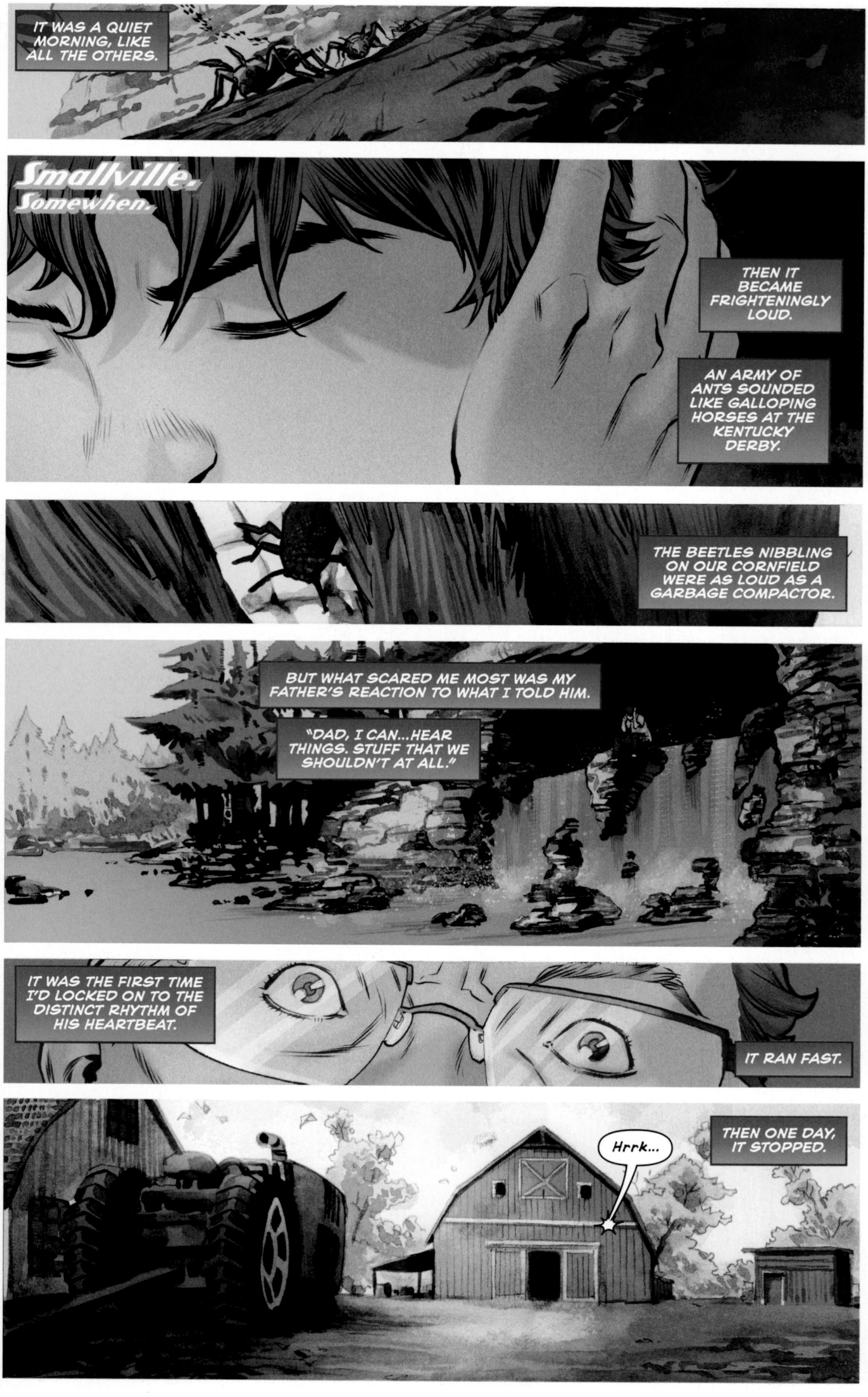
IT WAS A QUIET MORNING, LIKE ALL THE OTHERS.
Smallville. Somewhen.
THEN IT BECAME FRIGHTENINGLY LOUD.
AN ARMY OF ANTS SOUNDED LIKE GALLOPING HORSES AT THE KENTUCKY DERBY.
THE BEETLES NIBBLING ON OUR CORNFIELD WERE AS LOUD AS A GARBAGE COMPACTOR.
BUT WHAT SCARED ME MOST WAS MY FATHER'S REACTION TO WHAT I TOLD HIM.
"DAD, I CAN...HEAR THINGS. STUFF THAT WE SHOULDN'T AT ALL."
IT WAS THE FIRST TIME I'D LOCKED ON TO THE DISTINCT RHYTHM OF HIS HEARTBEAT.
IT RAN FAST.
THEN ONE DAY, IT STOPPED.
Hrrk...

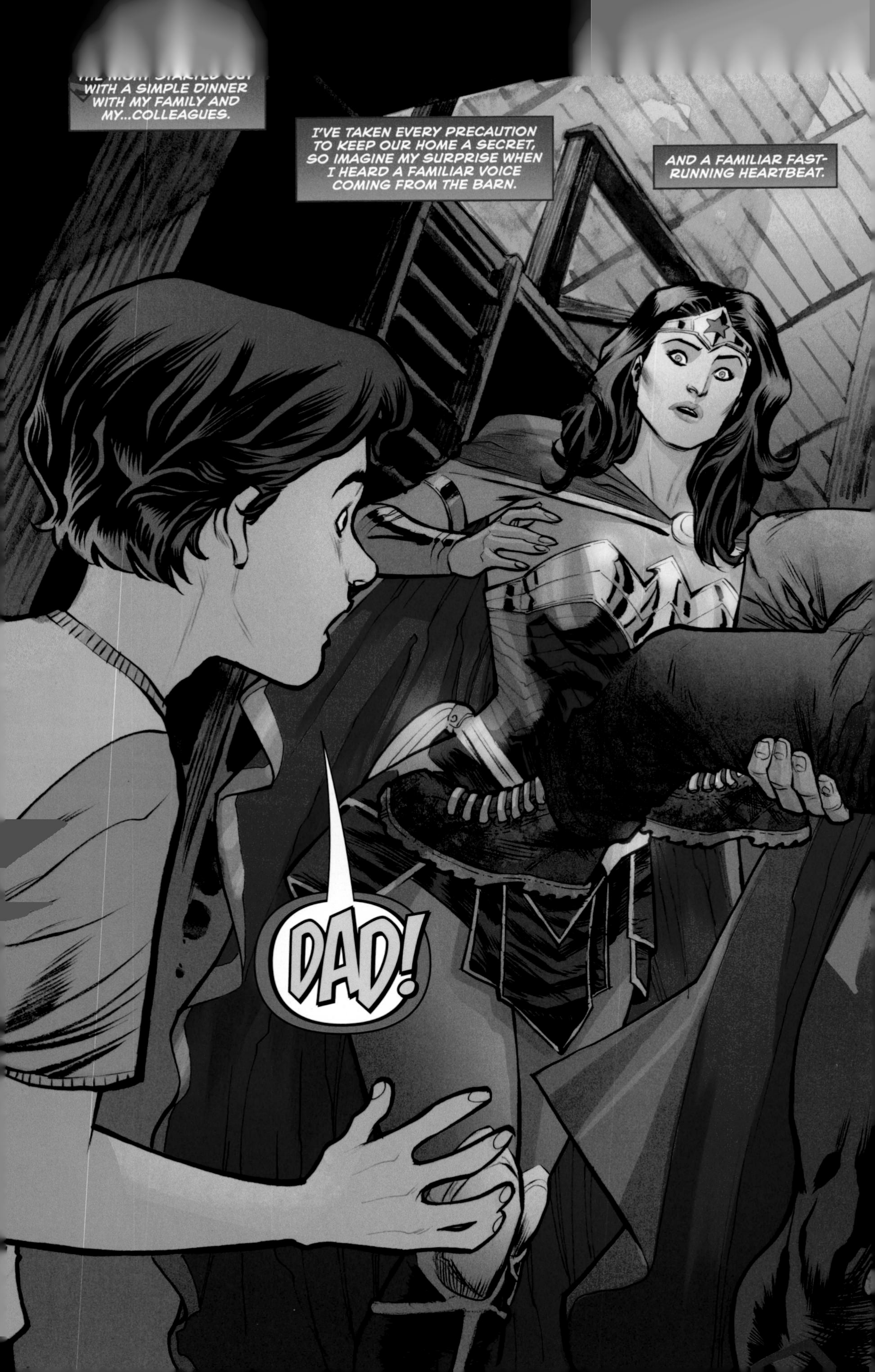
WITH A SIMPLE DINNER WITH MY FAMILY AND MY...COLLEAGUES.
I'VE TAKEN EVERY PRECAUTION TO KEEP OUR HOME A SECRET, SO IMAGINE MY SURPRISE WHEN I HEARD A FAMILIAR VOICE COMING FROM THE BARN.
AND A FAMILIAR FAST-RUNNING HEARTBEAT.
DAD!

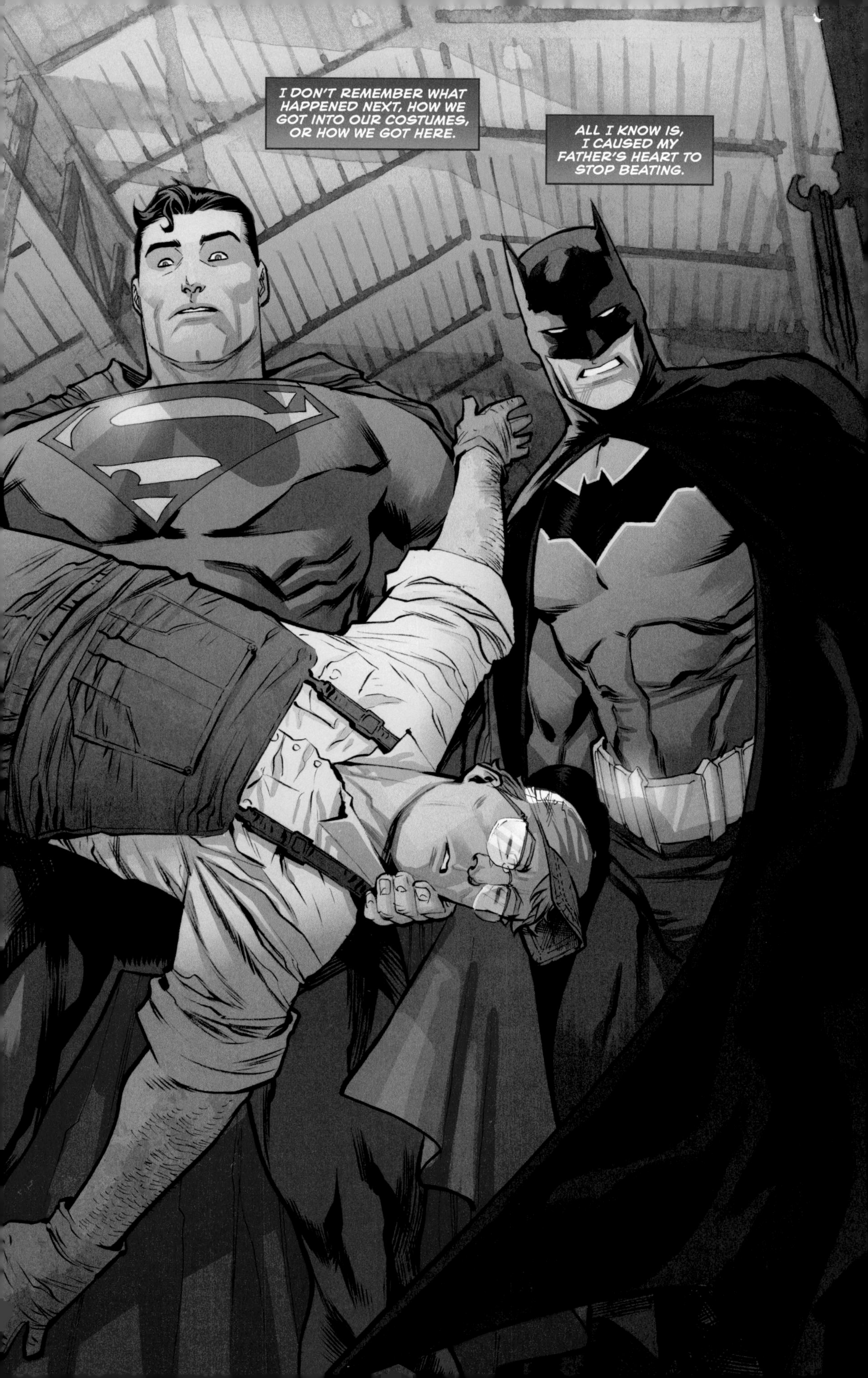
I DON'T REMEMBER WHAT HAPPENED NEXT, HOW WE GOT INTO OUR COSTUMES, OR HOW WE GOT HERE.
ALL I KNOW IS, I CAUSED MY FATHER'S HEART TO STOP BEATING.

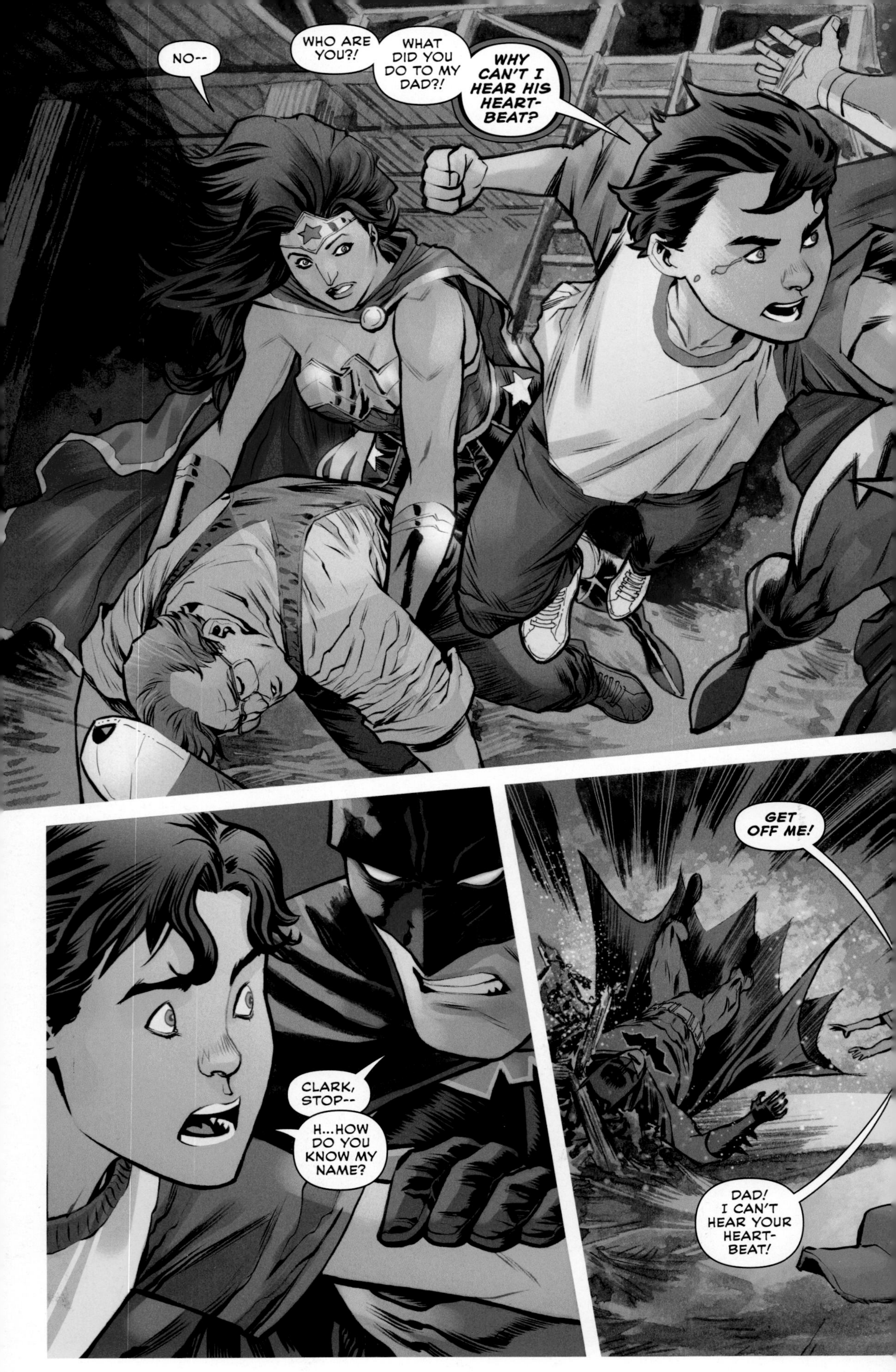
NO--
WHO ARE YOU?!
WHAT DID YOU DO TO MY DAD?!
WHY CAN'T I HEAR HIS HEART-BEAT?
CLARK, STOP--
H...HOW DO YOU KNOW MY NAME?
GET OFF ME!
DAD! I CAN'T HEAR YOUR HEART-BEAT!

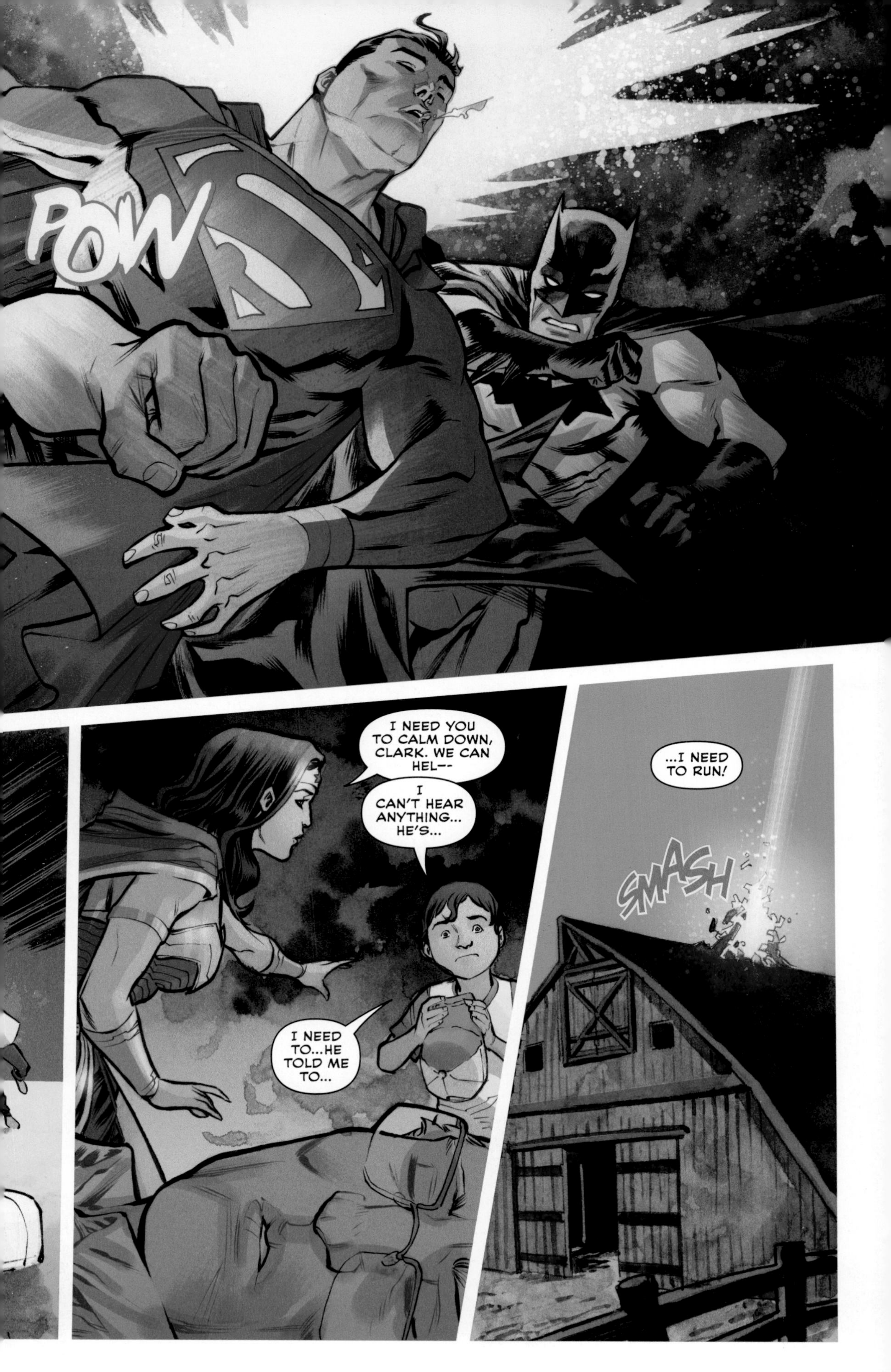
POW
I NEED YOU TO CALM DOWN, CLARK. WE CAN HEL--
I CAN'T HEAR ANYTHING... HE'S...
I NEED TO...HE TOLD ME TO...
SMASH
...I NEED TO RUN!

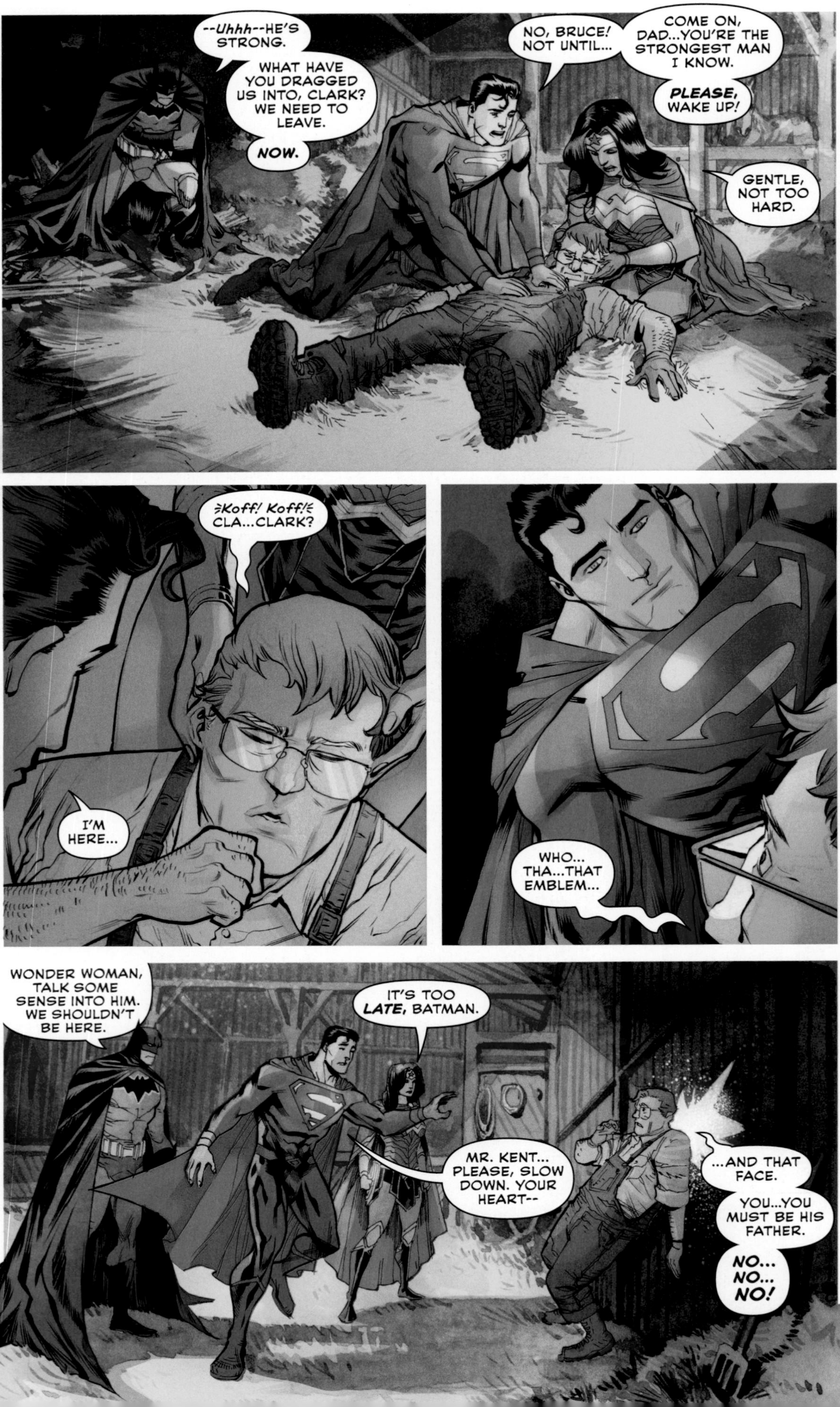
--*Uhhh*--HE'S STRONG.
WHAT HAVE YOU DRAGGED US INTO, CLARK? WE NEED TO LEAVE.
NOW.
NO, BRUCE! NOT UNTIL...
COME ON, DAD...YOU'RE THE STRONGEST MAN I KNOW.
PLEASE, WAKE UP!
GENTLE, NOT TOO HARD.
Koff! Koff! CLA...CLARK?
I'M HERE...
WHO... THA...THAT EMBLEM...
WONDER WOMAN, TALK SOME SENSE INTO HIM. WE SHOULDN'T BE HERE.
IT'S TOO **LATE,** BATMAN.
MR. KENT... PLEASE, SLOW DOWN. YOUR HEART--
...AND THAT FACE.
YOU...YOU MUST BE HIS FATHER.
NO... NO... NO!

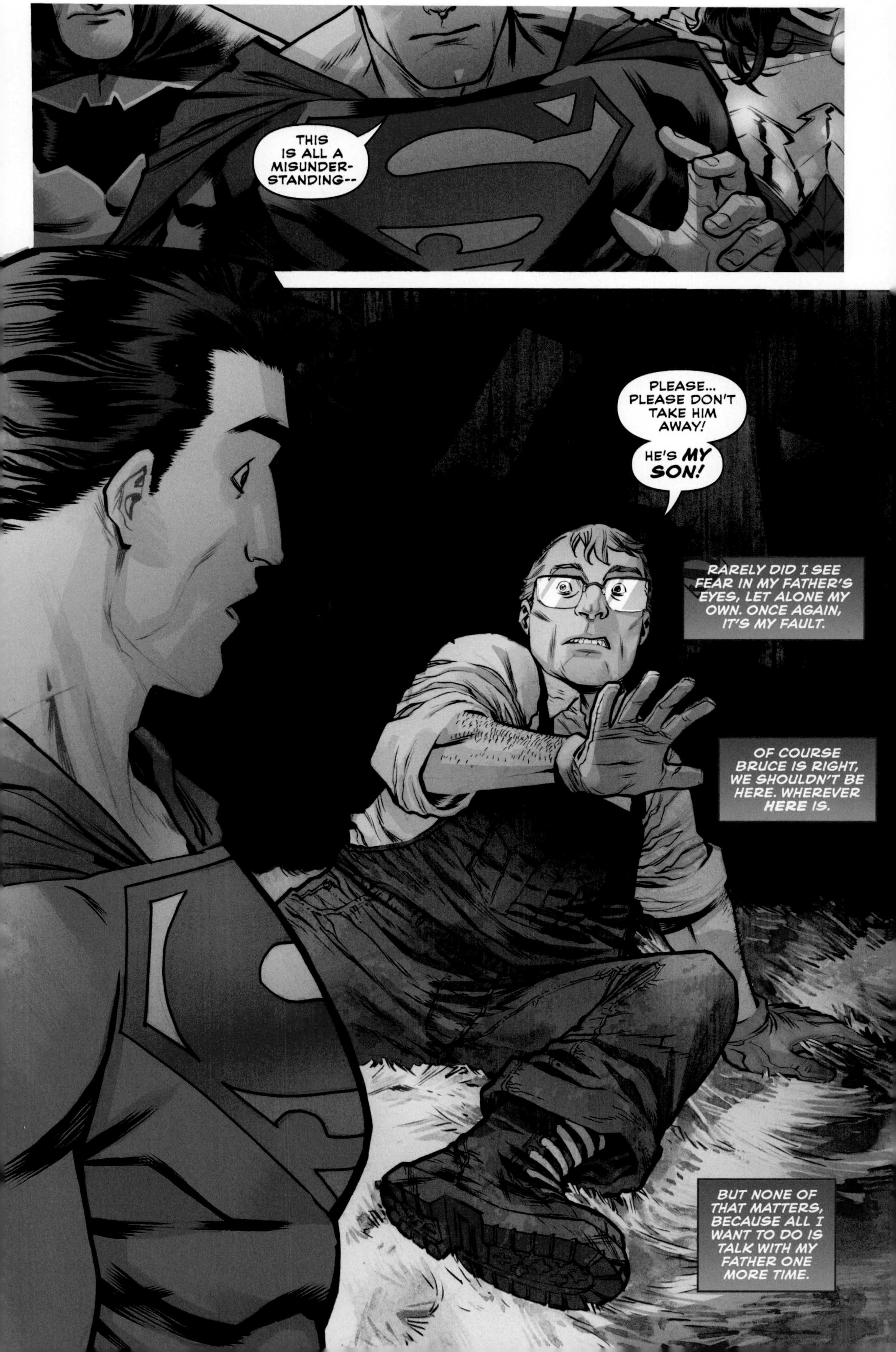

THIS IS ALL A MISUNDER-STANDING--
PLEASE... PLEASE DON'T TAKE HIM AWAY!
HE'S MY SON!
RARELY DID I SEE FEAR IN MY FATHER'S EYES, LET ALONE MY OWN. ONCE AGAIN, IT'S MY FAULT.
OF COURSE BRUCE IS RIGHT, WE SHOULDN'T BE HERE. WHEREVER HERE IS.
BUT NONE OF THAT MATTERS, BECAUSE ALL I WANT TO DO IS TALK WITH MY FATHER ONE MORE TIME.

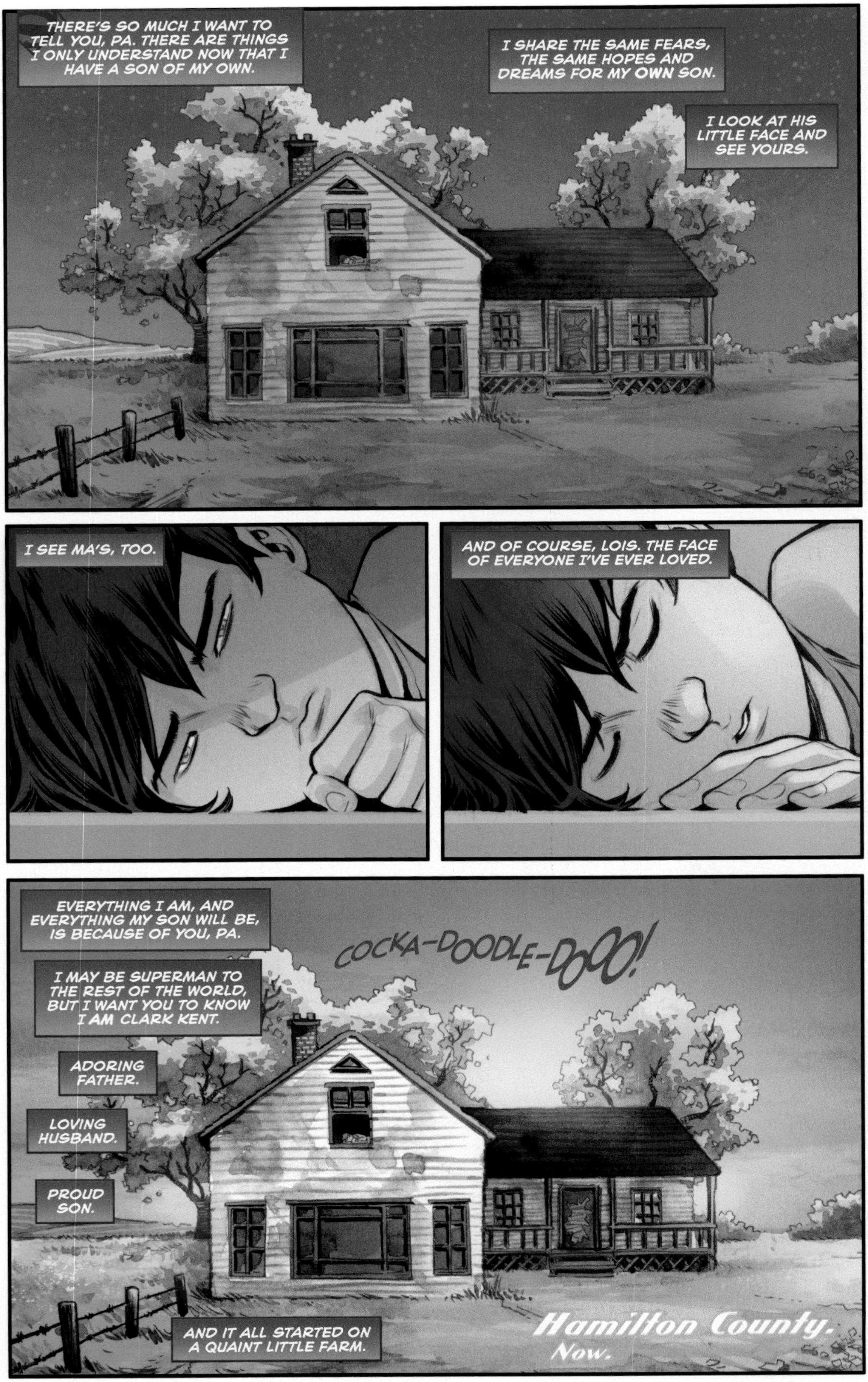
THERE'S SO MUCH I WANT TO TELL YOU, PA. THERE ARE THINGS I ONLY UNDERSTAND NOW THAT I HAVE A SON OF MY OWN.
I SHARE THE SAME FEARS, THE SAME HOPES AND DREAMS FOR MY OWN SON.
I LOOK AT HIS LITTLE FACE AND SEE YOURS.
I SEE MA'S, TOO.
AND OF COURSE, LOIS. THE FACE OF EVERYONE I'VE EVER LOVED.
EVERYTHING I AM, AND EVERYTHING MY SON WILL BE, IS BECAUSE OF YOU, PA.
COCKA-DOODLE-DOOO!
I MAY BE SUPERMAN TO THE REST OF THE WORLD, BUT I WANT YOU TO KNOW I AM CLARK KENT.
ADORING FATHER.
LOVING HUSBAND.
PROUD SON.
AND IT ALL STARTED ON A QUAINT LITTLE FARM.
Hamilton County.
Now.

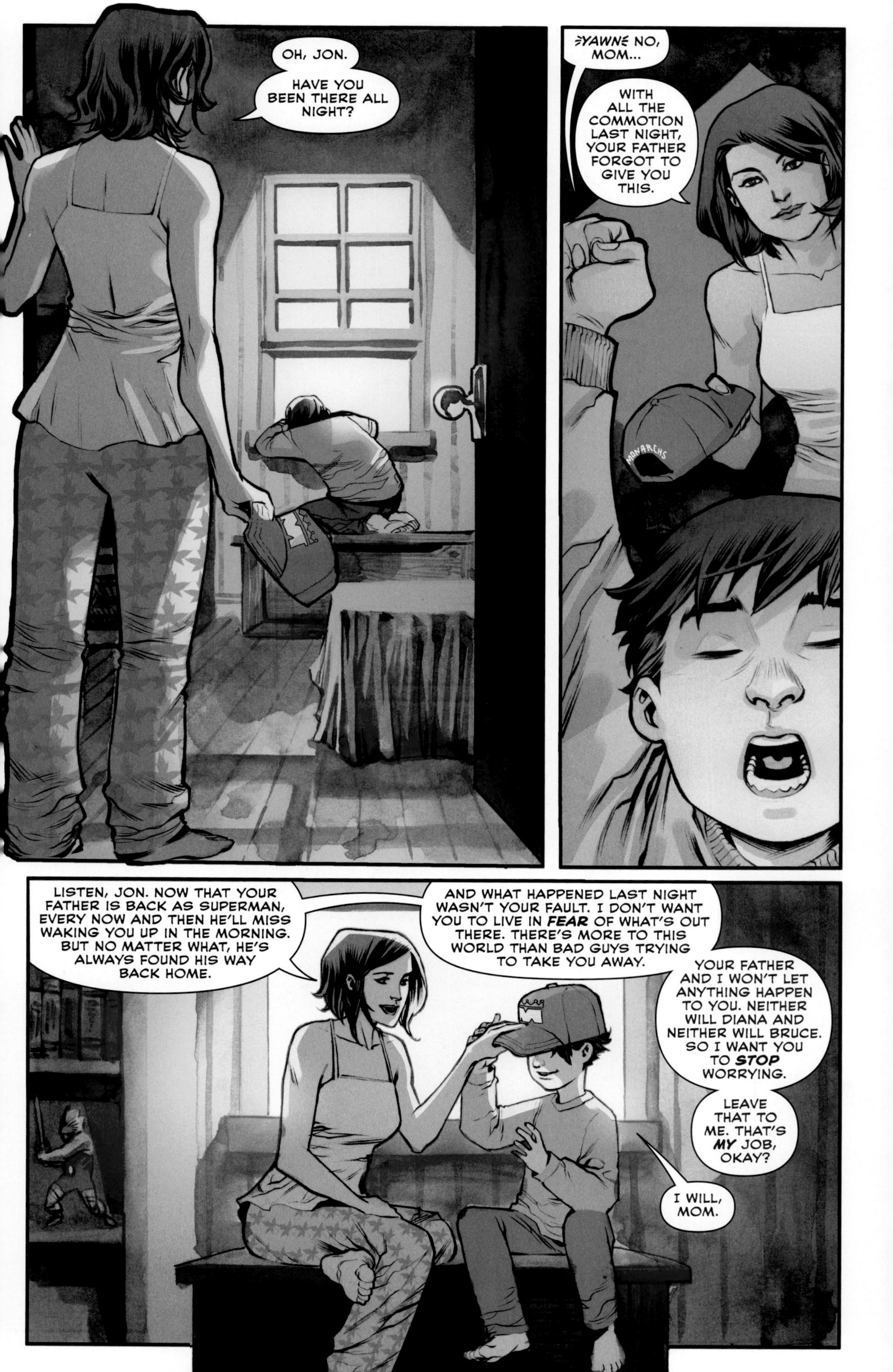
OH, JON.
HAVE YOU BEEN THERE ALL NIGHT?
YAWN NO, MOM...
WITH ALL THE COMMOTION LAST NIGHT, YOUR FATHER FORGOT TO GIVE YOU THIS.
MONARCHS
LISTEN, JON. NOW THAT YOUR FATHER IS BACK AS SUPERMAN, EVERY NOW AND THEN HE'LL MISS WAKING YOU UP IN THE MORNING. BUT NO MATTER WHAT, HE'S ALWAYS FOUND HIS WAY BACK HOME.
AND WHAT HAPPENED LAST NIGHT WASN'T YOUR FAULT. I DON'T WANT YOU TO LIVE IN FEAR OF WHAT'S OUT THERE. THERE'S MORE TO THIS WORLD THAN BAD GUYS TRYING TO TAKE YOU AWAY.
YOUR FATHER AND I WON'T LET ANYTHING HAPPEN TO YOU. NEITHER WILL DIANA AND NEITHER WILL BRUCE. SO I WANT YOU TO STOP WORRYING.
LEAVE THAT TO ME. THAT'S MY JOB, OKAY?
I WILL, MOM.

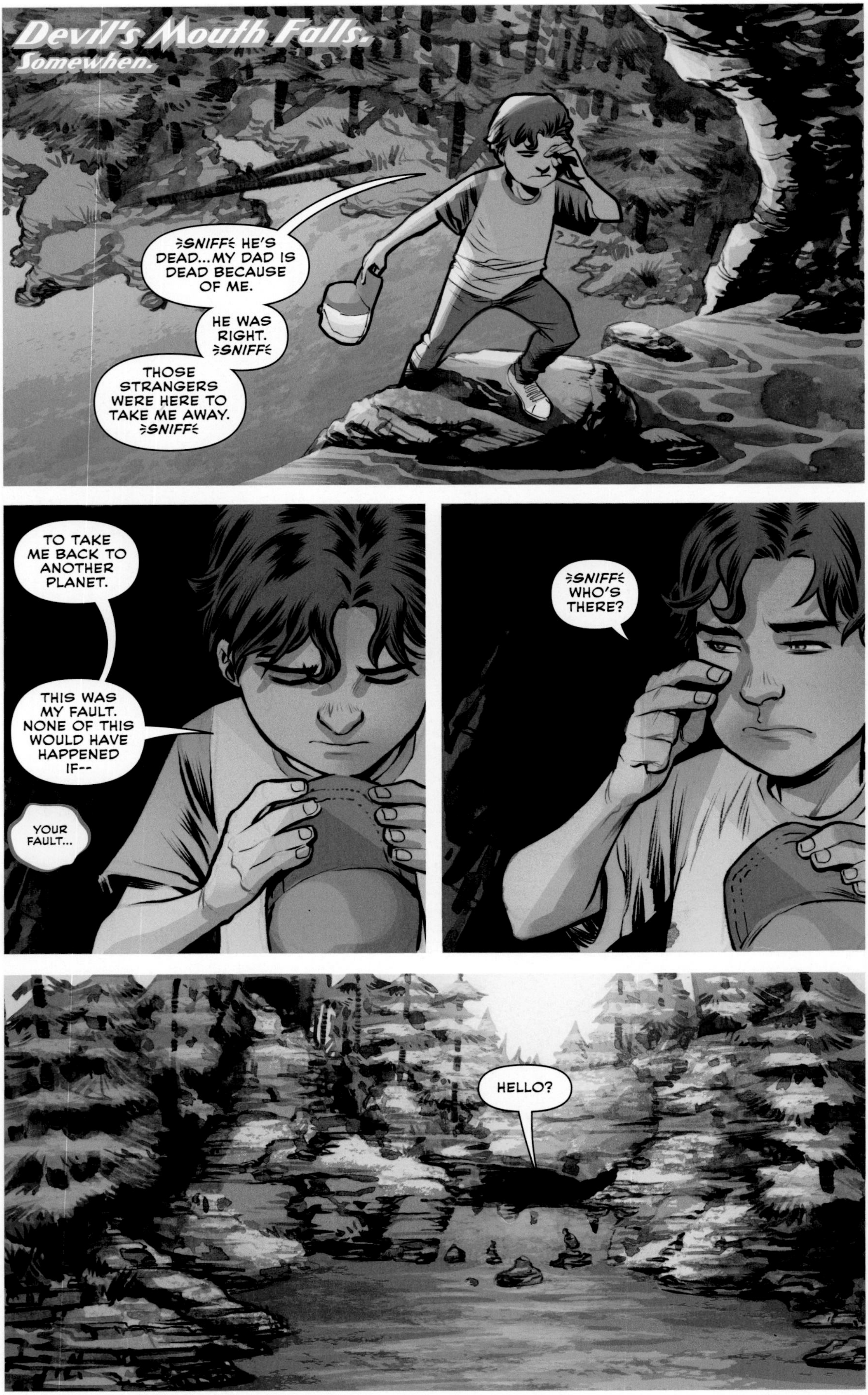
Devil's Mouth Falls.
Somewhen.
≠SNIFF≠ HE'S DEAD...MY DAD IS DEAD BECAUSE OF ME.
HE WAS RIGHT. ≠SNIFF≠
THOSE STRANGERS WERE HERE TO TAKE ME AWAY. ≠SNIFF≠
TO TAKE ME BACK TO ANOTHER PLANET.
THIS WAS MY FAULT. NONE OF THIS WOULD HAVE HAPPENED IF--
YOUR FAULT...
≠SNIFF≠ WHO'S THERE?
HELLO?

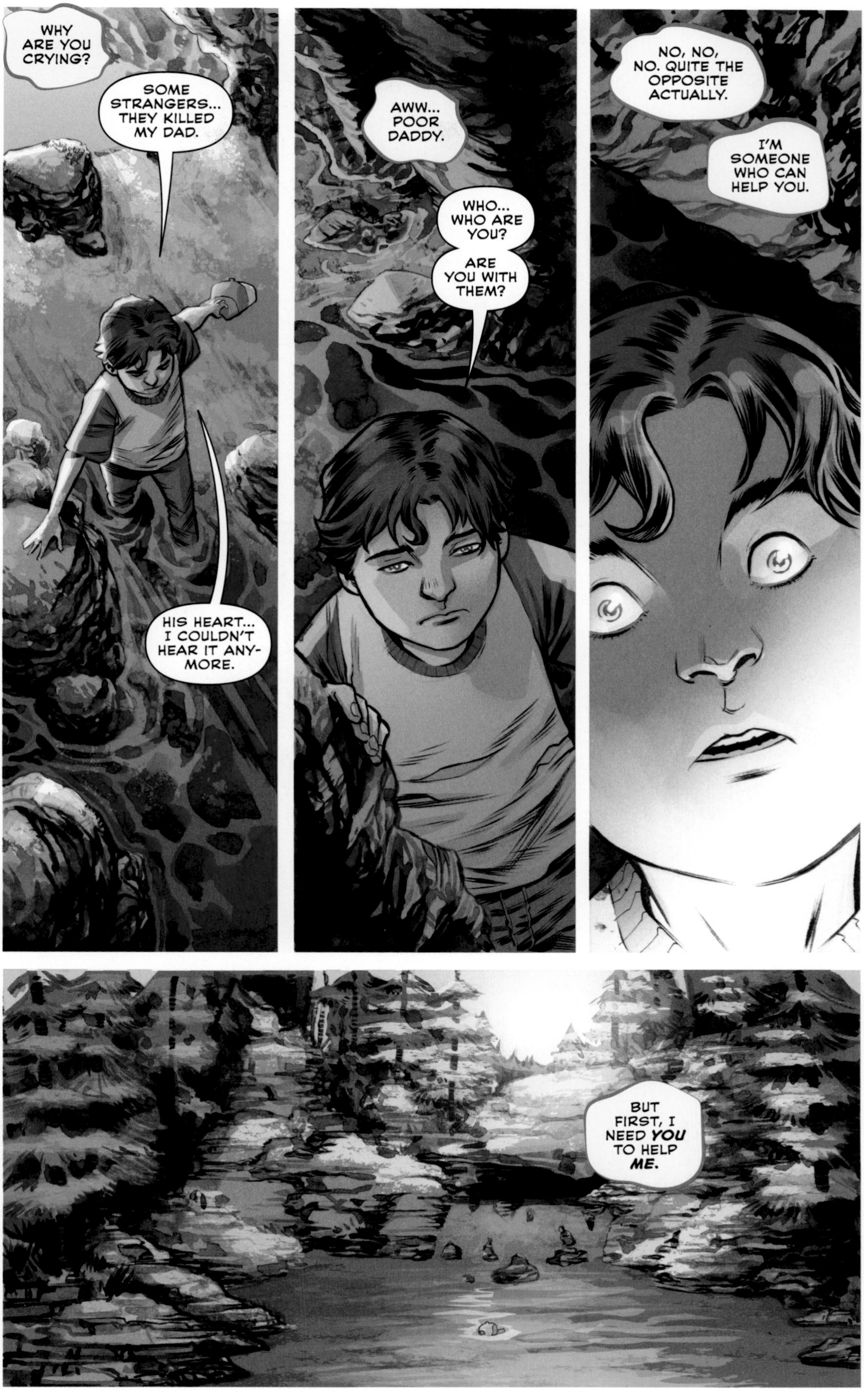
WHY ARE YOU CRYING?
SOME STRANGERS... THEY KILLED MY DAD.
HIS HEART... I COULDN'T HEAR IT ANY-MORE.
AWW... POOR DADDY.
WHO... WHO ARE YOU?
ARE YOU WITH THEM?
NO, NO, NO. QUITE THE OPPOSITE ACTUALLY.
I'M SOMEONE WHO CAN HELP YOU.
BUT FIRST, I NEED *YOU* TO HELP *ME*.

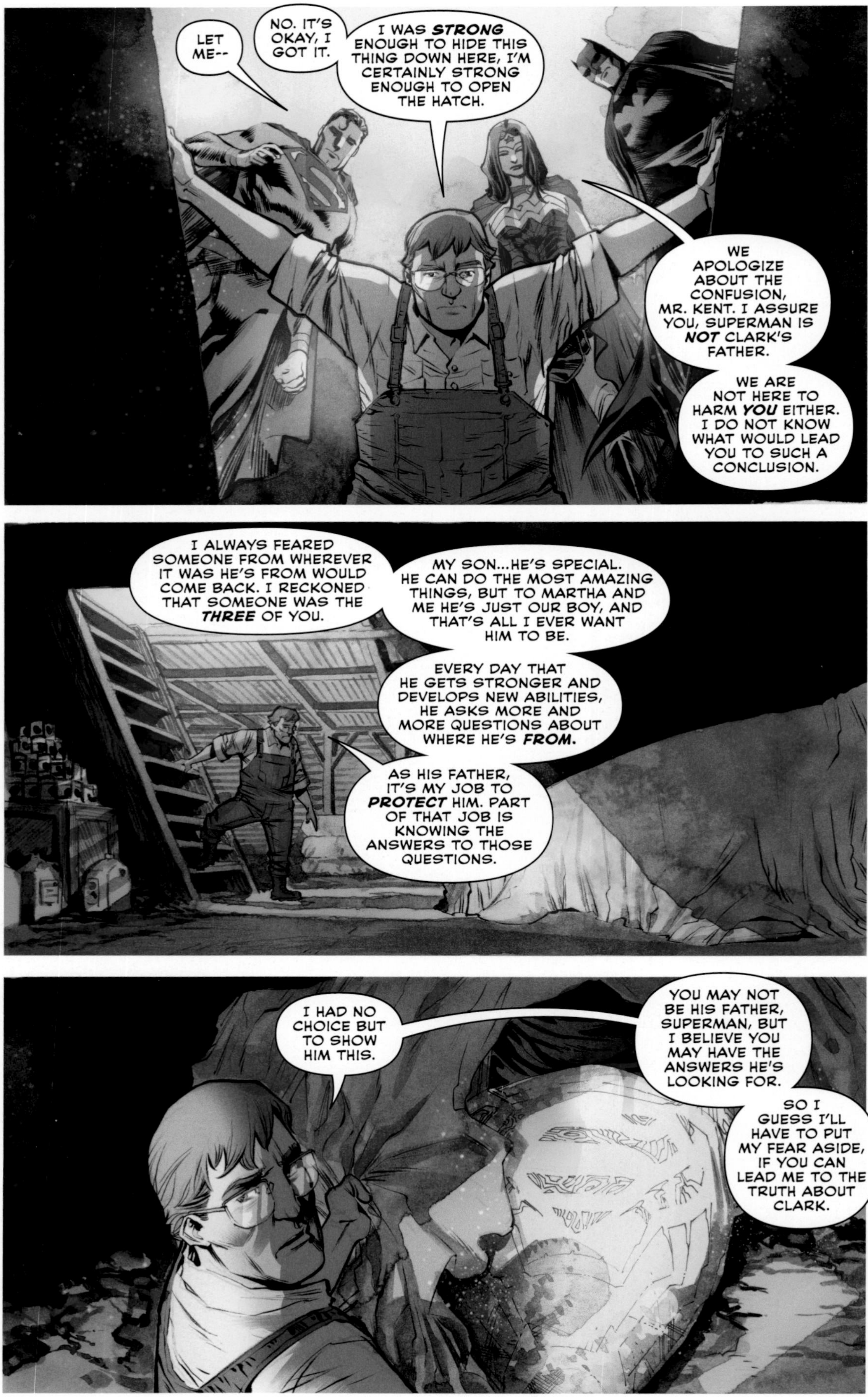

LET ME--
NO. IT'S OKAY, I GOT IT.
I WAS STRONG ENOUGH TO HIDE THIS THING DOWN HERE, I'M CERTAINLY STRONG ENOUGH TO OPEN THE HATCH.
WE APOLOGIZE ABOUT THE CONFUSION, MR. KENT. I ASSURE YOU, SUPERMAN IS NOT CLARK'S FATHER.
WE ARE NOT HERE TO HARM YOU EITHER. I DO NOT KNOW WHAT WOULD LEAD YOU TO SUCH A CONCLUSION.
I ALWAYS FEARED SOMEONE FROM WHEREVER IT WAS HE'S FROM WOULD COME BACK. I RECKONED THAT SOMEONE WAS THE THREE OF YOU.
MY SON...HE'S SPECIAL. HE CAN DO THE MOST AMAZING THINGS, BUT TO MARTHA AND ME HE'S JUST OUR BOY, AND THAT'S ALL I EVER WANT HIM TO BE.
EVERY DAY THAT HE GETS STRONGER AND DEVELOPS NEW ABILITIES, HE ASKS MORE AND MORE QUESTIONS ABOUT WHERE HE'S FROM.
AS HIS FATHER, IT'S MY JOB TO PROTECT HIM. PART OF THAT JOB IS KNOWING THE ANSWERS TO THOSE QUESTIONS.
I HAD NO CHOICE BUT TO SHOW HIM THIS.
YOU MAY NOT BE HIS FATHER, SUPERMAN, BUT I BELIEVE YOU MAY HAVE THE ANSWERS HE'S LOOKING FOR.
SO I GUESS I'LL HAVE TO PUT MY FEAR ASIDE, IF YOU CAN LEAD ME TO THE TRUTH ABOUT CLARK.

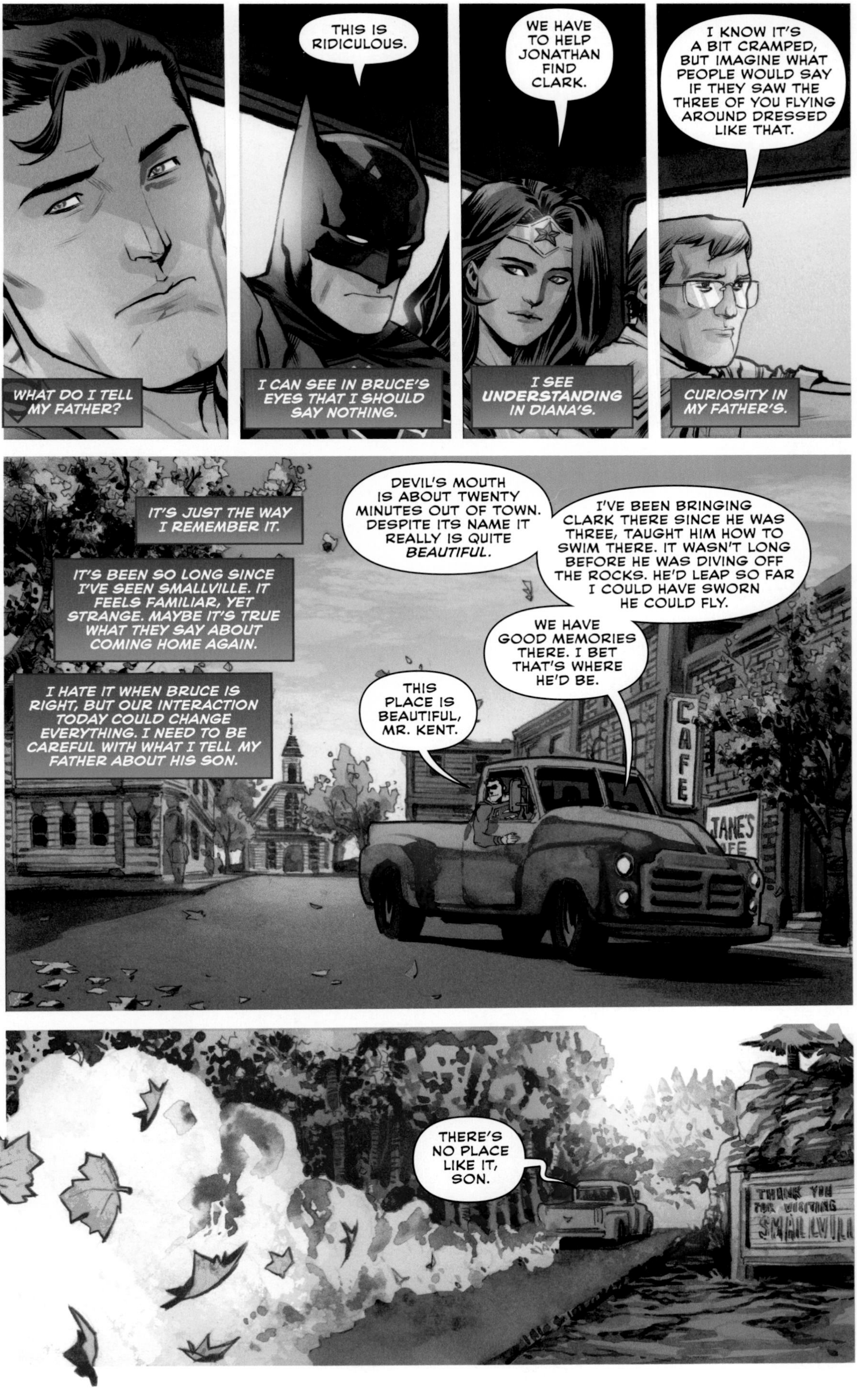
WHAT DO I TELL MY FATHER?
THIS IS RIDICULOUS.
I CAN SEE IN BRUCE'S EYES THAT I SHOULD SAY NOTHING.
WE HAVE TO HELP JONATHAN FIND CLARK.
I SEE UNDERSTANDING IN DIANA'S.
I KNOW IT'S A BIT CRAMPED, BUT IMAGINE WHAT PEOPLE WOULD SAY IF THEY SAW THE THREE OF YOU FLYING AROUND DRESSED LIKE THAT.
CURIOSITY IN MY FATHER'S.
IT'S JUST THE WAY I REMEMBER IT.
IT'S BEEN SO LONG SINCE I'VE SEEN SMALLVILLE. IT FEELS FAMILIAR, YET STRANGE. MAYBE IT'S TRUE WHAT THEY SAY ABOUT COMING HOME AGAIN.
I HATE IT WHEN BRUCE IS RIGHT, BUT OUR INTERACTION TODAY COULD CHANGE EVERYTHING. I NEED TO BE CAREFUL WITH WHAT I TELL MY FATHER ABOUT HIS SON.
DEVIL'S MOUTH IS ABOUT TWENTY MINUTES OUT OF TOWN. DESPITE ITS NAME IT REALLY IS QUITE BEAUTIFUL.
I'VE BEEN BRINGING CLARK THERE SINCE HE WAS THREE, TAUGHT HIM HOW TO SWIM THERE. IT WASN'T LONG BEFORE HE WAS DIVING OFF THE ROCKS. HE'D LEAP SO FAR I COULD HAVE SWORN HE COULD FLY.
WE HAVE GOOD MEMORIES THERE. I BET THAT'S WHERE HE'D BE.
THIS PLACE IS BEAUTIFUL, MR. KENT.
CAFE
JANE'S
THERE'S NO PLACE LIKE IT, SON.

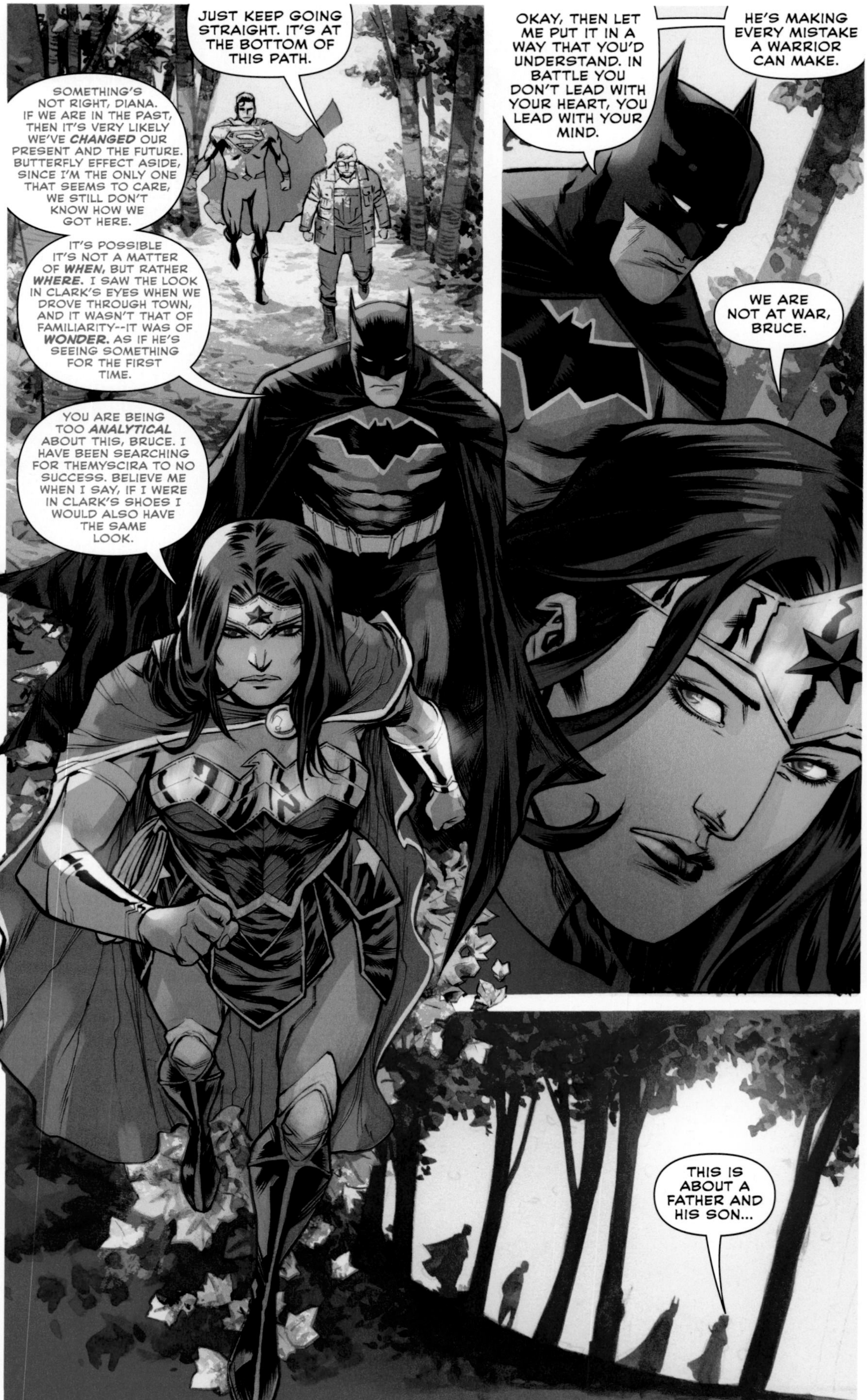
JUST KEEP GOING STRAIGHT. IT'S AT THE BOTTOM OF THIS PATH.
SOMETHING'S NOT RIGHT, DIANA. IF WE ARE IN THE PAST, THEN IT'S VERY LIKELY WE'VE CHANGED OUR PRESENT AND THE FUTURE. BUTTERFLY EFFECT ASIDE, SINCE I'M THE ONLY ONE THAT SEEMS TO CARE, WE STILL DON'T KNOW HOW WE GOT HERE.
IT'S POSSIBLE IT'S NOT A MATTER OF WHEN, BUT RATHER WHERE. I SAW THE LOOK IN CLARK'S EYES WHEN WE DROVE THROUGH TOWN, AND IT WASN'T THAT OF FAMILIARITY--IT WAS OF WONDER. AS IF HE'S SEEING SOMETHING FOR THE FIRST TIME.
YOU ARE BEING TOO ANALYTICAL ABOUT THIS, BRUCE. I HAVE BEEN SEARCHING FOR THEMYSCIRA TO NO SUCCESS. BELIEVE ME WHEN I SAY, IF I WERE IN CLARK'S SHOES I WOULD ALSO HAVE THE SAME LOOK.
OKAY, THEN LET ME PUT IT IN A WAY THAT YOU'D UNDERSTAND. IN BATTLE YOU DON'T LEAD WITH YOUR HEART, YOU LEAD WITH YOUR MIND.
HE'S MAKING EVERY MISTAKE A WARRIOR CAN MAKE.
WE ARE NOT AT WAR, BRUCE.
THIS IS ABOUT A FATHER AND HIS SON...

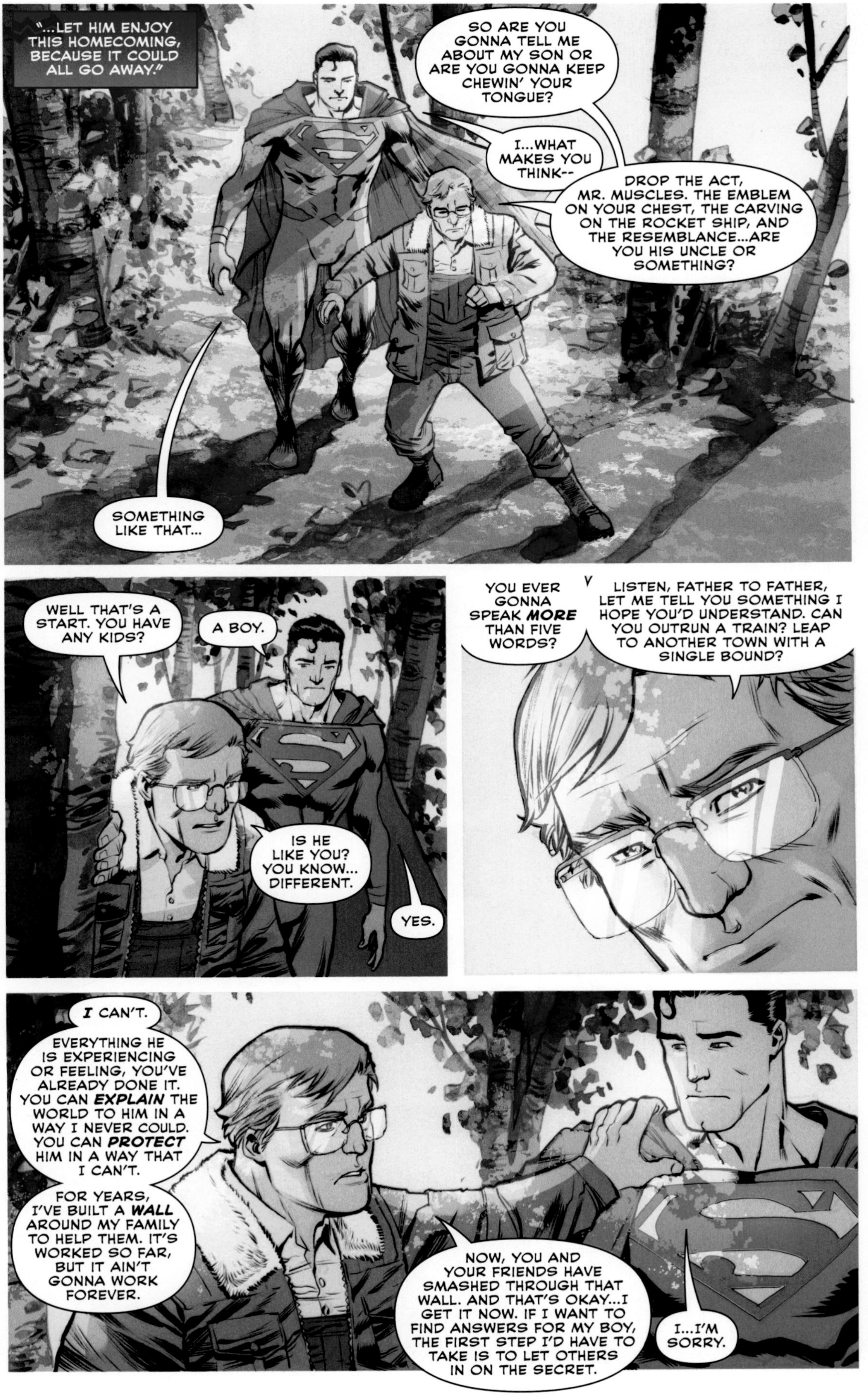
"...LET HIM ENJOY THIS HOMECOMING, BECAUSE IT COULD ALL GO AWAY."
SO ARE YOU GONNA TELL ME ABOUT MY SON OR ARE YOU GONNA KEEP CHEWIN' YOUR TONGUE?
I...WHAT MAKES YOU THINK--
DROP THE ACT, MR. MUSCLES. THE EMBLEM ON YOUR CHEST, THE CARVING ON THE ROCKET SHIP, AND THE RESEMBLANCE...ARE YOU HIS UNCLE OR SOMETHING?
SOMETHING LIKE THAT...
WELL THAT'S A START. YOU HAVE ANY KIDS?
A BOY.
IS HE LIKE YOU? YOU KNOW... DIFFERENT.
YES.
YOU EVER GONNA SPEAK MORE THAN FIVE WORDS?
LISTEN, FATHER TO FATHER, LET ME TELL YOU SOMETHING I HOPE YOU'D UNDERSTAND. CAN YOU OUTRUN A TRAIN? LEAP TO ANOTHER TOWN WITH A SINGLE BOUND?
I CAN'T.
EVERYTHING HE IS EXPERIENCING OR FEELING, YOU'VE ALREADY DONE IT. YOU CAN EXPLAIN THE WORLD TO HIM IN A WAY I NEVER COULD. YOU CAN PROTECT HIM IN A WAY THAT I CAN'T.
FOR YEARS, I'VE BUILT A WALL AROUND MY FAMILY TO HELP THEM. IT'S WORKED SO FAR, BUT IT AIN'T GONNA WORK FOREVER.
NOW, YOU AND YOUR FRIENDS HAVE SMASHED THROUGH THAT WALL. AND THAT'S OKAY...I GET IT NOW. IF I WANT TO FIND ANSWERS FOR MY BOY, THE FIRST STEP I'D HAVE TO TAKE IS TO LET OTHERS IN ON THE SECRET.
I...I'M SORRY.

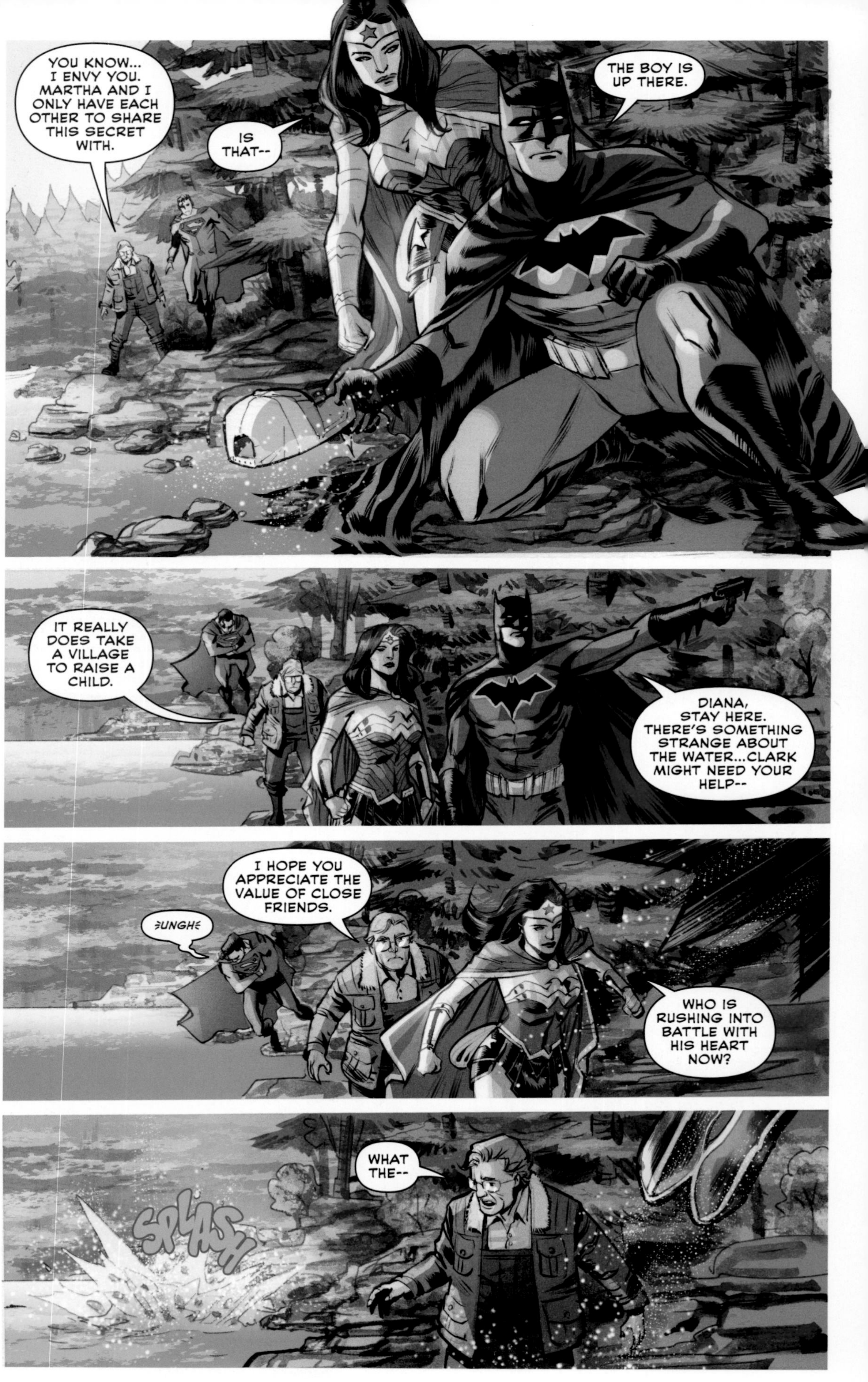
YOU KNOW... I ENVY YOU. MARTHA AND I ONLY HAVE EACH OTHER TO SHARE THIS SECRET WITH.
IS THAT--
THE BOY IS UP THERE.
IT REALLY DOES TAKE A VILLAGE TO RAISE A CHILD.
DIANA, STAY HERE. THERE'S SOMETHING STRANGE ABOUT THE WATER...CLARK MIGHT NEED YOUR HELP--
I HOPE YOU APPRECIATE THE VALUE OF CLOSE FRIENDS.
UNGH
WHO IS RUSHING INTO BATTLE WITH HIS HEART NOW?
WHAT THE--
SPLASH

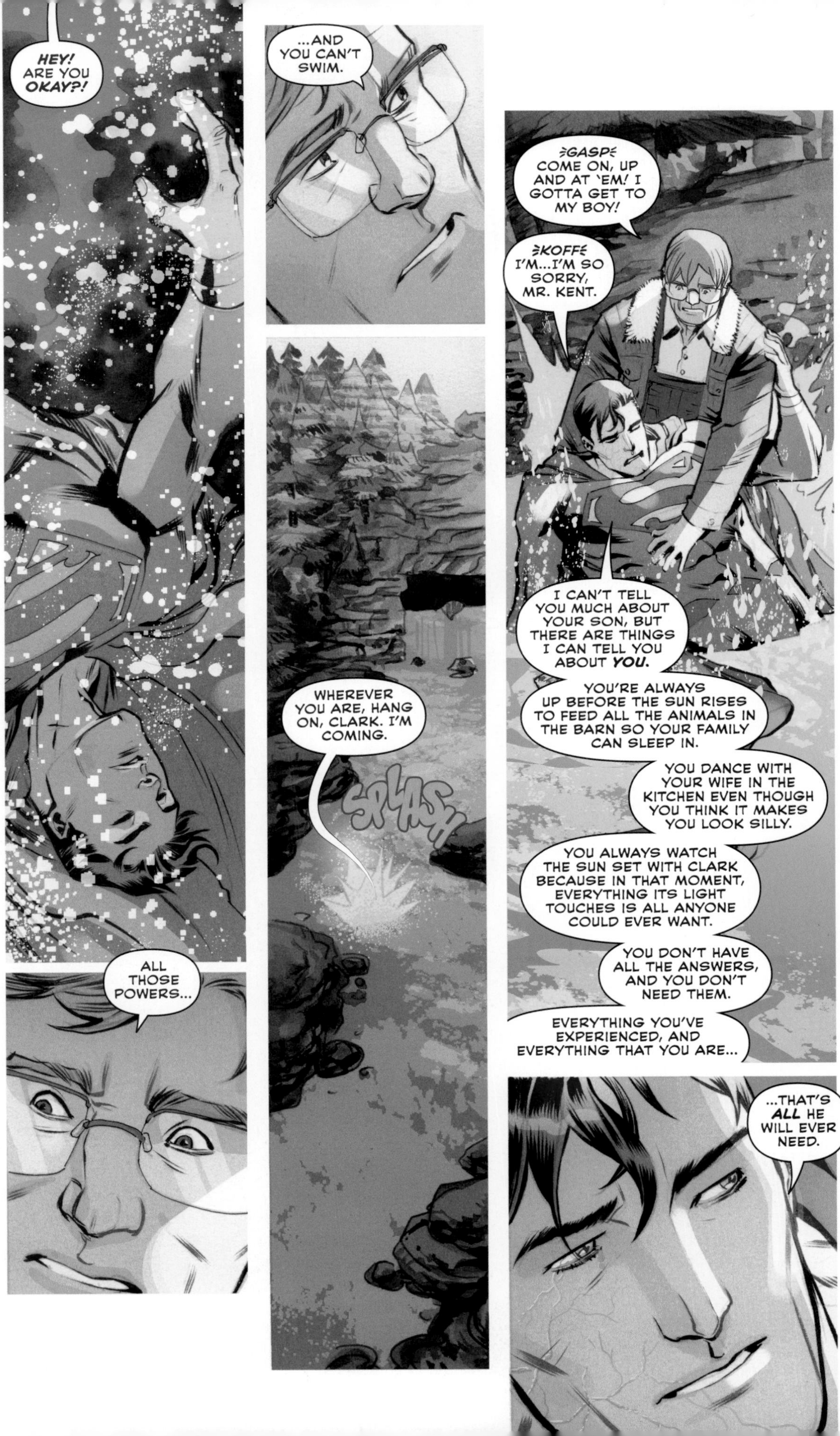

HEY! ARE YOU OKAY?!
ALL THOSE POWERS...
...AND YOU CAN'T SWIM.
WHEREVER YOU ARE, HANG ON, CLARK. I'M COMING.
SPLASH
GASP COME ON, UP AND AT 'EM! I GOTTA GET TO MY BOY!
KOFF I'M...I'M SO SORRY, MR. KENT.
I CAN'T TELL YOU MUCH ABOUT YOUR SON, BUT THERE ARE THINGS I CAN TELL YOU ABOUT YOU.
YOU'RE ALWAYS UP BEFORE THE SUN RISES TO FEED ALL THE ANIMALS IN THE BARN SO YOUR FAMILY CAN SLEEP IN.
YOU DANCE WITH YOUR WIFE IN THE KITCHEN EVEN THOUGH YOU THINK IT MAKES YOU LOOK SILLY.
YOU ALWAYS WATCH THE SUN SET WITH CLARK BECAUSE IN THAT MOMENT, EVERYTHING ITS LIGHT TOUCHES IS ALL ANYONE COULD EVER WANT.
YOU DON'T HAVE ALL THE ANSWERS, AND YOU DON'T NEED THEM.
EVERYTHING YOU'VE EXPERIENCED, AND EVERYTHING THAT YOU ARE...
...THAT'S ALL HE WILL EVER NEED.

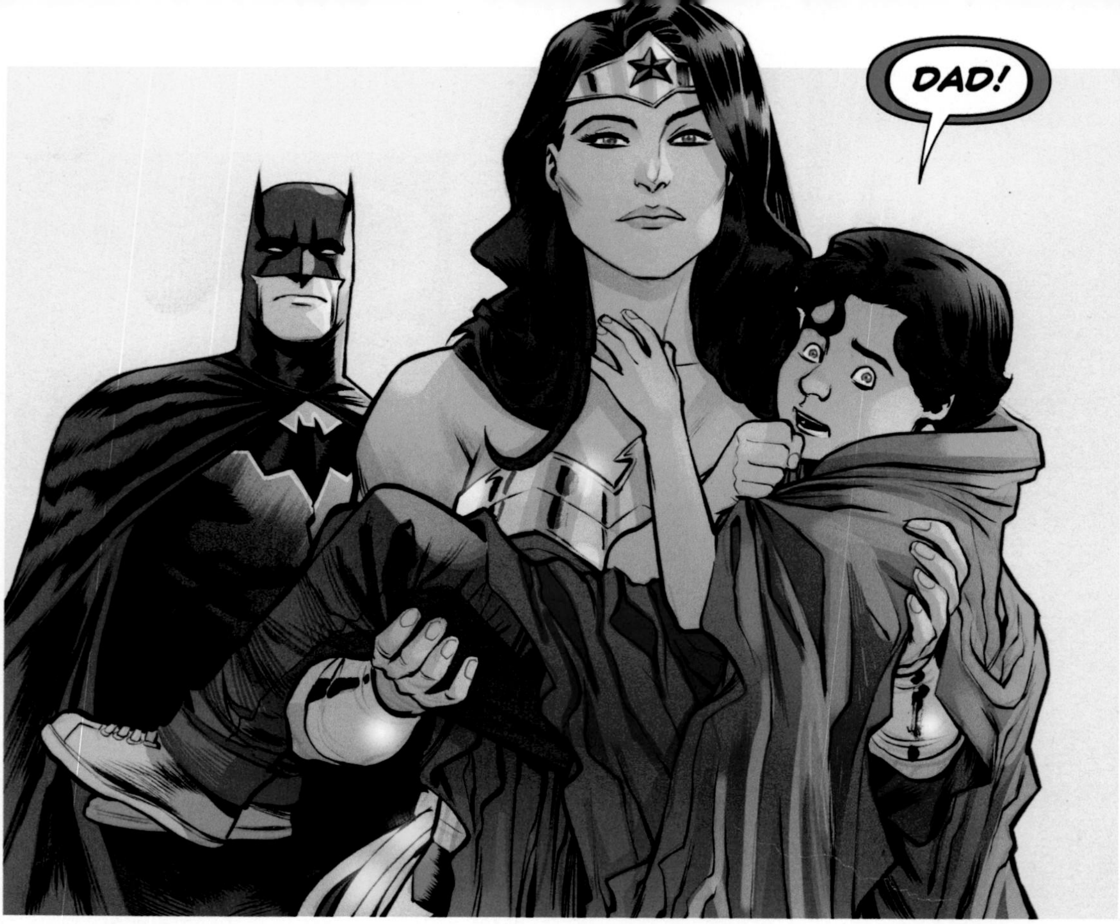
DAD!

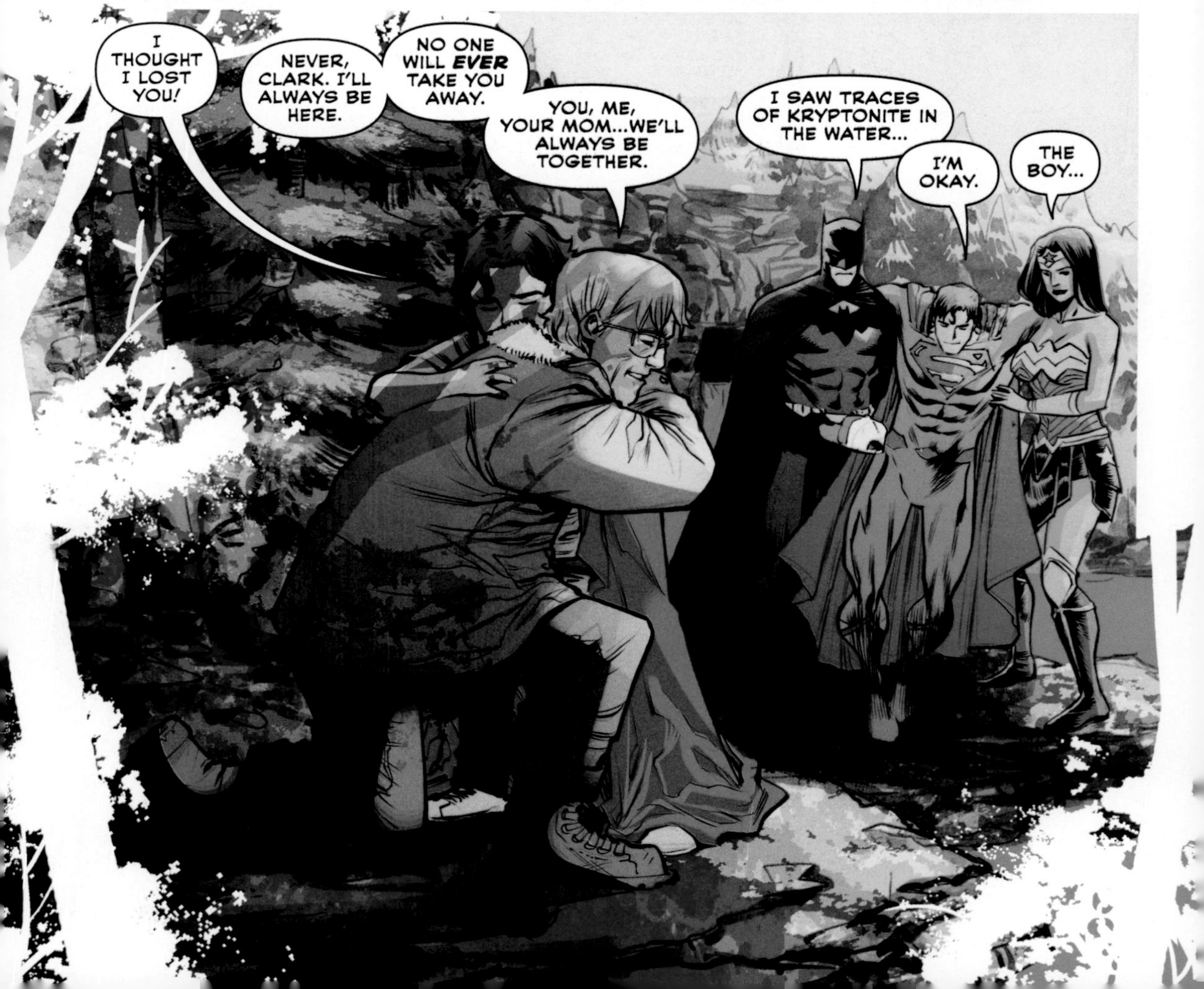
I THOUGHT I LOST YOU!
NEVER, CLARK. I'LL ALWAYS BE HERE.
NO ONE WILL EVER TAKE YOU AWAY.
YOU, ME, YOUR MOM...WE'LL ALWAYS BE TOGETHER.
I SAW TRACES OF KRYPTONITE IN THE WATER...
I'M OKAY.
THE BOY...

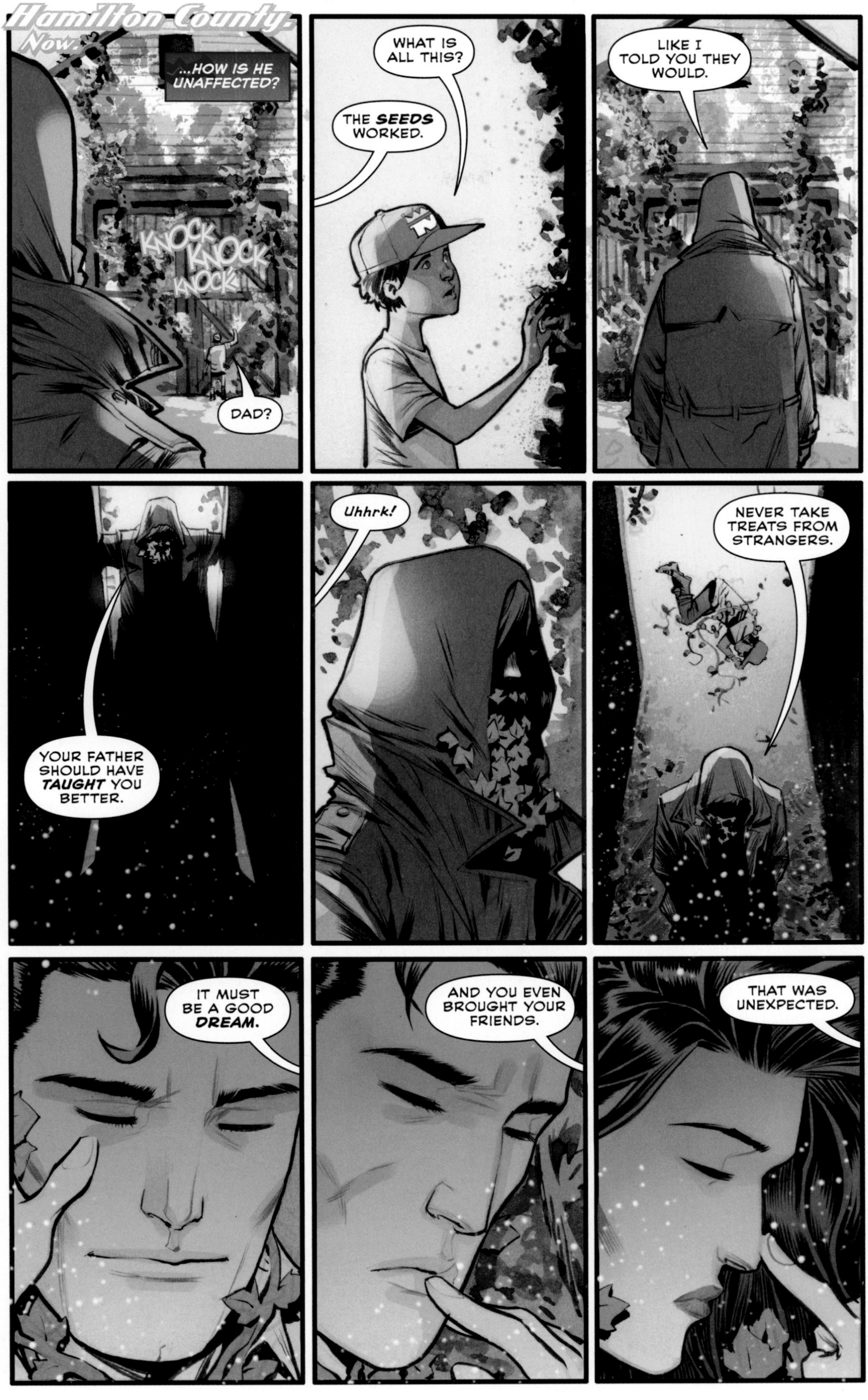

Hamilton County. Now.
...HOW IS HE UNAFFECTED?
KNOCK KNOCK KNOCK
DAD?
WHAT IS ALL THIS?
THE SEEDS WORKED.
LIKE I TOLD YOU THEY WOULD.
YOUR FATHER SHOULD HAVE TAUGHT YOU BETTER.
Uhhrk!
NEVER TAKE TREATS FROM STRANGERS.
IT MUST BE A GOOD DREAM.
AND YOU EVEN BROUGHT YOUR FRIENDS.
THAT WAS UNEXPECTED.

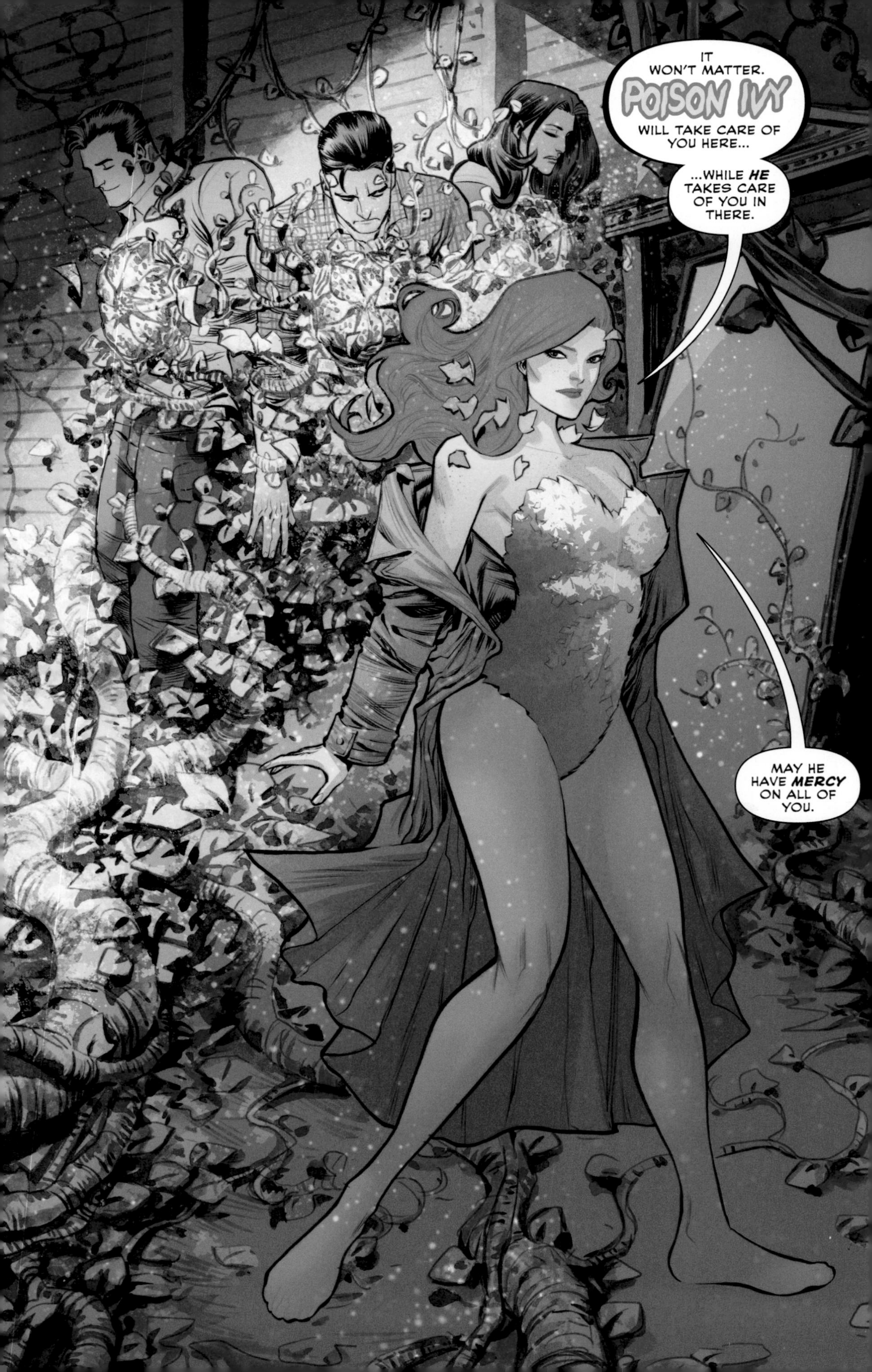
IT WON'T MATTER. POISON IVY WILL TAKE CARE OF YOU HERE...
...WHILE HE TAKES CARE OF YOU IN THERE.
MAY HE HAVE MERCY ON ALL OF YOU.

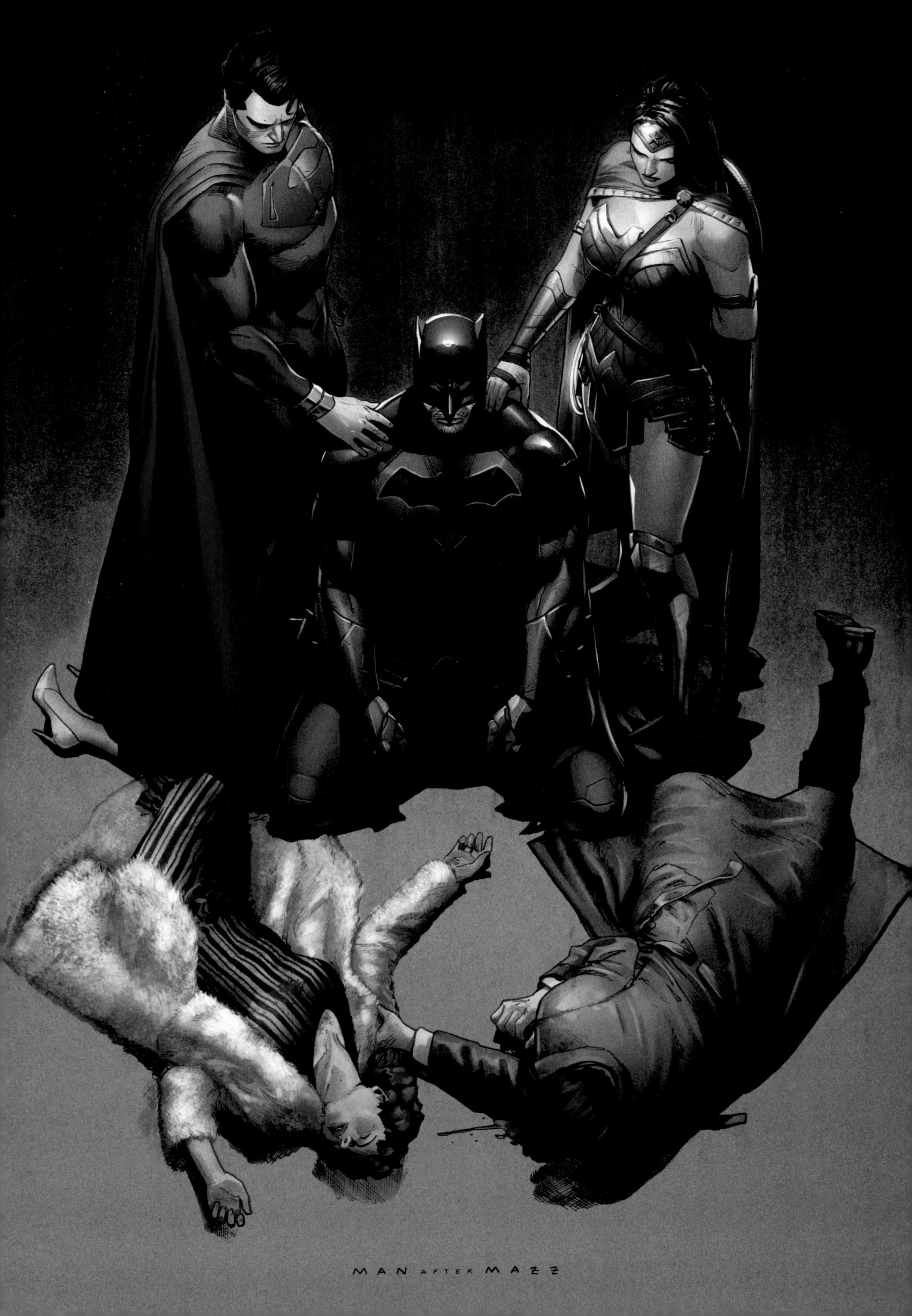
MAN AFTER MAZZ

BETTER TOGETHER Part Three: NOBODY DIES TONIGHT

CLAY MANN, SETH MANN artists * BRAD ANDERSON colorist

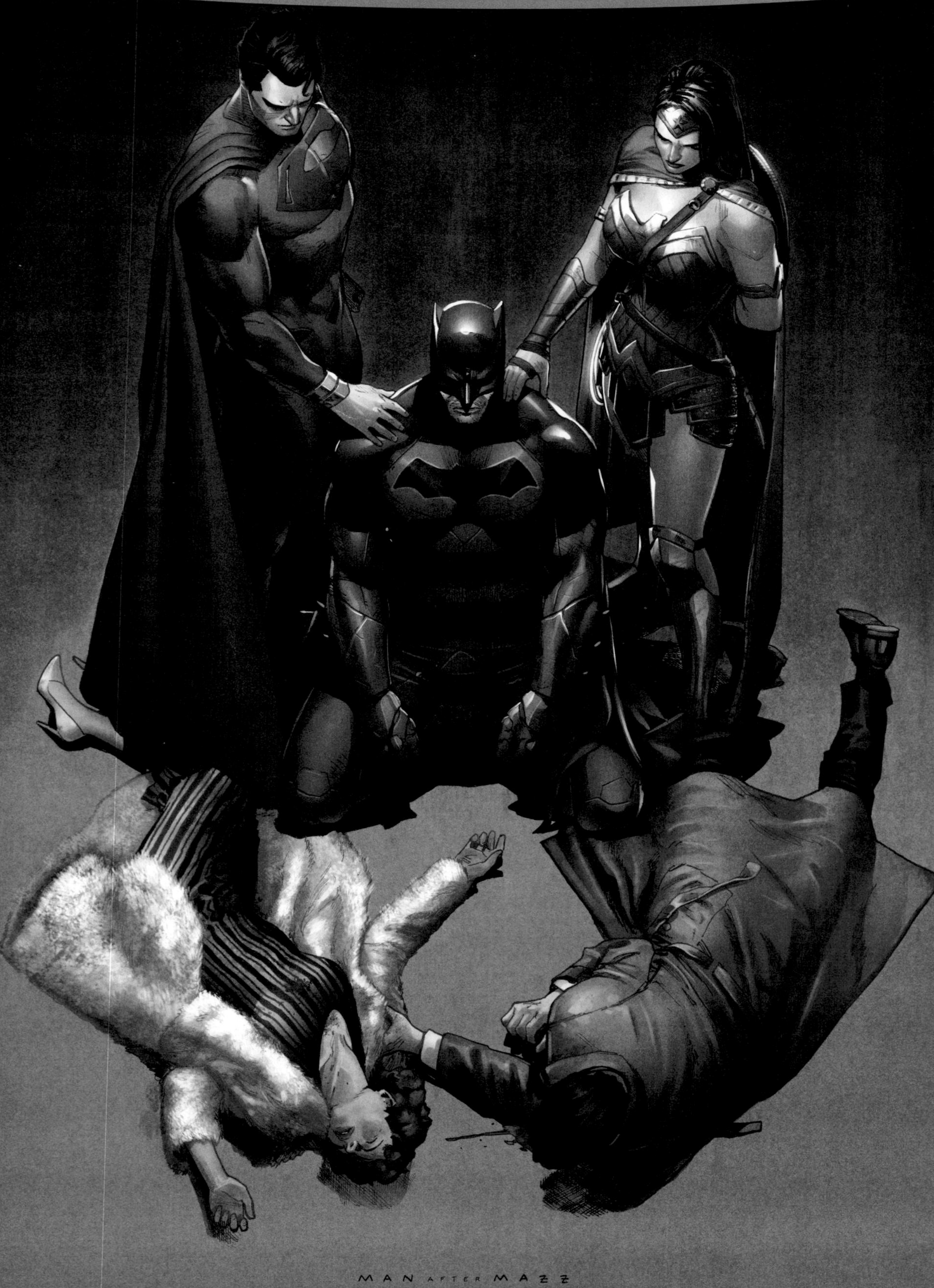
MAN AFTER MAZZ

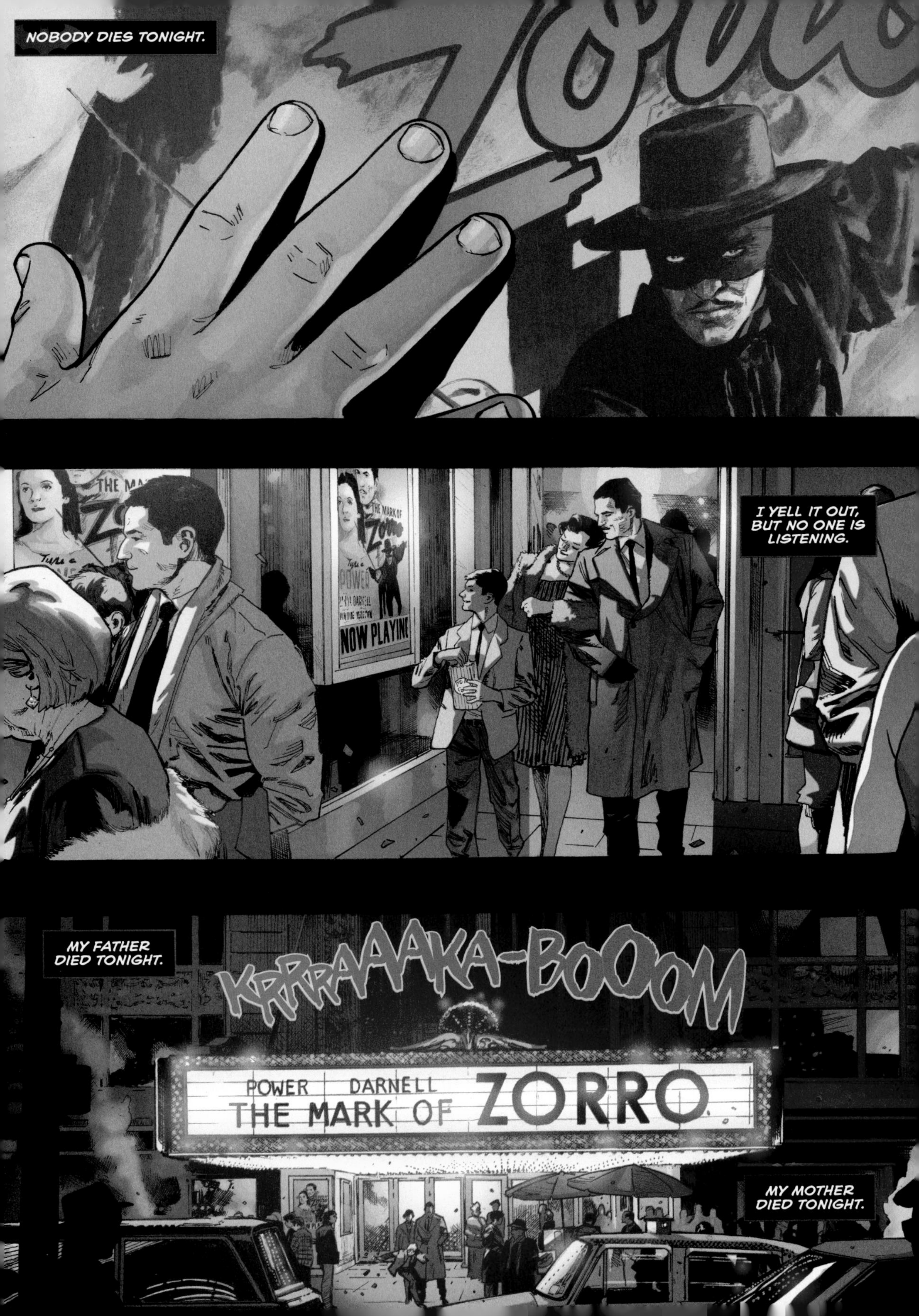
NOBODY DIES TONIGHT.
THE MARK OF ZORRO
POWER
NOW PLAYING
I YELL IT OUT, BUT NO ONE IS LISTENING.
MY FATHER DIED TONIGHT.
KRRRAAAAKA-BOOOOM
POWER DARNELL
THE MARK OF ZORRO
MY MOTHER DIED TONIGHT.

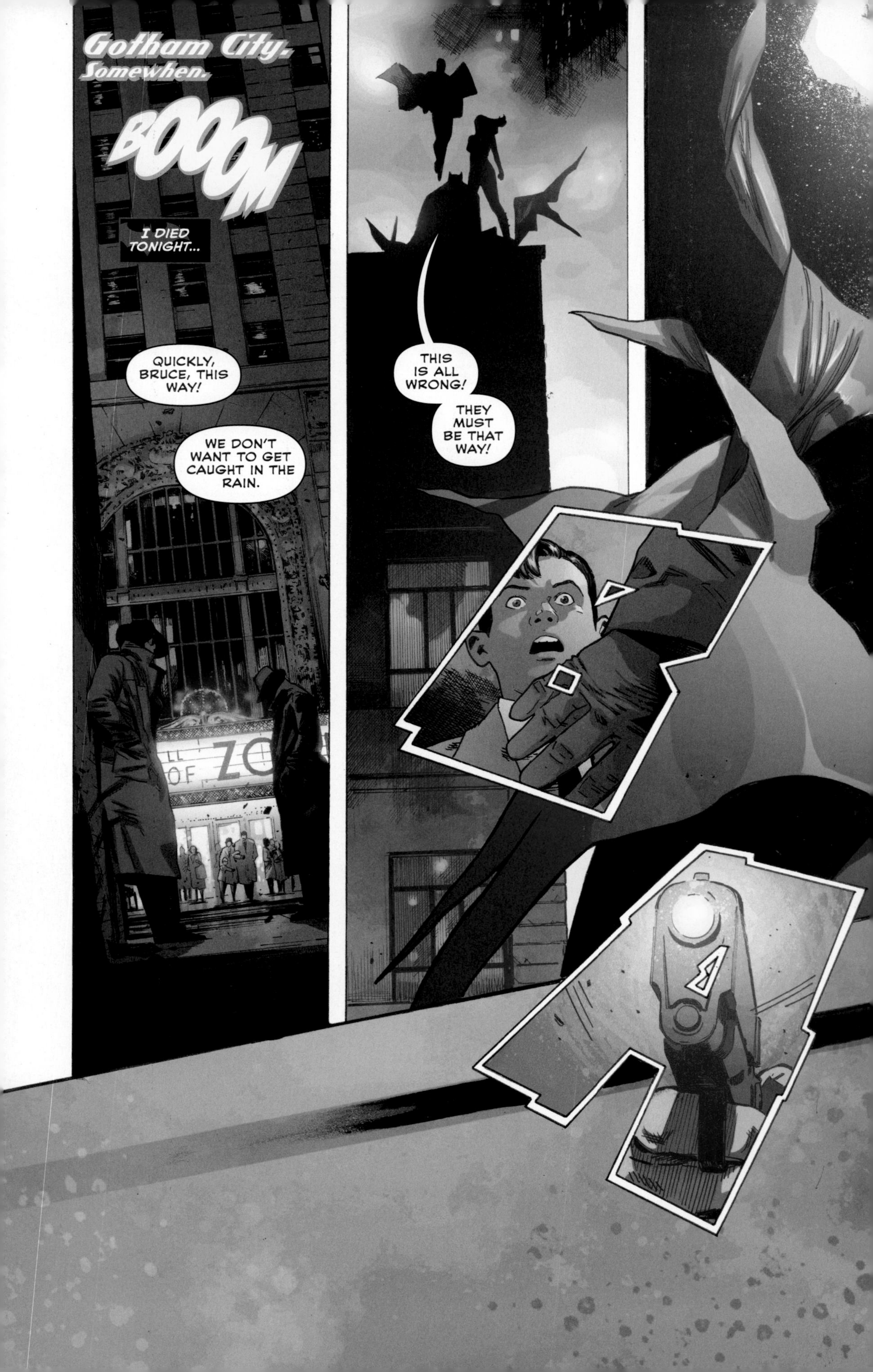
Gotham City. Somewhen.
BOOOM
I DIED TONIGHT...
QUICKLY, BRUCE, THIS WAY!
WE DON'T WANT TO GET CAUGHT IN THE RAIN.
THIS IS ALL WRONG!
THEY MUST BE THAT WAY!

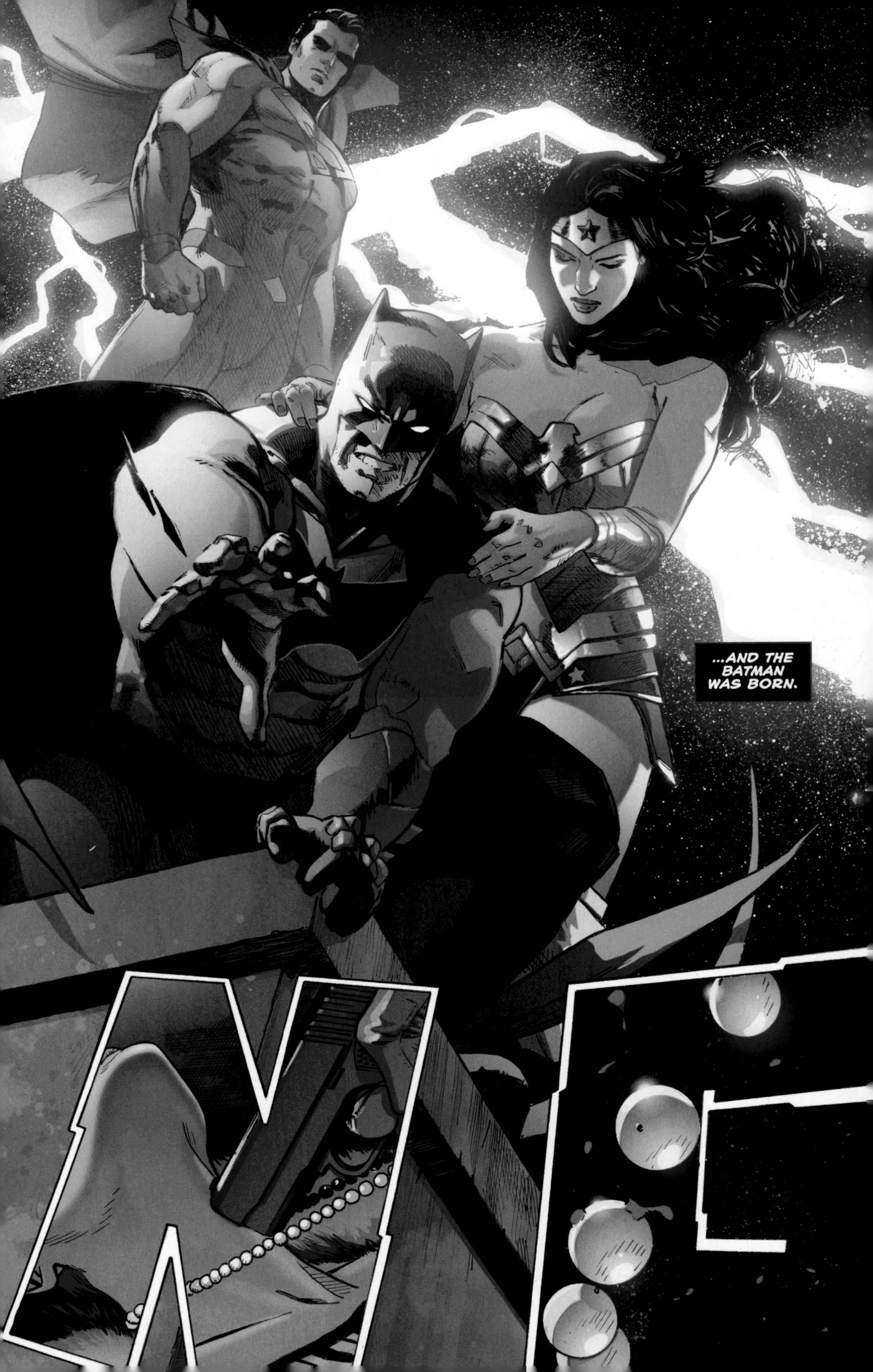
...AND THE BATMAN WAS BORN.

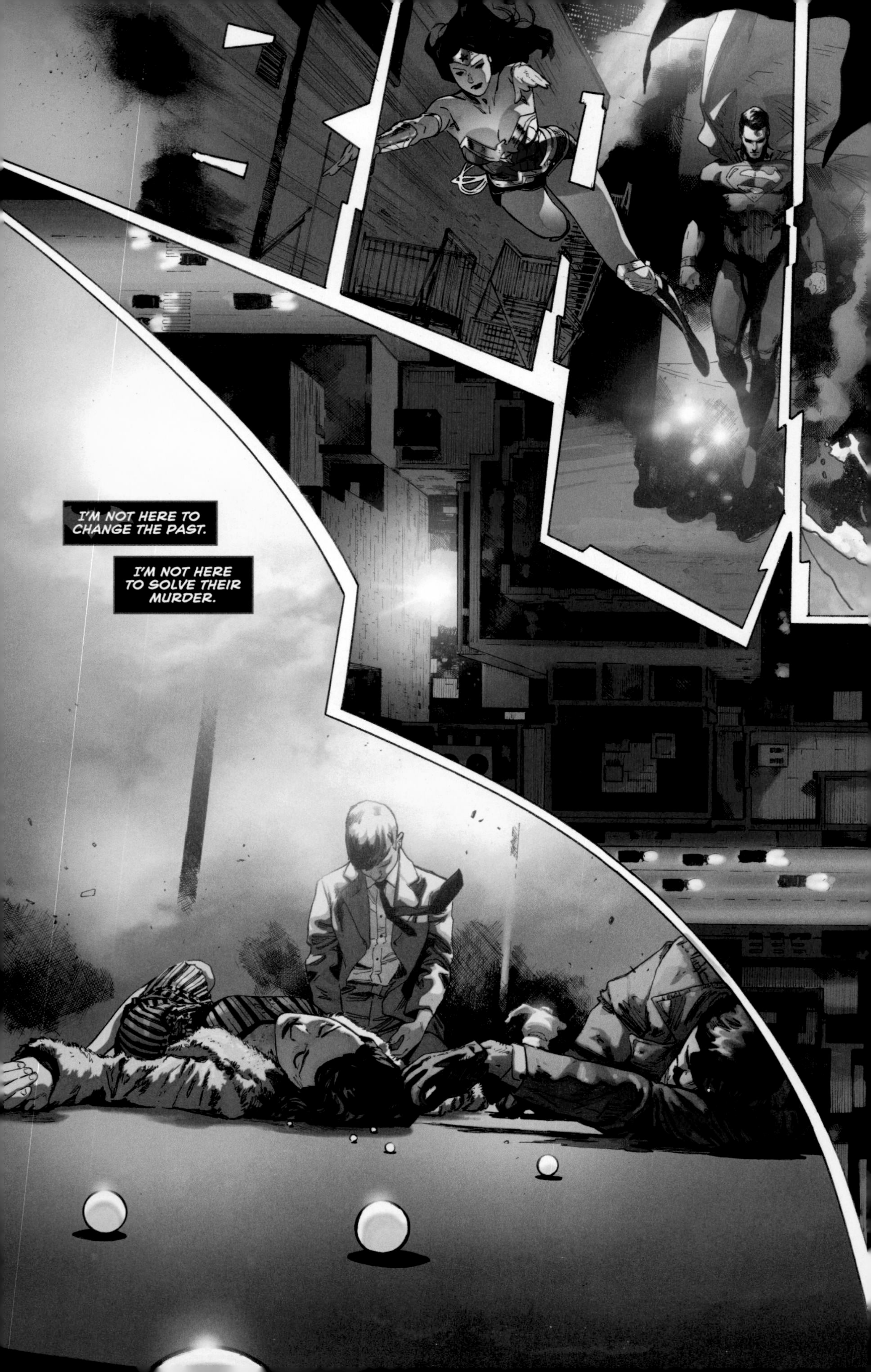
I'M NOT HERE TO CHANGE THE PAST.
I'M NOT HERE TO SOLVE THEIR MURDER.

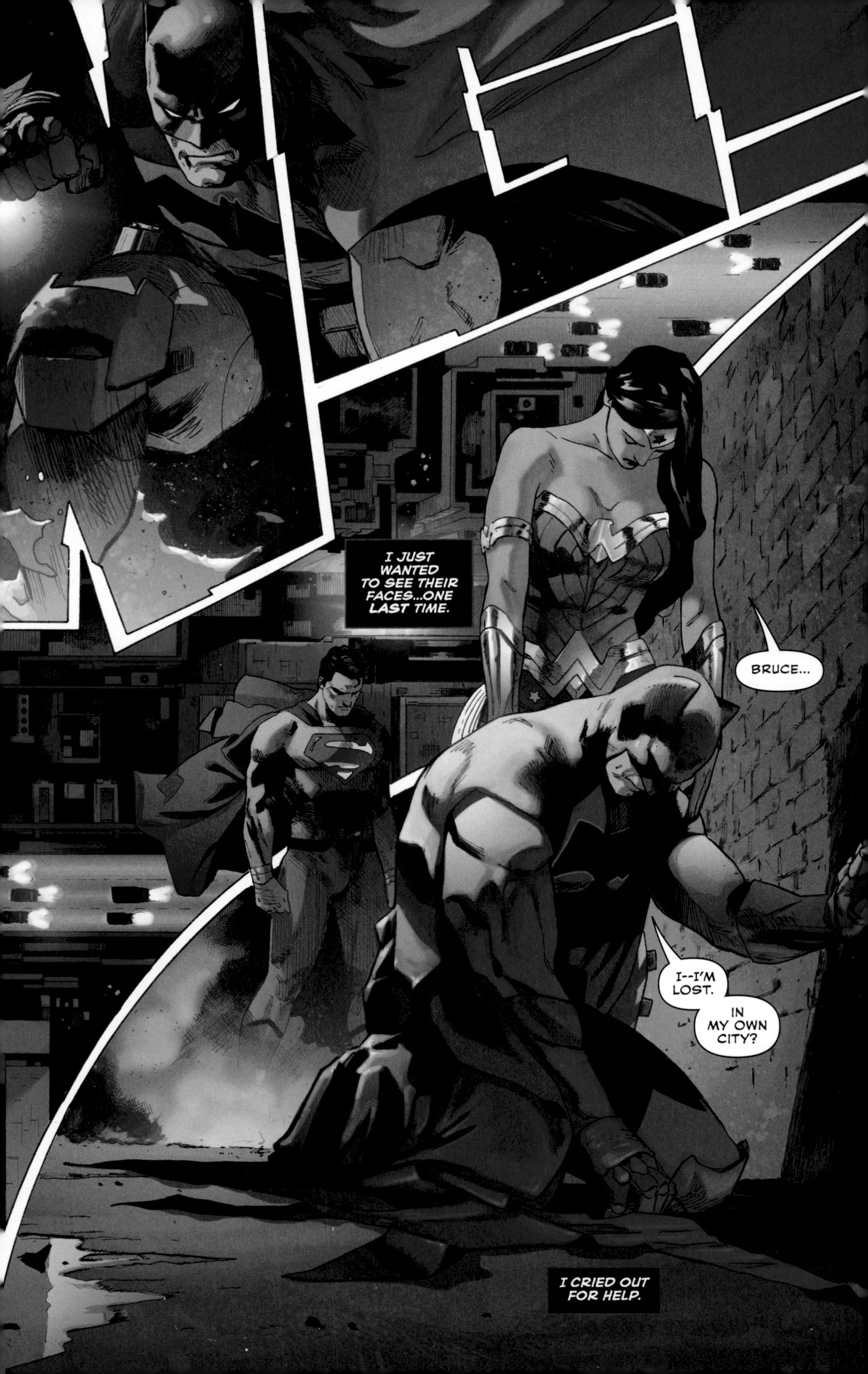
I JUST WANTED TO SEE THEIR FACES...ONE LAST TIME.
BRUCE...
I--I'M LOST.
IN MY OWN CITY?
I CRIED OUT FOR HELP.

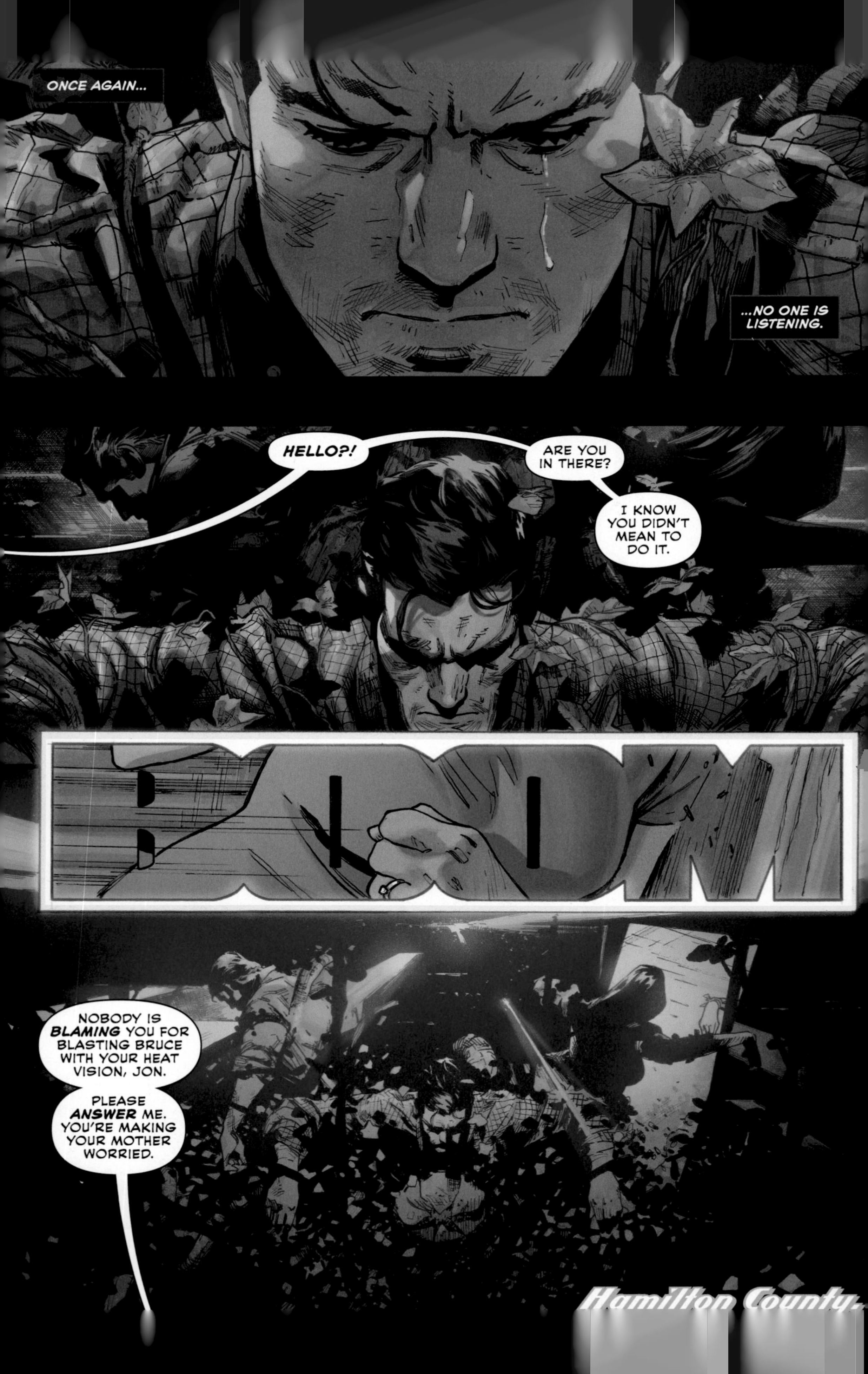
ONCE AGAIN...
...NO ONE IS LISTENING.
HELLO?!
ARE YOU IN THERE?
I KNOW YOU DIDN'T MEAN TO DO IT.
BOOM
NOBODY IS BLAMING YOU FOR BLASTING BRUCE WITH YOUR HEAT VISION, JON.
PLEASE ANSWER ME. YOU'RE MAKING YOUR MOTHER WORRIED.
Hamilton County.

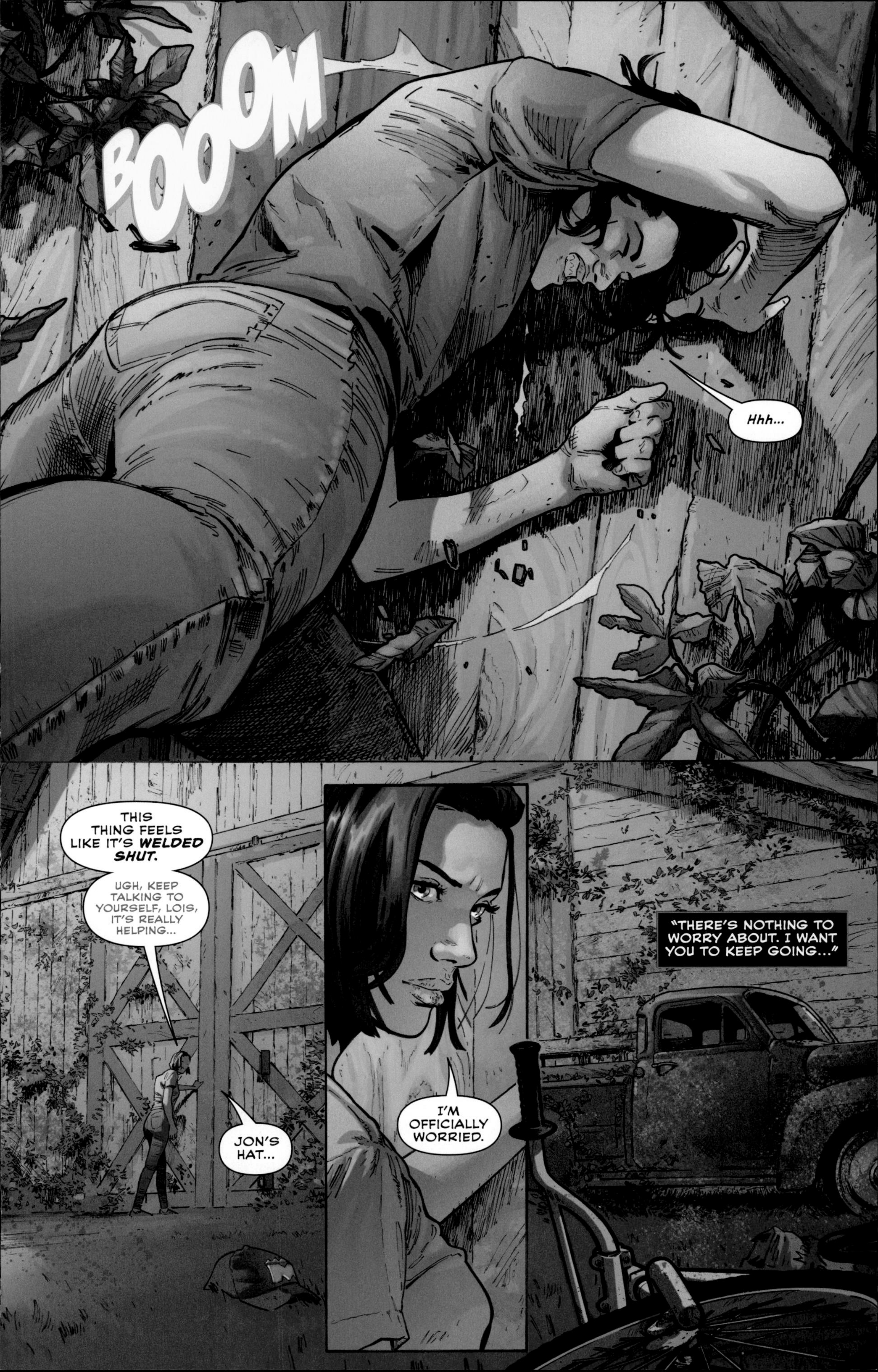
BOOOM
Hhh...
THIS THING FEELS LIKE IT'S *WELDED SHUT*.
UGH, KEEP TALKING TO YOURSELF, LOIS, IT'S REALLY HELPING...
JON'S HAT...
I'M OFFICIALLY WORRIED.
"THERE'S NOTHING TO WORRY ABOUT. I WANT YOU TO KEEP GOING..."

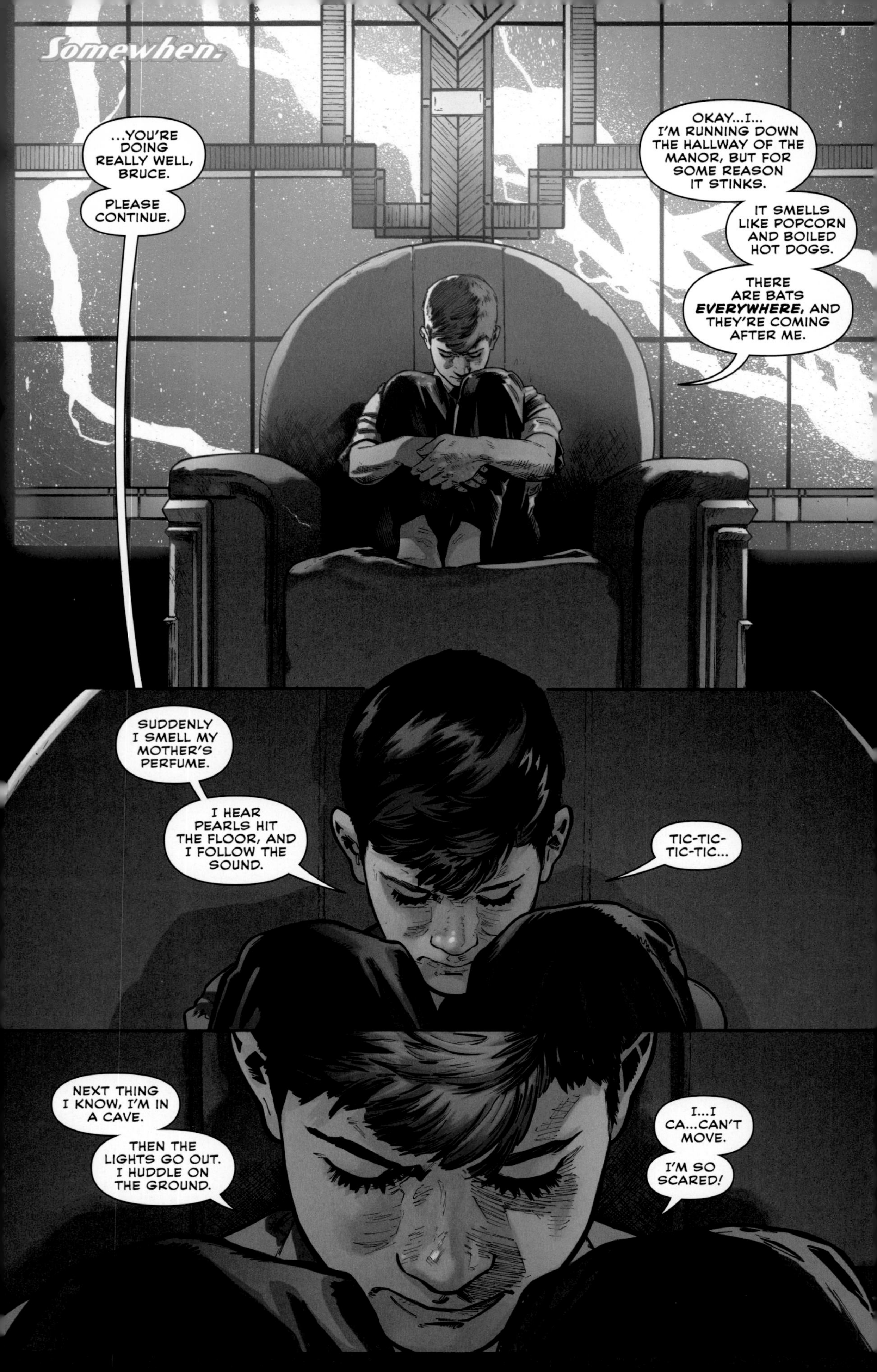
Somewhen.
...YOU'RE DOING REALLY WELL, BRUCE.
PLEASE CONTINUE.
OKAY...I... I'M RUNNING DOWN THE HALLWAY OF THE MANOR, BUT FOR SOME REASON IT STINKS.
IT SMELLS LIKE POPCORN AND BOILED HOT DOGS.
THERE ARE BATS EVERYWHERE, AND THEY'RE COMING AFTER ME.
SUDDENLY I SMELL MY MOTHER'S PERFUME.
I HEAR PEARLS HIT THE FLOOR, AND I FOLLOW THE SOUND.
TIC-TIC-TIC-TIC...
NEXT THING I KNOW, I'M IN A CAVE.
THEN THE LIGHTS GO OUT. I HUDDLE ON THE GROUND.
I...I CA...CAN'T MOVE.
I'M SO SCARED!

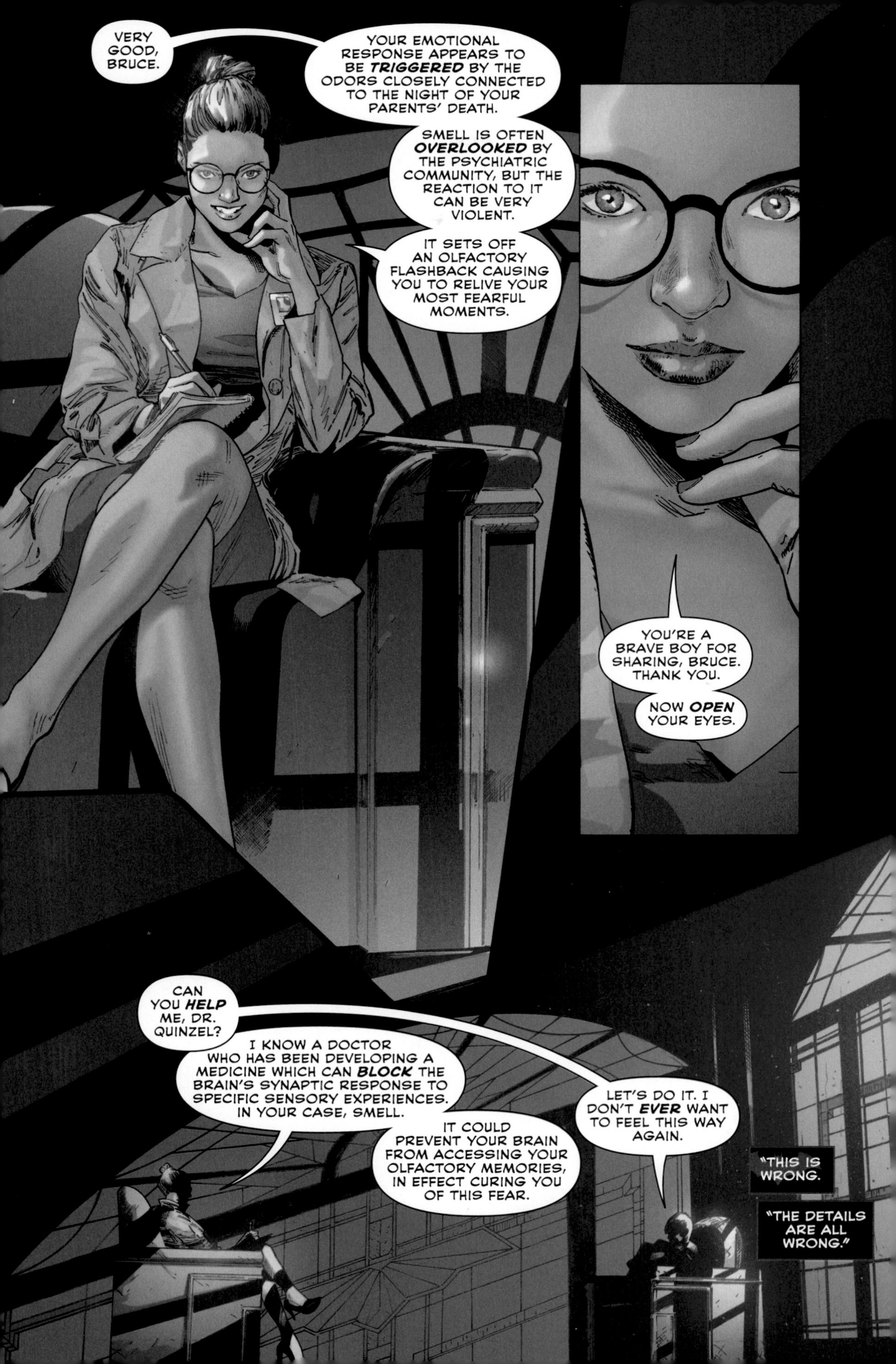
VERY GOOD, BRUCE.
YOUR EMOTIONAL RESPONSE APPEARS TO BE TRIGGERED BY THE ODORS CLOSELY CONNECTED TO THE NIGHT OF YOUR PARENTS' DEATH.
SMELL IS OFTEN OVERLOOKED BY THE PSYCHIATRIC COMMUNITY, BUT THE REACTION TO IT CAN BE VERY VIOLENT.
IT SETS OFF AN OLFACTORY FLASHBACK CAUSING YOU TO RELIVE YOUR MOST FEARFUL MOMENTS.
YOU'RE A BRAVE BOY FOR SHARING, BRUCE. THANK YOU.
NOW OPEN YOUR EYES.
CAN YOU HELP ME, DR. QUINZEL?
I KNOW A DOCTOR WHO HAS BEEN DEVELOPING A MEDICINE WHICH CAN BLOCK THE BRAIN'S SYNAPTIC RESPONSE TO SPECIFIC SENSORY EXPERIENCES. IN YOUR CASE, SMELL.
IT COULD PREVENT YOUR BRAIN FROM ACCESSING YOUR OLFACTORY MEMORIES, IN EFFECT CURING YOU OF THIS FEAR.
LET'S DO IT. I DON'T EVER WANT TO FEEL THIS WAY AGAIN.
"THIS IS WRONG.
"THE DETAILS ARE ALL WRONG."

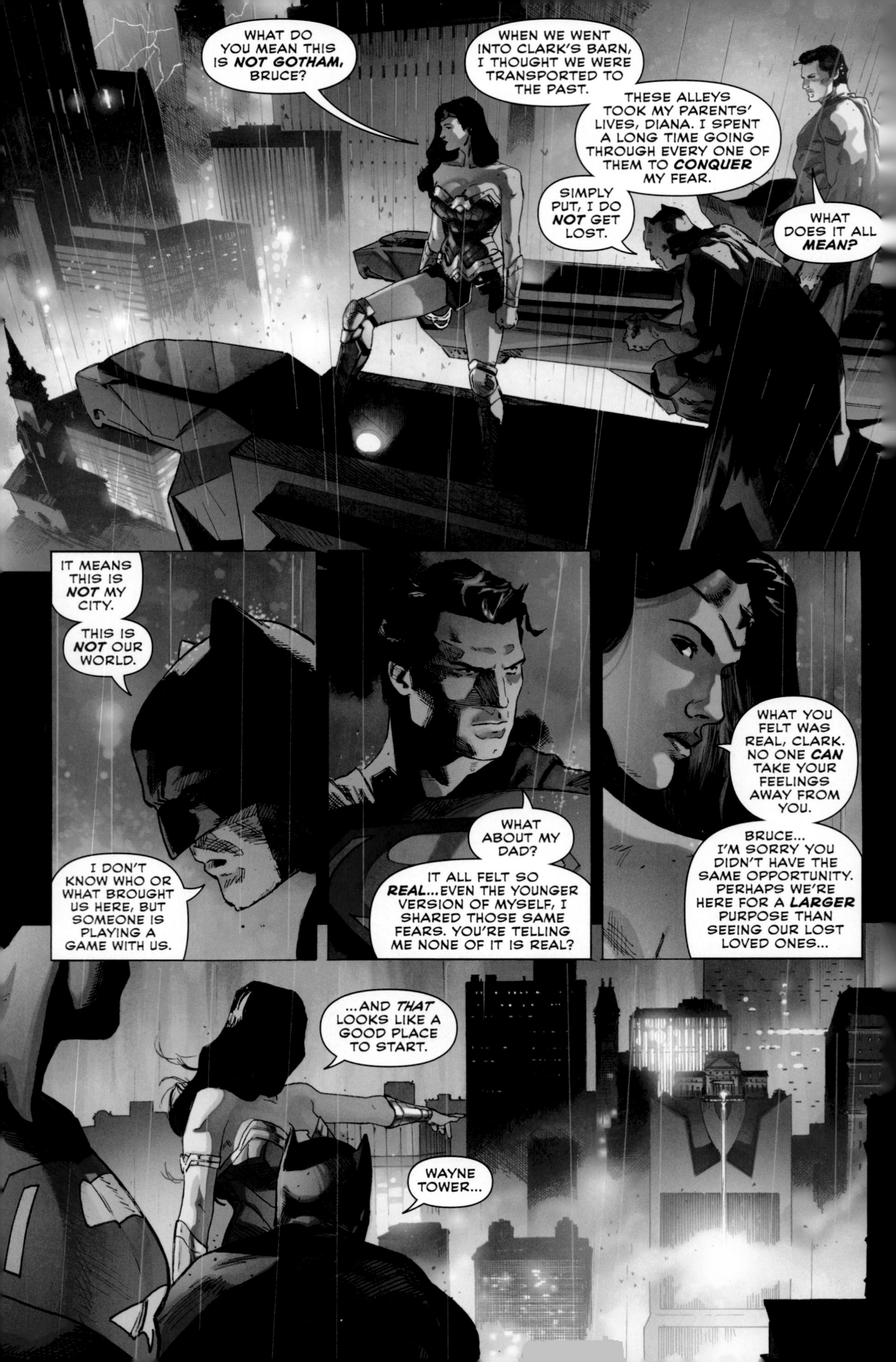
WHAT DO YOU MEAN THIS IS NOT GOTHAM, BRUCE?
WHEN WE WENT INTO CLARK'S BARN, I THOUGHT WE WERE TRANSPORTED TO THE PAST.
THESE ALLEYS TOOK MY PARENTS' LIVES, DIANA. I SPENT A LONG TIME GOING THROUGH EVERY ONE OF THEM TO CONQUER MY FEAR.
SIMPLY PUT, I DO NOT GET LOST.
WHAT DOES IT ALL MEAN?
IT MEANS THIS IS NOT MY CITY.
THIS IS NOT OUR WORLD.
I DON'T KNOW WHO OR WHAT BROUGHT US HERE, BUT SOMEONE IS PLAYING A GAME WITH US.
WHAT ABOUT MY DAD?
IT ALL FELT SO REAL...EVEN THE YOUNGER VERSION OF MYSELF, I SHARED THOSE SAME FEARS. YOU'RE TELLING ME NONE OF IT IS REAL?
WHAT YOU FELT WAS REAL, CLARK. NO ONE CAN TAKE YOUR FEELINGS AWAY FROM YOU.
BRUCE... I'M SORRY YOU DIDN'T HAVE THE SAME OPPORTUNITY. PERHAPS WE'RE HERE FOR A LARGER PURPOSE THAN SEEING OUR LOST LOVED ONES...
...AND THAT LOOKS LIKE A GOOD PLACE TO START.
WAYNE TOWER...

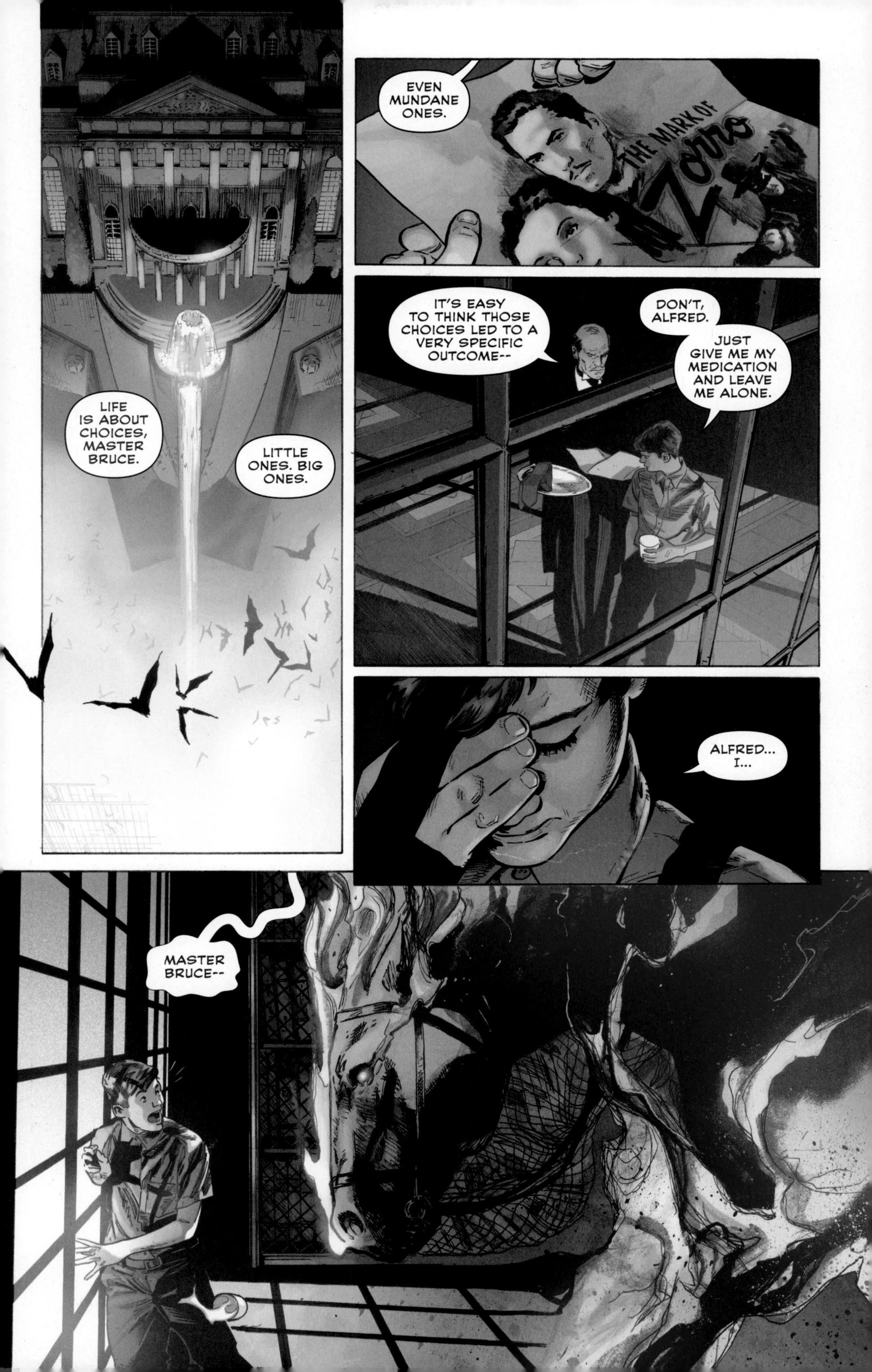
LIFE IS ABOUT CHOICES, MASTER BRUCE.
LITTLE ONES. BIG ONES.
EVEN MUNDANE ONES.
THE MARK OF Zorro
IT'S EASY TO THINK THOSE CHOICES LED TO A VERY SPECIFIC OUTCOME--
DON'T, ALFRED.
JUST GIVE ME MY MEDICATION AND LEAVE ME ALONE.
ALFRED... I...
MASTER BRUCE--

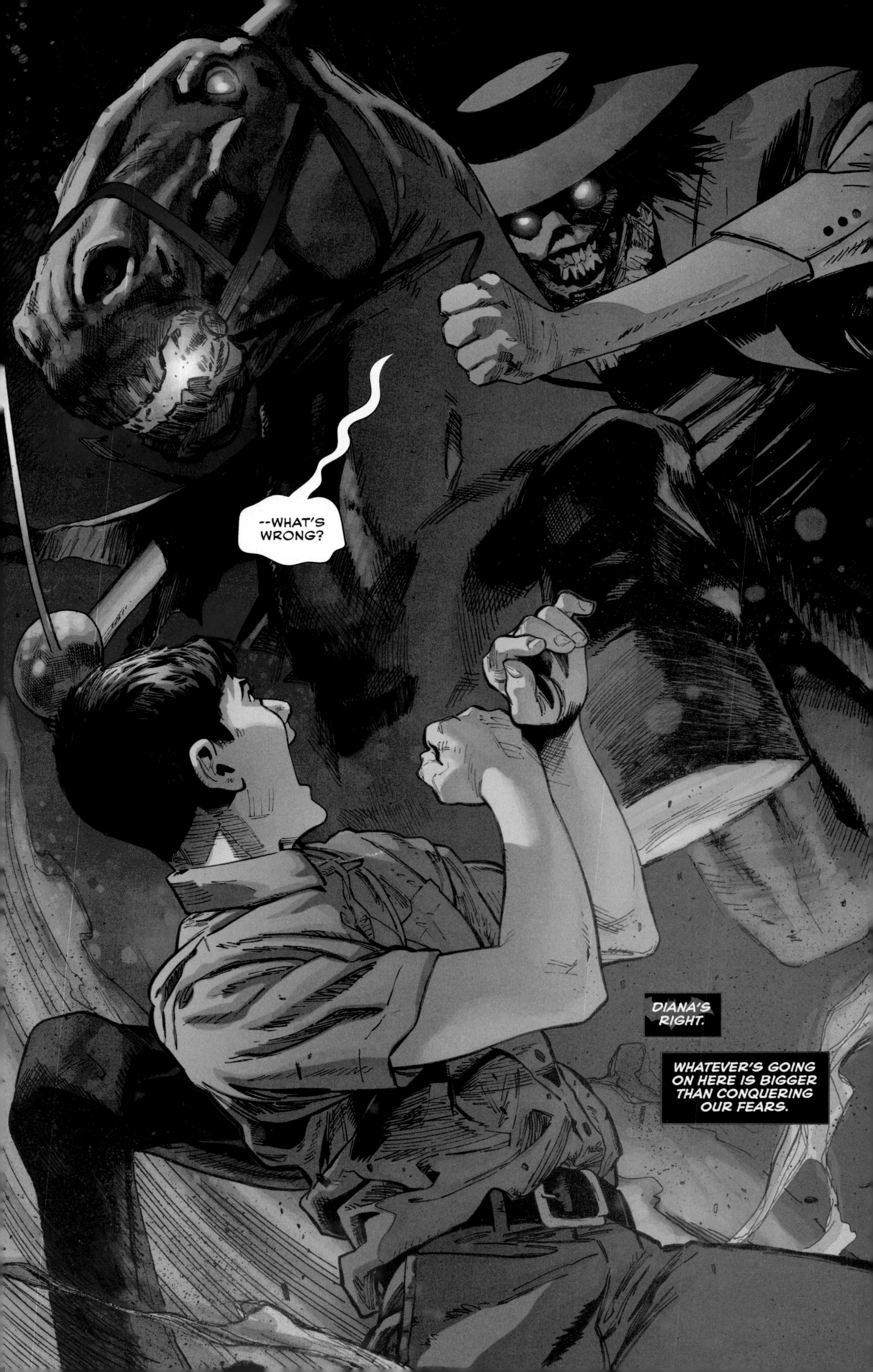
--WHAT'S WRONG?
DIANA'S RIGHT.
WHATEVER'S GOING ON HERE IS BIGGER THAN CONQUERING OUR FEARS.

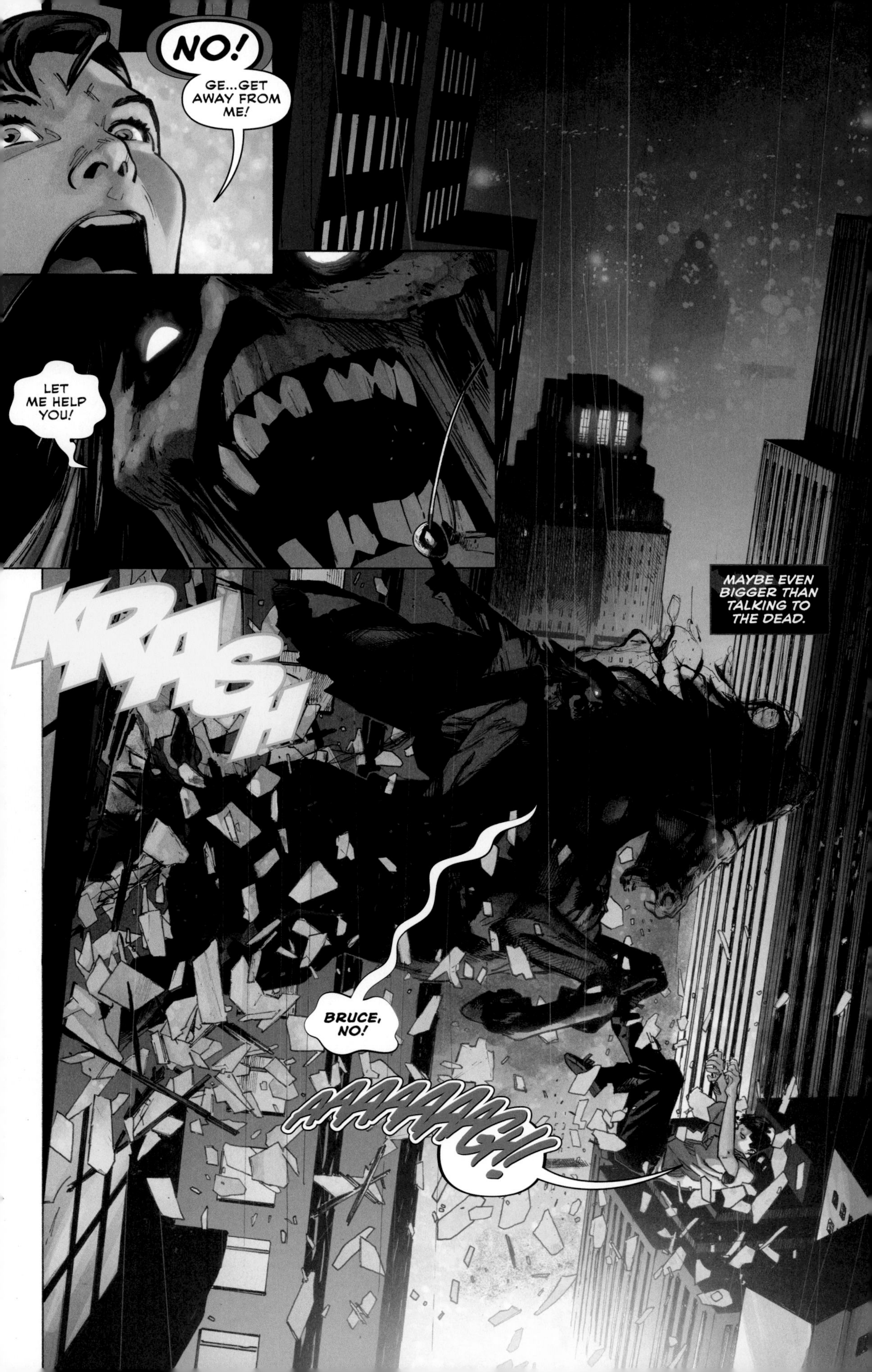
NO!
GE...GET AWAY FROM ME!
LET ME HELP YOU!
KRASH
MAYBE EVEN BIGGER THAN TALKING TO THE DEAD.
BRUCE, NO!
AAAAAAAGH!!

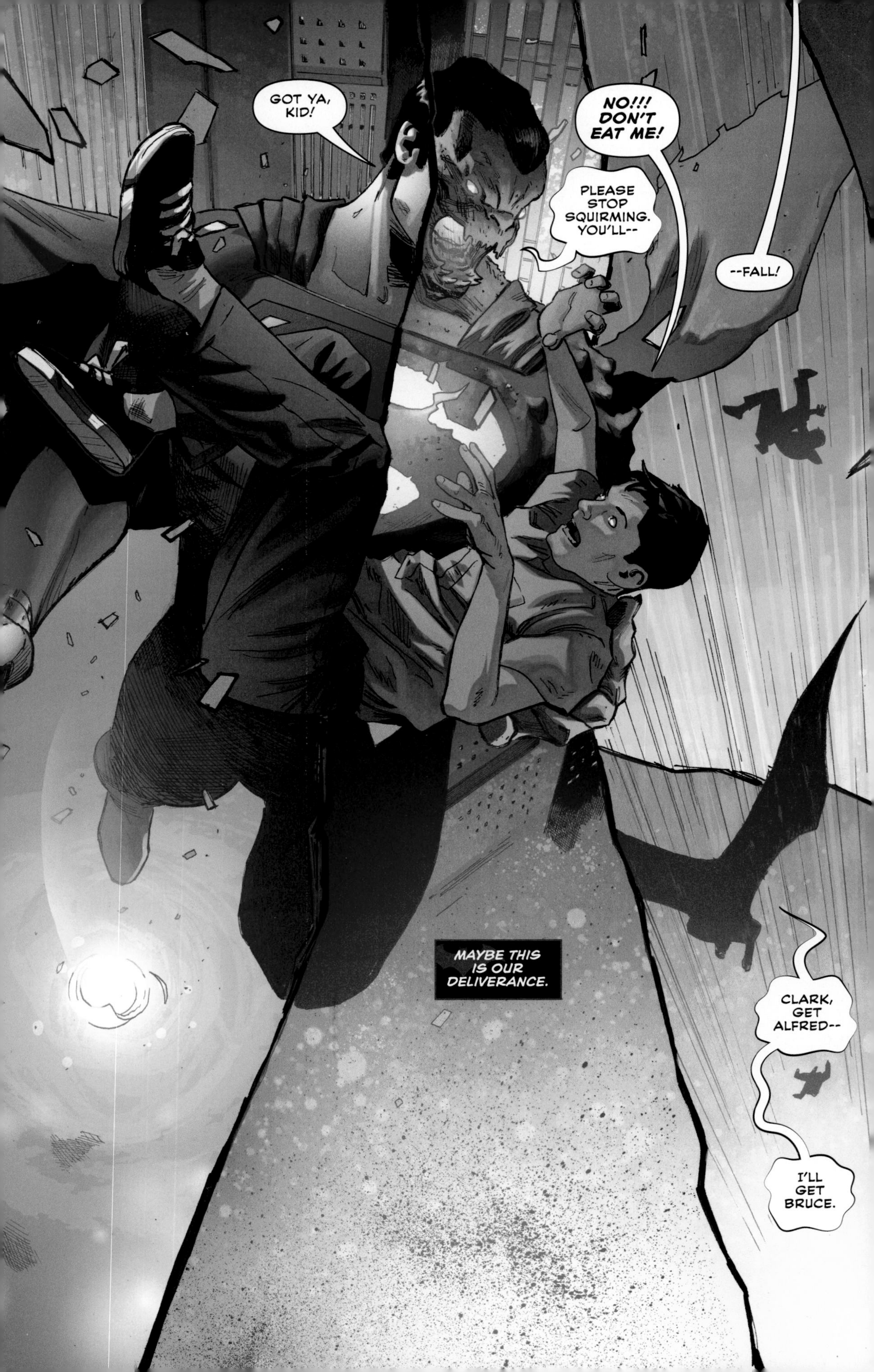
GOT YA, KID!
NO!!! DON'T EAT ME!
PLEASE STOP SQUIRMING. YOU'LL--
--FALL!
MAYBE THIS IS OUR DELIVERANCE.
CLARK, GET ALFRED--
I'LL GET BRUCE.

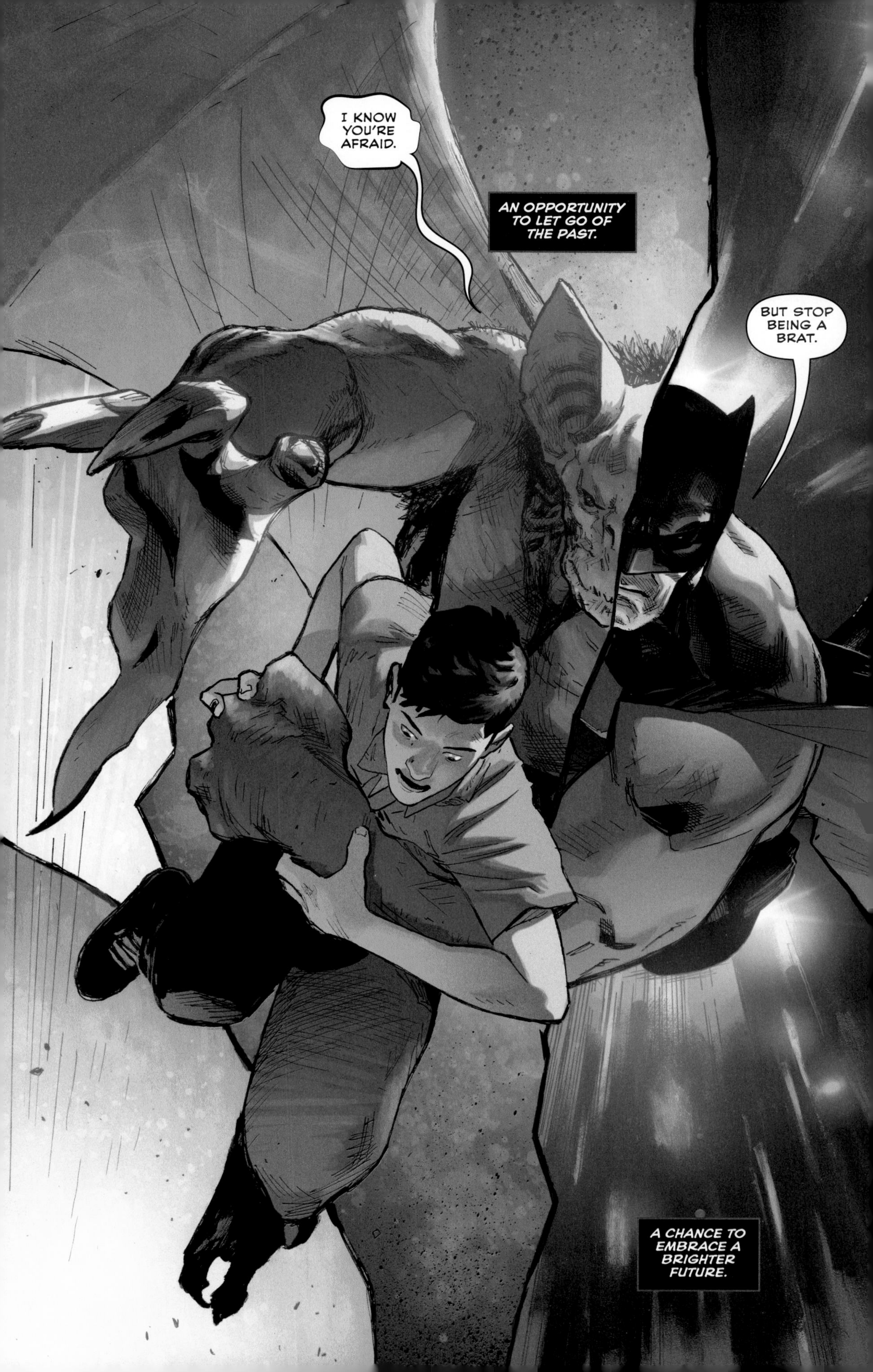

I KNOW YOU'RE AFRAID.
AN OPPORTUNITY TO LET GO OF THE PAST.
BUT STOP BEING A BRAT.
A CHANCE TO EMBRACE A BRIGHTER FUTURE.

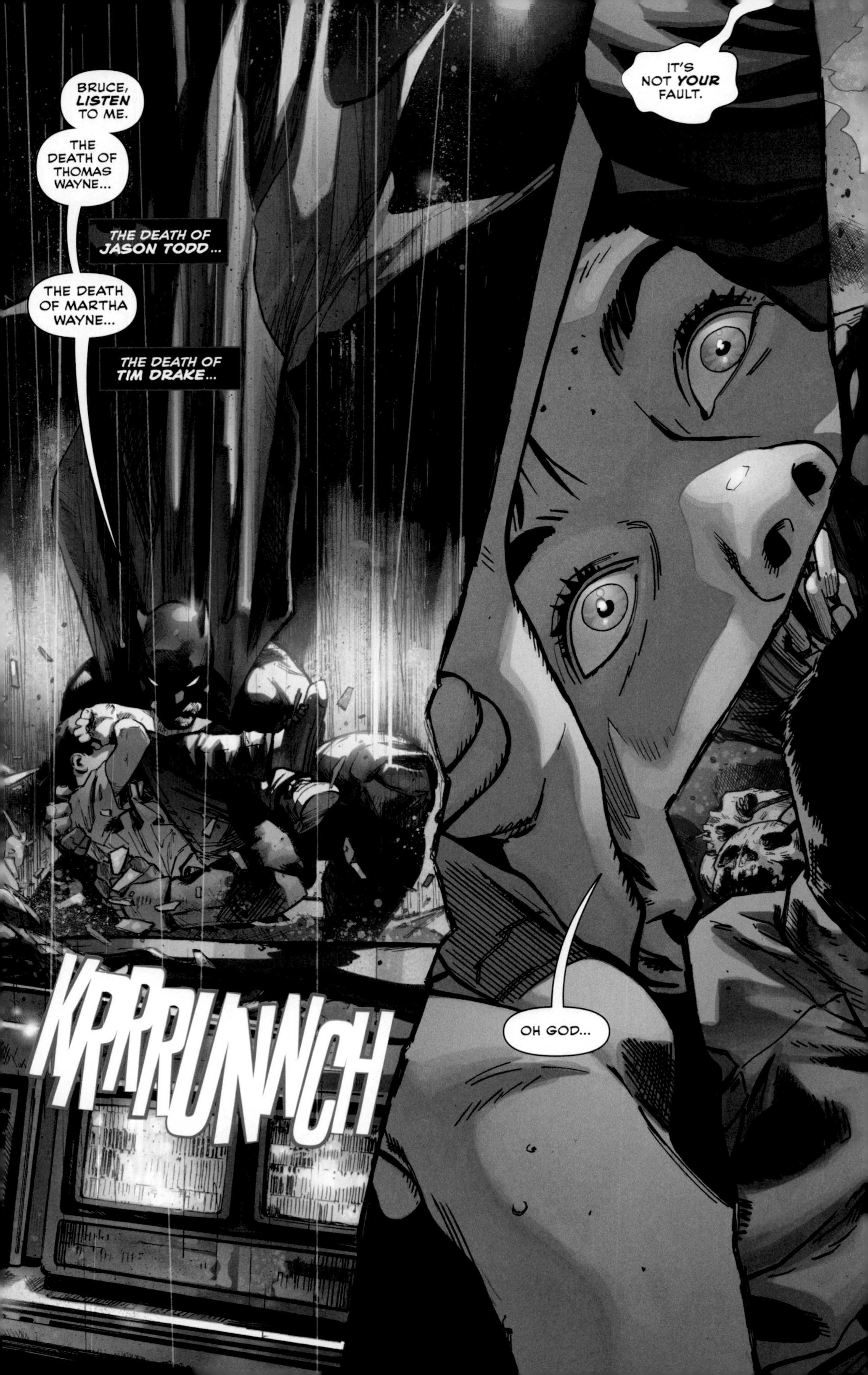
BRUCE, LISTEN TO ME.
THE DEATH OF THOMAS WAYNE...
THE DEATH OF JASON TODD...
THE DEATH OF MARTHA WAYNE...
THE DEATH OF TIM DRAKE...
IT'S NOT YOUR FAULT.
KRRRUNNCH
OH GOD...

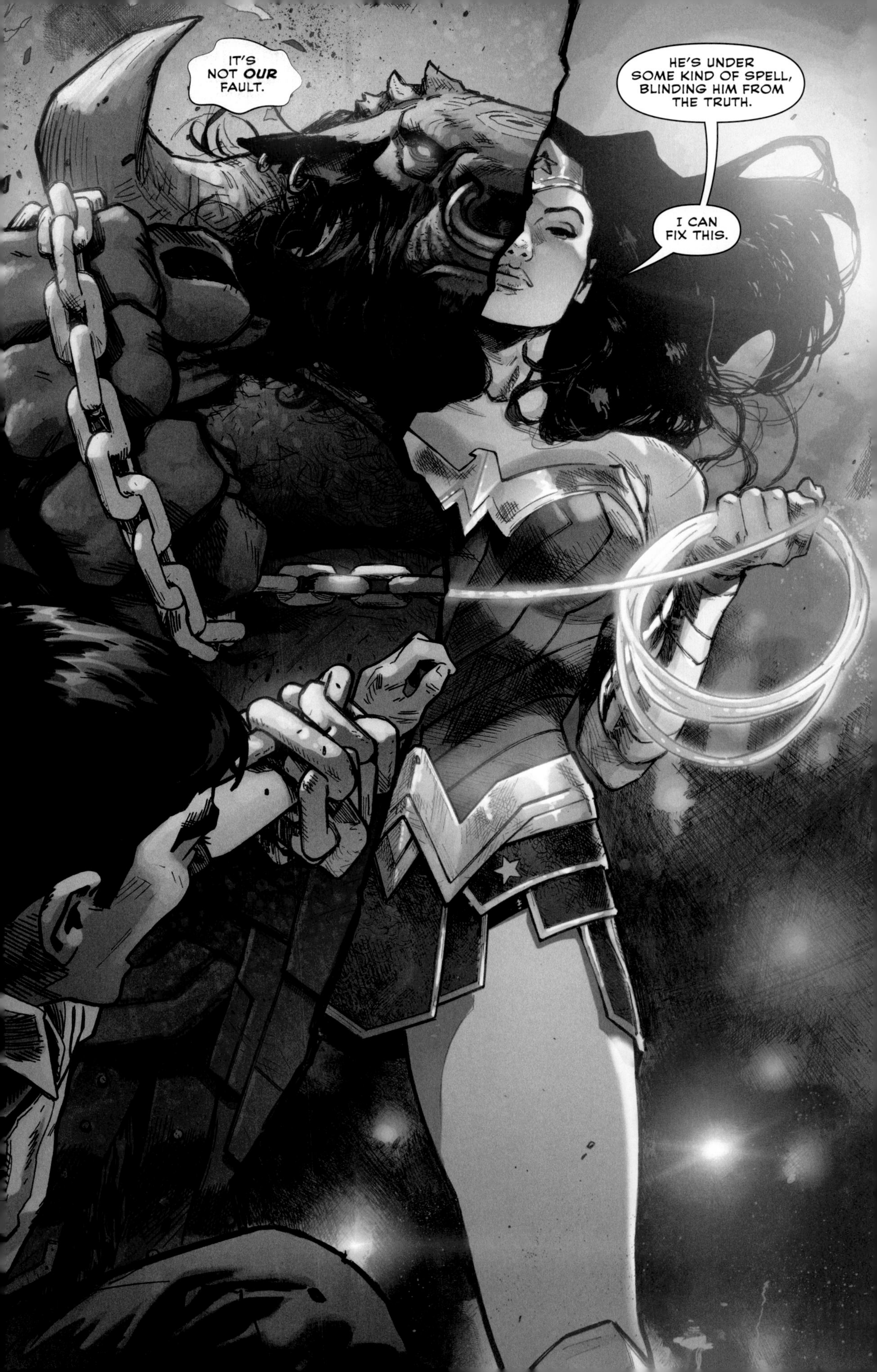
IT'S NOT OUR FAULT.
HE'S UNDER SOME KIND OF SPELL, BLINDING HIM FROM THE TRUTH.
I CAN FIX THIS.

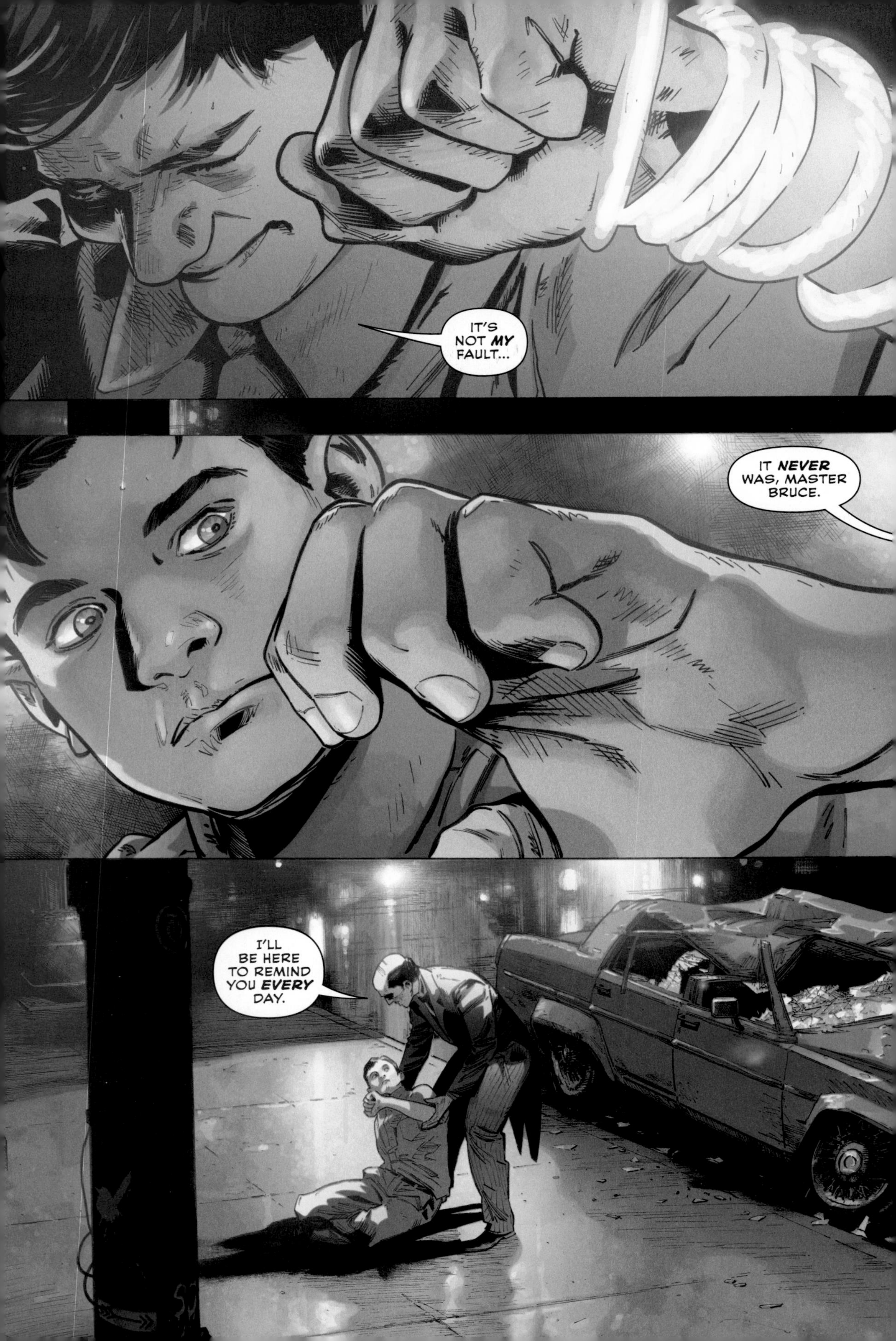
IT'S NOT MY FAULT...
IT NEVER WAS, MASTER BRUCE.
I'LL BE HERE TO REMIND YOU EVERY DAY.

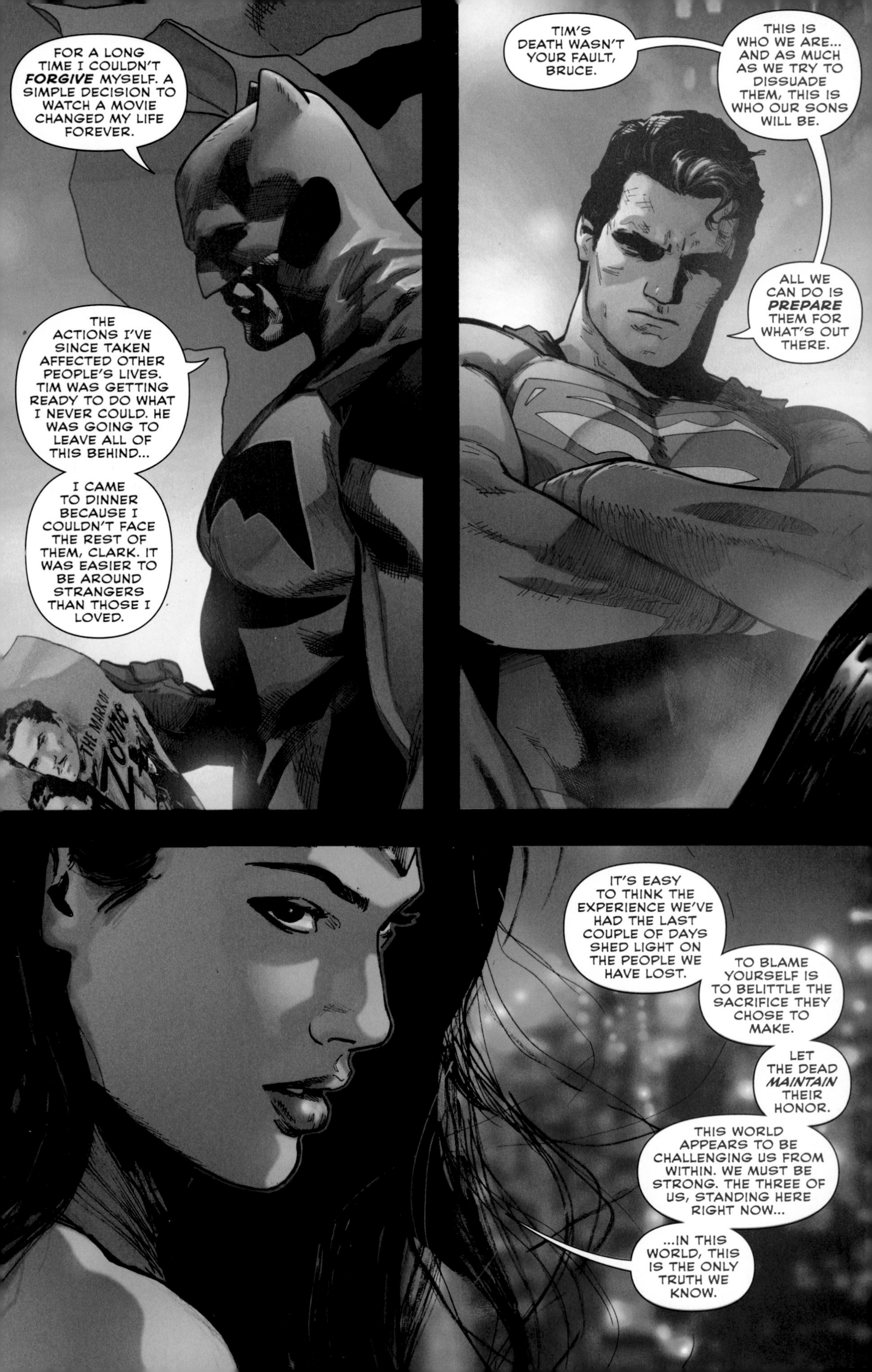
FOR A LONG TIME I COULDN'T FORGIVE MYSELF. A SIMPLE DECISION TO WATCH A MOVIE CHANGED MY LIFE FOREVER.
THE ACTIONS I'VE SINCE TAKEN AFFECTED OTHER PEOPLE'S LIVES. TIM WAS GETTING READY TO DO WHAT I NEVER COULD. HE WAS GOING TO LEAVE ALL OF THIS BEHIND...
I CAME TO DINNER BECAUSE I COULDN'T FACE THE REST OF THEM, CLARK. IT WAS EASIER TO BE AROUND STRANGERS THAN THOSE I LOVED.
THE MARK OF ZORRO
TIM'S DEATH WASN'T YOUR FAULT, BRUCE.
THIS IS WHO WE ARE... AND AS MUCH AS WE TRY TO DISSUADE THEM, THIS IS WHO OUR SONS WILL BE.
ALL WE CAN DO IS PREPARE THEM FOR WHAT'S OUT THERE.
IT'S EASY TO THINK THE EXPERIENCE WE'VE HAD THE LAST COUPLE OF DAYS SHED LIGHT ON THE PEOPLE WE HAVE LOST.
TO BLAME YOURSELF IS TO BELITTLE THE SACRIFICE THEY CHOSE TO MAKE.
LET THE DEAD MAINTAIN THEIR HONOR.
THIS WORLD APPEARS TO BE CHALLENGING US FROM WITHIN. WE MUST BE STRONG. THE THREE OF US, STANDING HERE RIGHT NOW...
...IN THIS WORLD, THIS IS THE ONLY TRUTH WE KNOW.

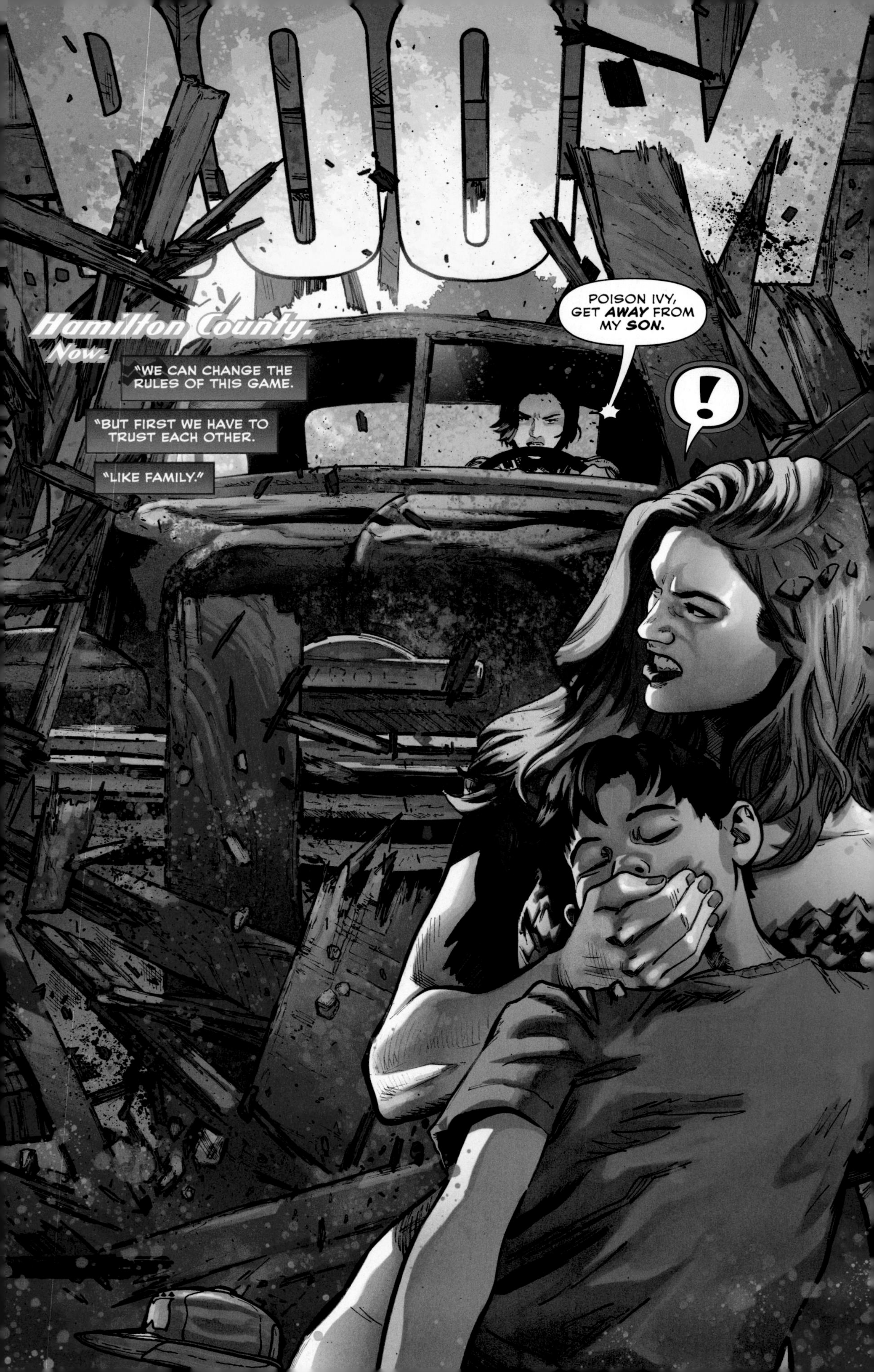

Hamilton County.
Now.
"WE CAN CHANGE THE RULES OF THIS GAME.
"BUT FIRST WE HAVE TO TRUST EACH OTHER.
"LIKE FAMILY."
POISON IVY, GET AWAY FROM MY SON.
!

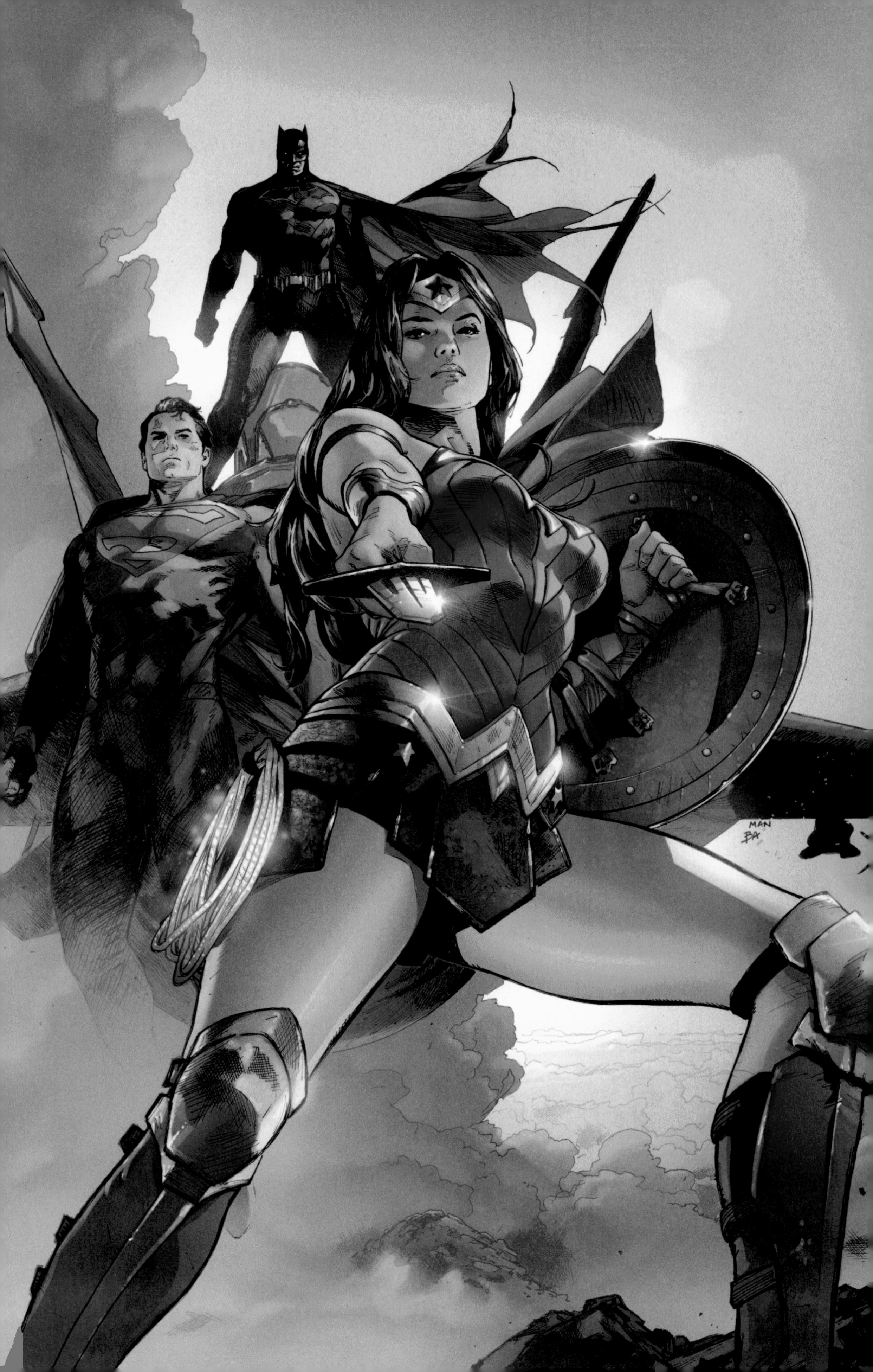
MAN
BA

BETTER TOGETHER Part Four: NOTHING IS REAL

EMANUELA LUPACCHINO penciller * RAY McCARTHY inker * HI-FI colorist

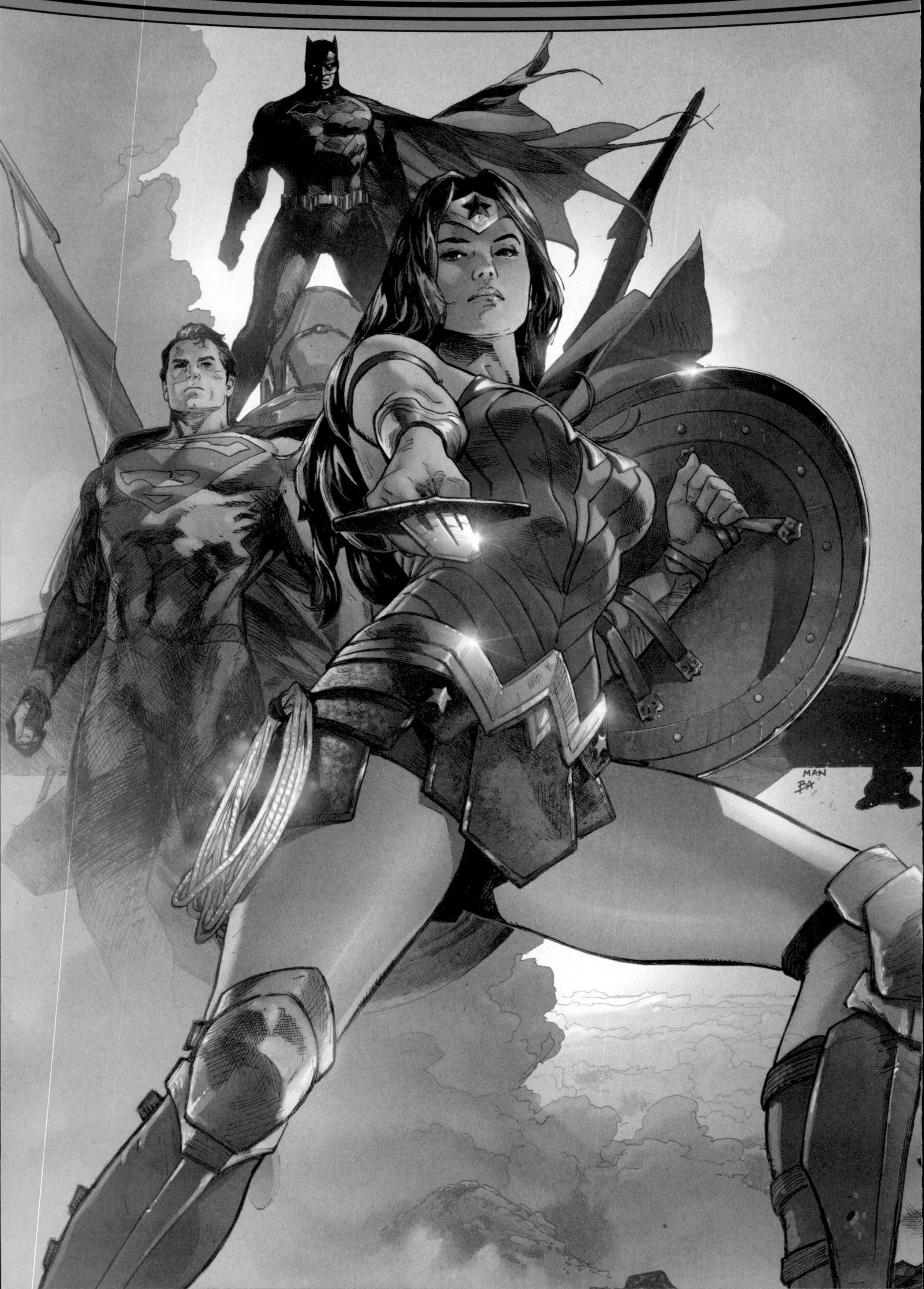

Somewhen.

NONE OF THIS IS REAL.

IT COULD ALL BE A DREAM.

IF THIS IS TRUE, WHY ARE WE IN CONTROL OF OUR OWN ACTIONS AND OUR OWN THOUGHTS?

FORWARD! I CAN FEEL IT.

THIS REALITY APPEARS TO BE ALTERED BY OUR EMOTIONS. PROVIDING US WITH MOMENTS WE HAVE LONG WANTED... AND RESOLUTIONS WE HAVE ALWAYS NEEDED.

BUT WHY?

AND FOR WHAT PURPOSE?

CLARK HAD AN OPPORTUNITY TO RECONNECT WITH HIS FATHER IN SMALLVILLE. A MUCH NEEDED ENCOUNTER WHICH WOULD HOPEFULLY ALLOW HIM TO TEAR DOWN HIS WALLS AND LET US IN.

BRUCE...POOR BRUCE. HE FAILED TO SEE HIS PARENTS BEFORE THEIR DEATH, BUT I BELIEVE THERE WAS GREATER IMPORTANCE IN FACING *HIMSELF.*

AS FOR ME...

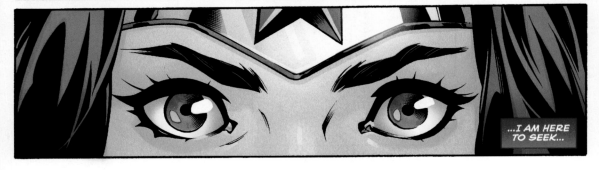

...I AM HERE TO SEEK...

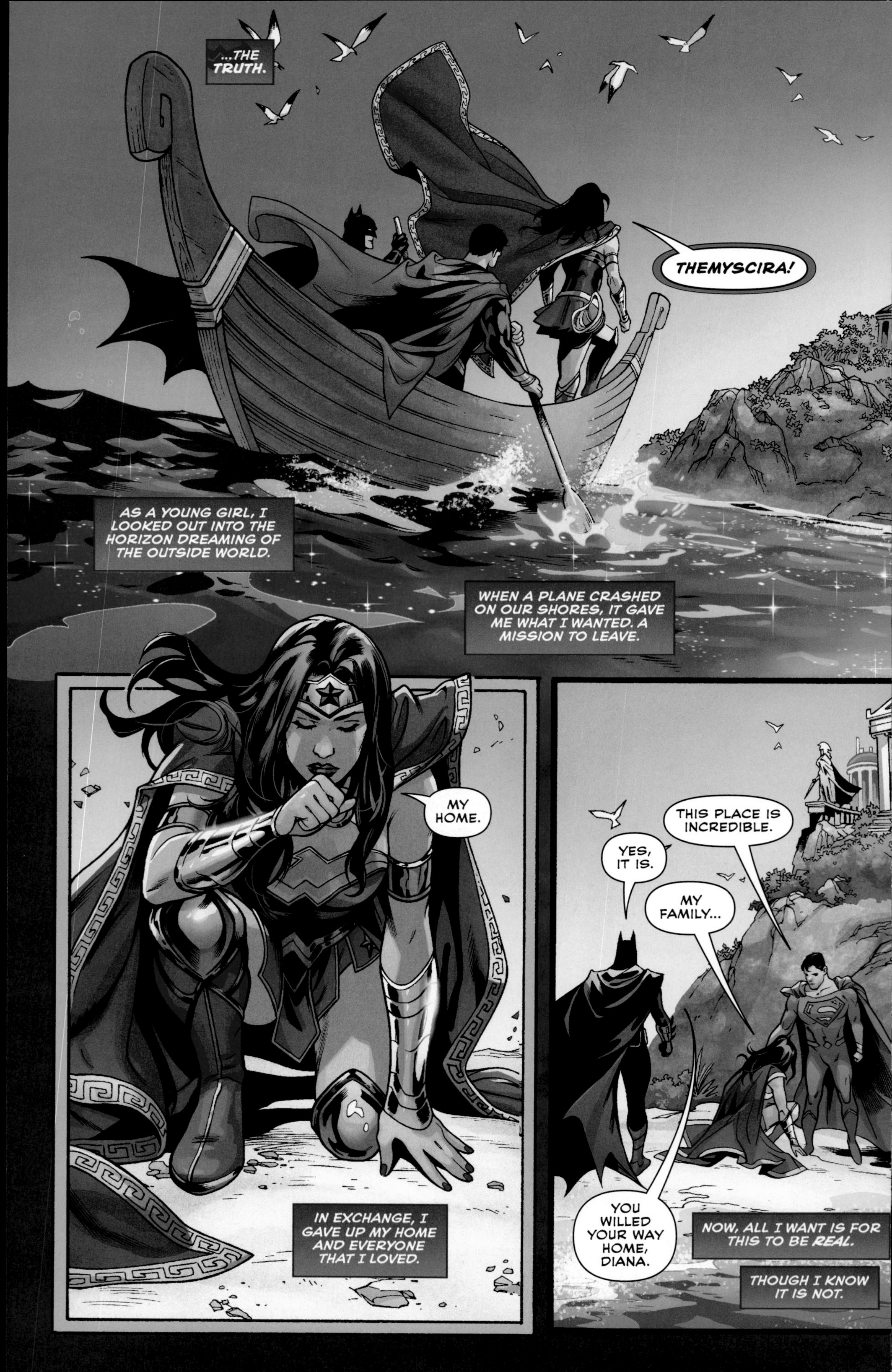

...THE TRUTH.
THEMYSCIRA!
AS A YOUNG GIRL, I LOOKED OUT INTO THE HORIZON DREAMING OF THE OUTSIDE WORLD.
WHEN A PLANE CRASHED ON OUR SHORES, IT GAVE ME WHAT I WANTED. A MISSION TO LEAVE.
MY HOME.
IN EXCHANGE, I GAVE UP MY HOME AND EVERYONE THAT I LOVED.
THIS PLACE IS INCREDIBLE.
YES, IT IS.
MY FAMILY...
YOU WILLED YOUR WAY HOME, DIANA.
NOW, ALL I WANT IS FOR THIS TO BE REAL.
THOUGH I KNOW IT IS NOT.

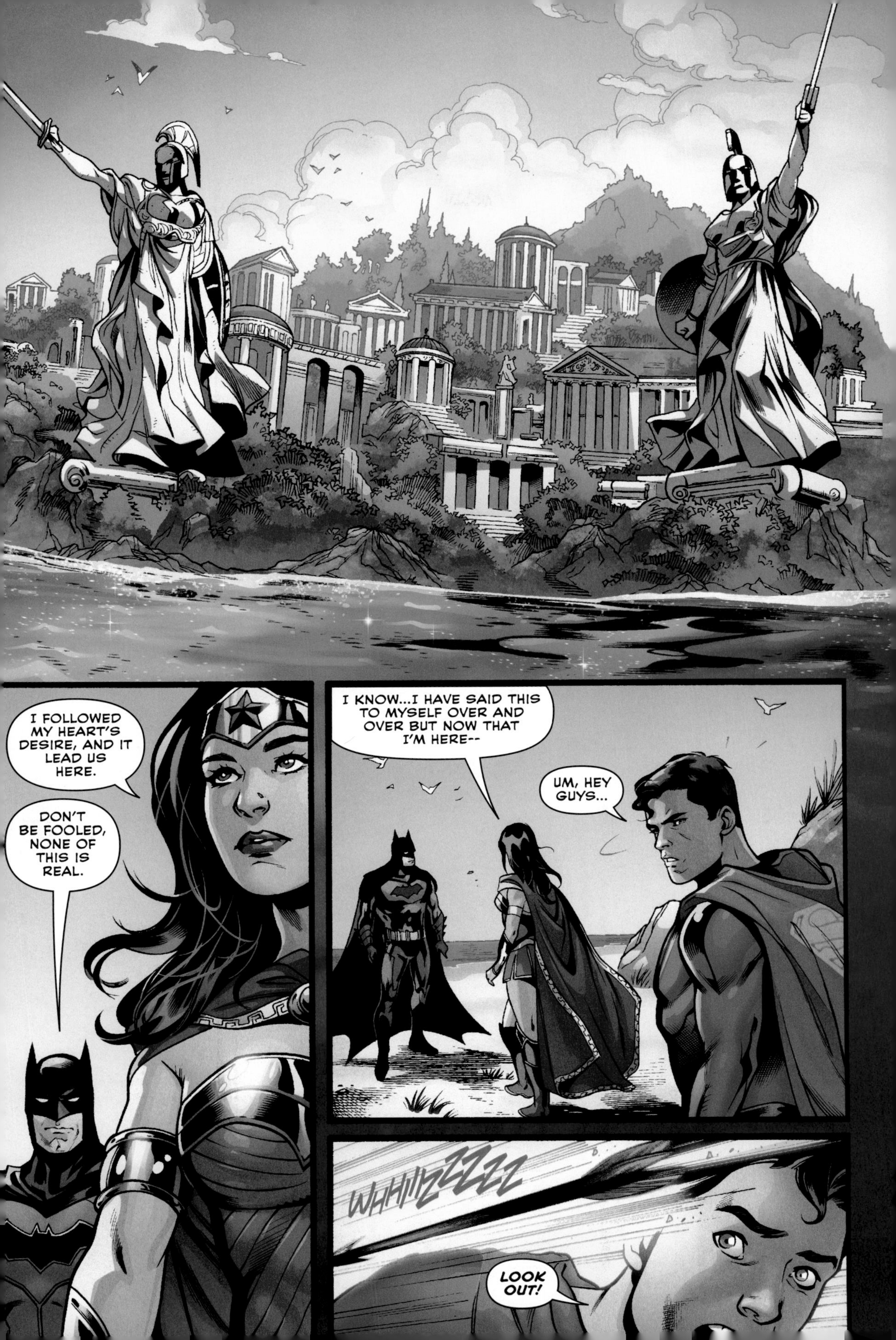
I FOLLOWED MY HEART'S DESIRE, AND IT LEAD US HERE.
DON'T BE FOOLED, NONE OF THIS IS REAL.
I KNOW...I HAVE SAID THIS TO MYSELF OVER AND OVER BUT NOW THAT I'M HERE--
UM, HEY GUYS...
WHHHZZZZZ
LOOK OUT!

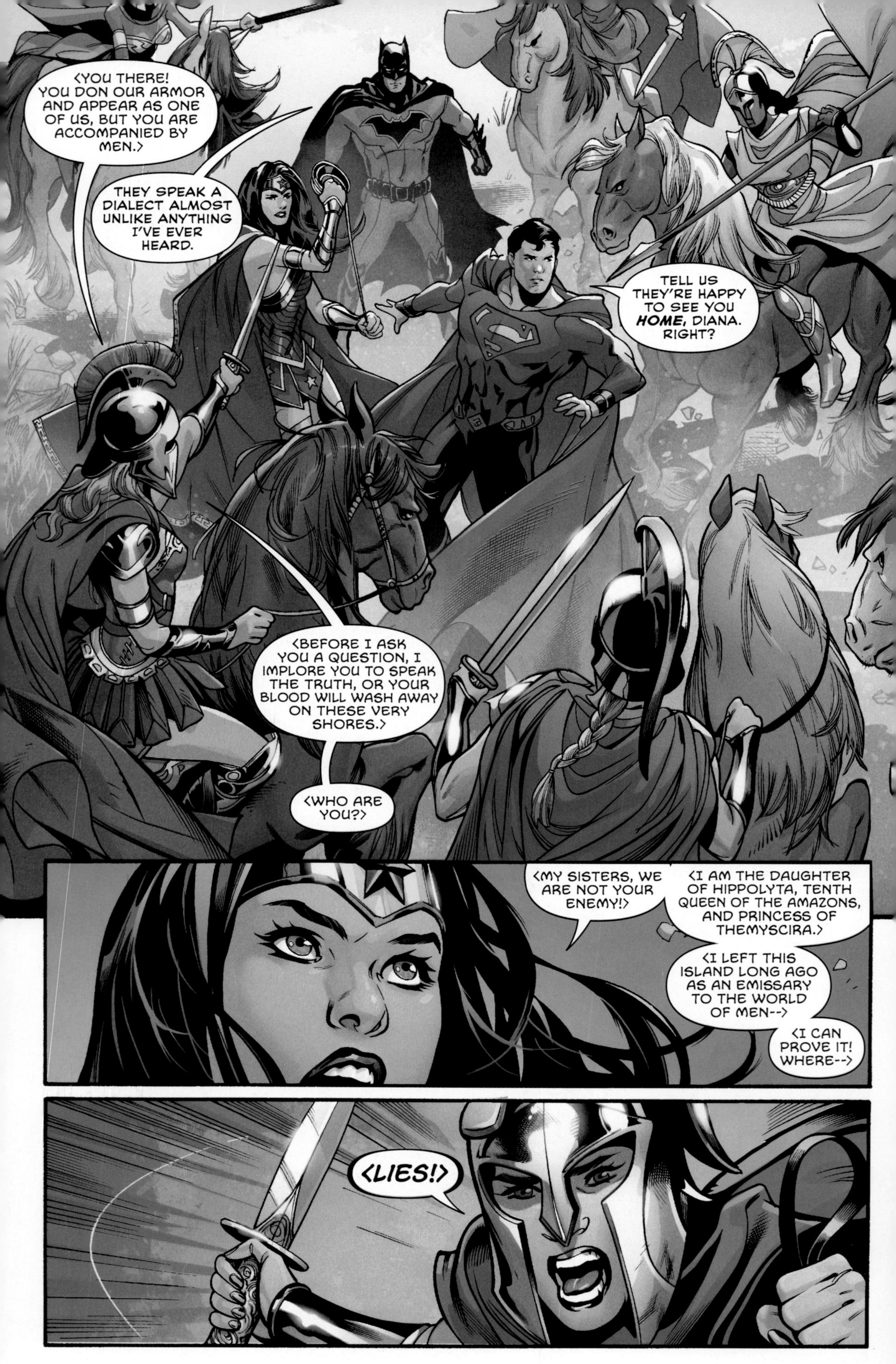
<YOU THERE! YOU DON OUR ARMOR AND APPEAR AS ONE OF US, BUT YOU ARE ACCOMPANIED BY MEN.>
THEY SPEAK A DIALECT ALMOST UNLIKE ANYTHING I'VE EVER HEARD.
TELL US THEY'RE HAPPY TO SEE YOU HOME, DIANA. RIGHT?
<BEFORE I ASK YOU A QUESTION, I IMPLORE YOU TO SPEAK THE TRUTH, OR YOUR BLOOD WILL WASH AWAY ON THESE VERY SHORES.>
<WHO ARE YOU?>
<MY SISTERS, WE ARE NOT YOUR ENEMY!>
<I AM THE DAUGHTER OF HIPPOLYTA, TENTH QUEEN OF THE AMAZONS, AND PRINCESS OF THEMYSCIRA.>
<I LEFT THIS ISLAND LONG AGO AS AN EMISSARY TO THE WORLD OF MEN-->
<I CAN PROVE IT! WHERE-->
<LIES!>

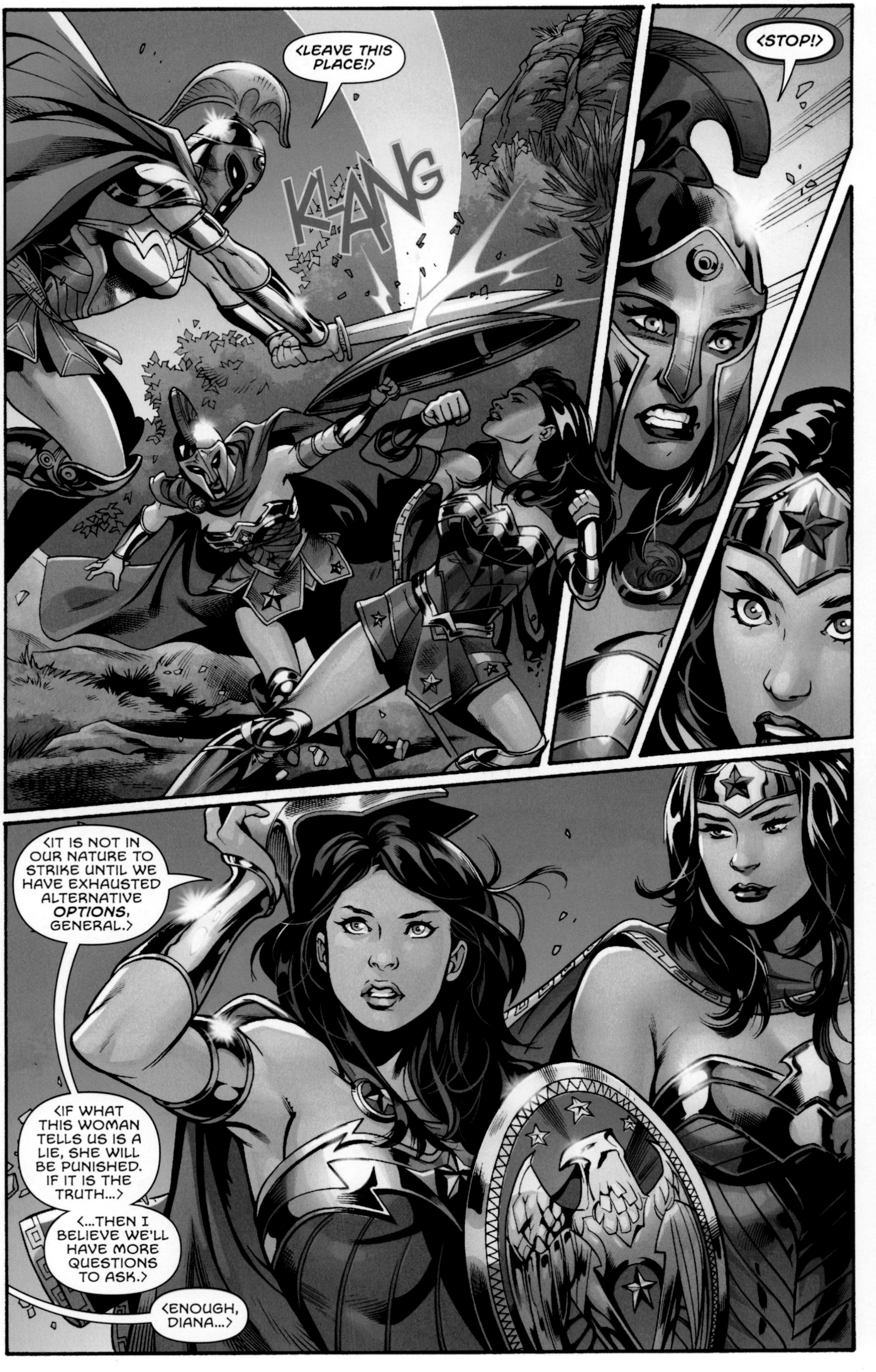
<LEAVE THIS PLACE!>
KLANG
<STOP!>
<IT IS NOT IN OUR NATURE TO STRIKE UNTIL WE HAVE EXHAUSTED ALTERNATIVE *OPTIONS*, GENERAL.>
<IF WHAT THIS WOMAN TELLS US IS A LIE, SHE WILL BE PUNISHED. IF IT IS THE TRUTH...>
<...THEN I BELIEVE WE'LL HAVE MORE QUESTIONS TO ASK.>
<ENOUGH, DIANA...>

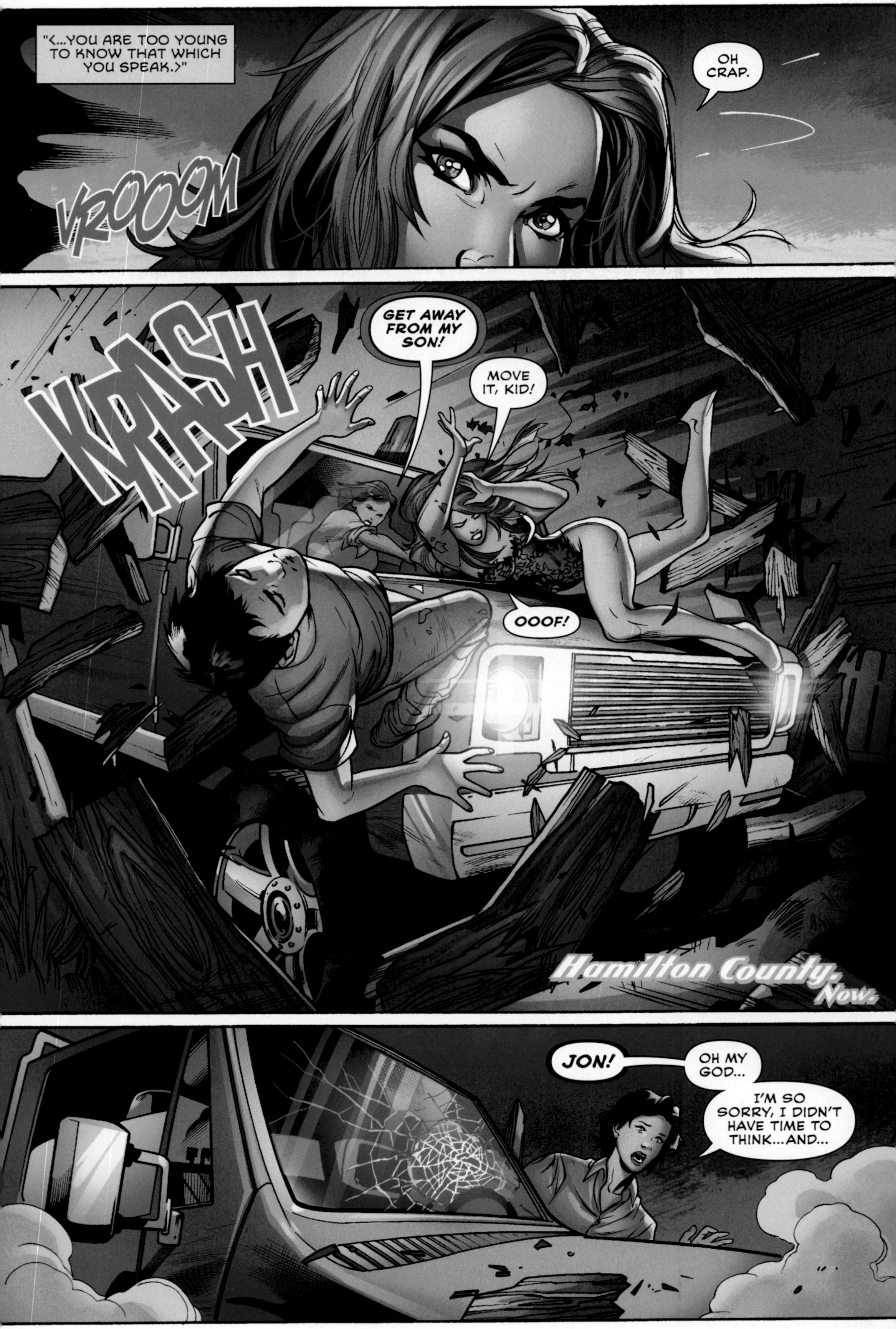
"<...YOU ARE TOO YOUNG TO KNOW THAT WHICH YOU SPEAK.>"
OH CRAP.
VROOOM
KRASH
GET AWAY FROM MY SON!
MOVE IT, KID!
OOOF!
Hamilton County. Now.
JON!
OH MY GOD...
I'M SO SORRY, I DIDN'T HAVE TIME TO THINK...AND...

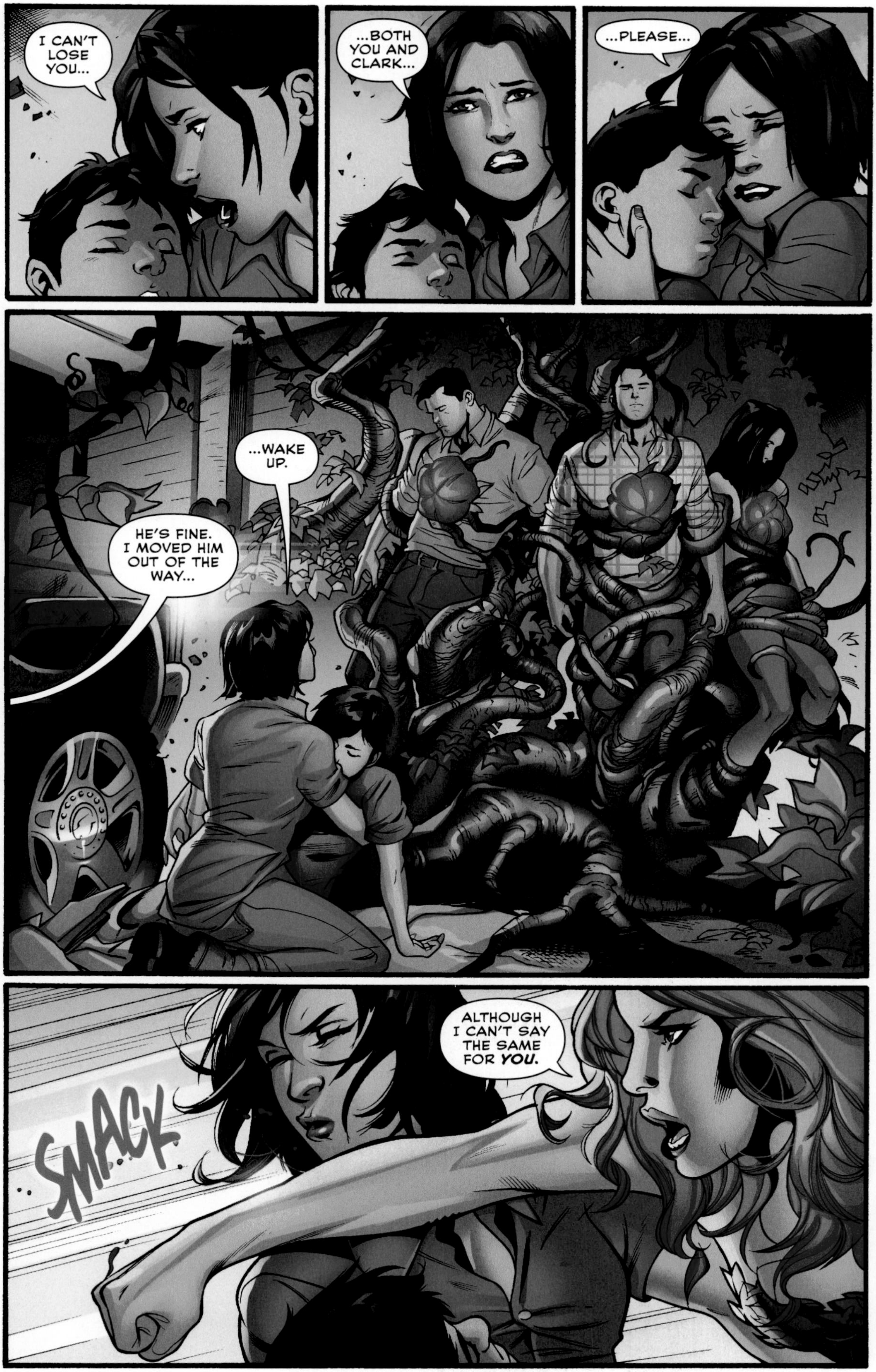
I CAN'T LOSE YOU...
...BOTH YOU AND CLARK...
...PLEASE...
...WAKE UP.
HE'S FINE. I MOVED HIM OUT OF THE WAY...
ALTHOUGH I CAN'T SAY THE SAME FOR *YOU.*
SMACK

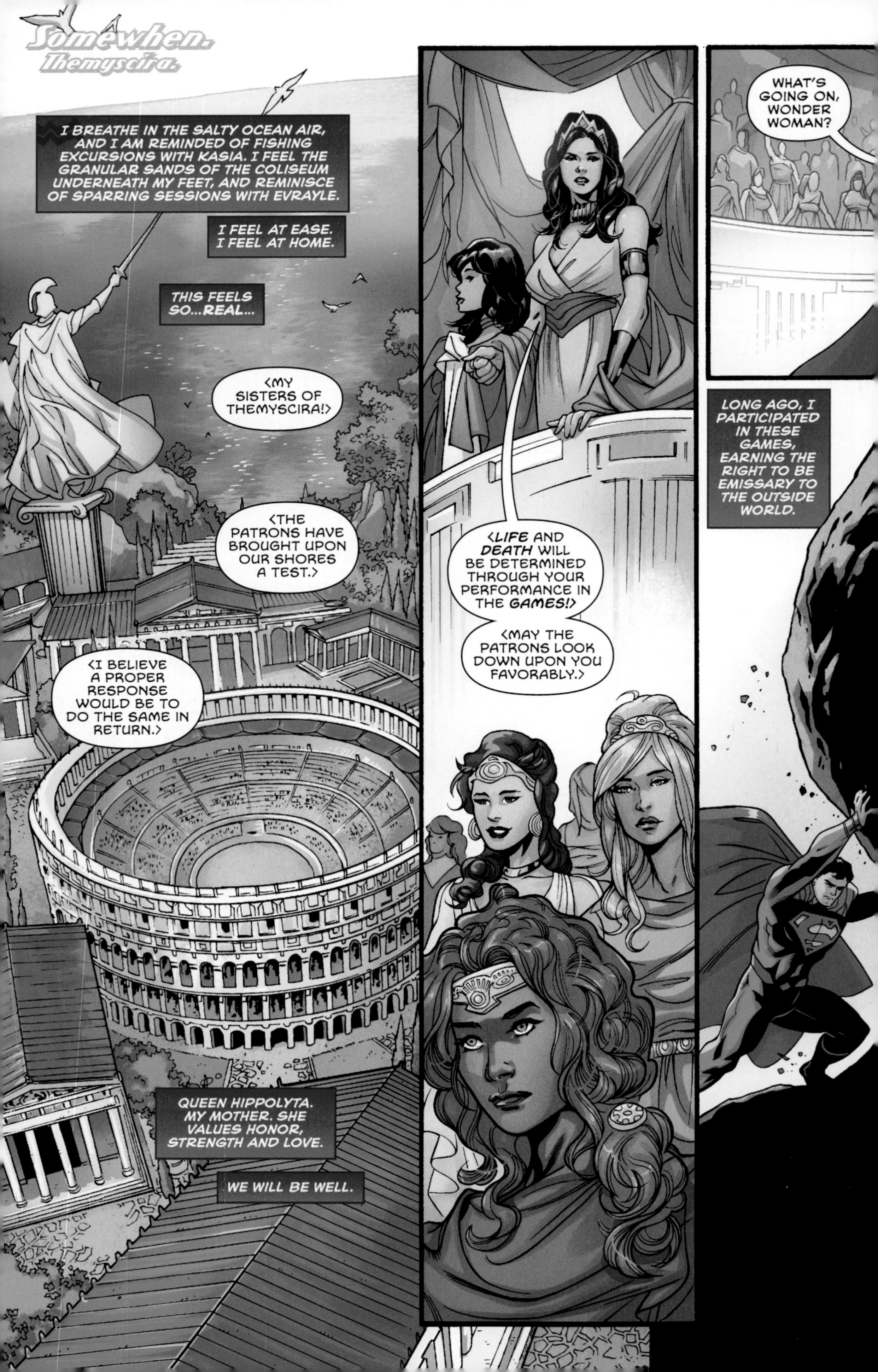
Somewhen. Themyscira.
I BREATHE IN THE SALTY OCEAN AIR, AND I AM REMINDED OF FISHING EXCURSIONS WITH KASIA. I FEEL THE GRANULAR SANDS OF THE COLISEUM UNDERNEATH MY FEET, AND REMINISCE OF SPARRING SESSIONS WITH EVRAYLE.
I FEEL AT EASE. I FEEL AT HOME.
THIS FEELS SO...REAL...
<MY SISTERS OF THEMYSCIRA!>
<THE PATRONS HAVE BROUGHT UPON OUR SHORES A TEST.>
<I BELIEVE A PROPER RESPONSE WOULD BE TO DO THE SAME IN RETURN.>
QUEEN HIPPOLYTA. MY MOTHER. SHE VALUES HONOR, STRENGTH AND LOVE.
WE WILL BE WELL.
<LIFE AND DEATH WILL BE DETERMINED THROUGH YOUR PERFORMANCE IN THE GAMES!>
<MAY THE PATRONS LOOK DOWN UPON YOU FAVORABLY.>
WHAT'S GOING ON, WONDER WOMAN?
LONG AGO, I PARTICIPATED IN THESE GAMES, EARNING THE RIGHT TO BE EMISSARY TO THE OUTSIDE WORLD.

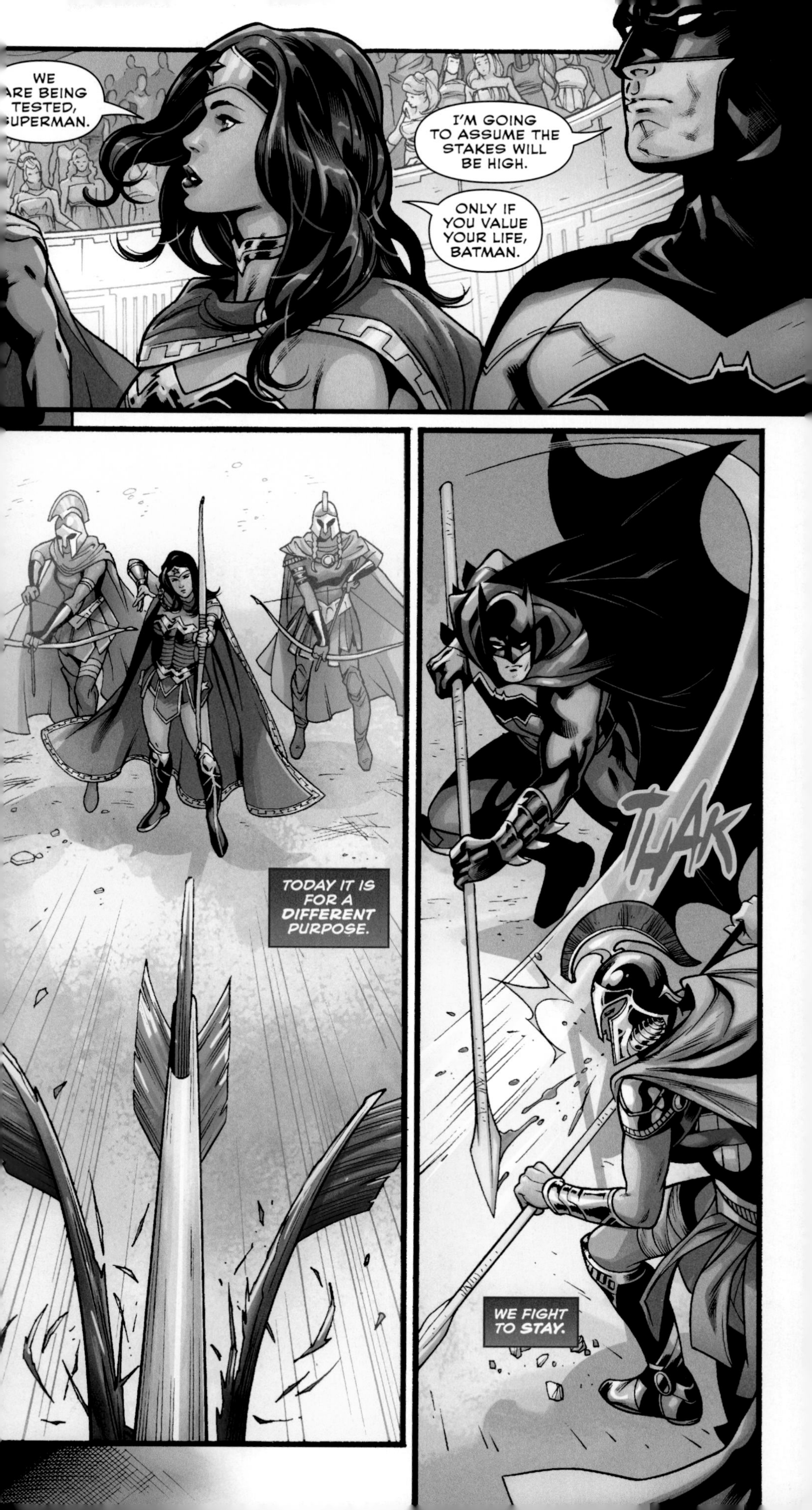
WE ARE BEING TESTED, SUPERMAN.
I'M GOING TO ASSUME THE STAKES WILL BE HIGH.
ONLY IF YOU VALUE YOUR LIFE, BATMAN.
TODAY IT IS FOR A DIFFERENT PURPOSE.
THAK
WE FIGHT TO STAY.

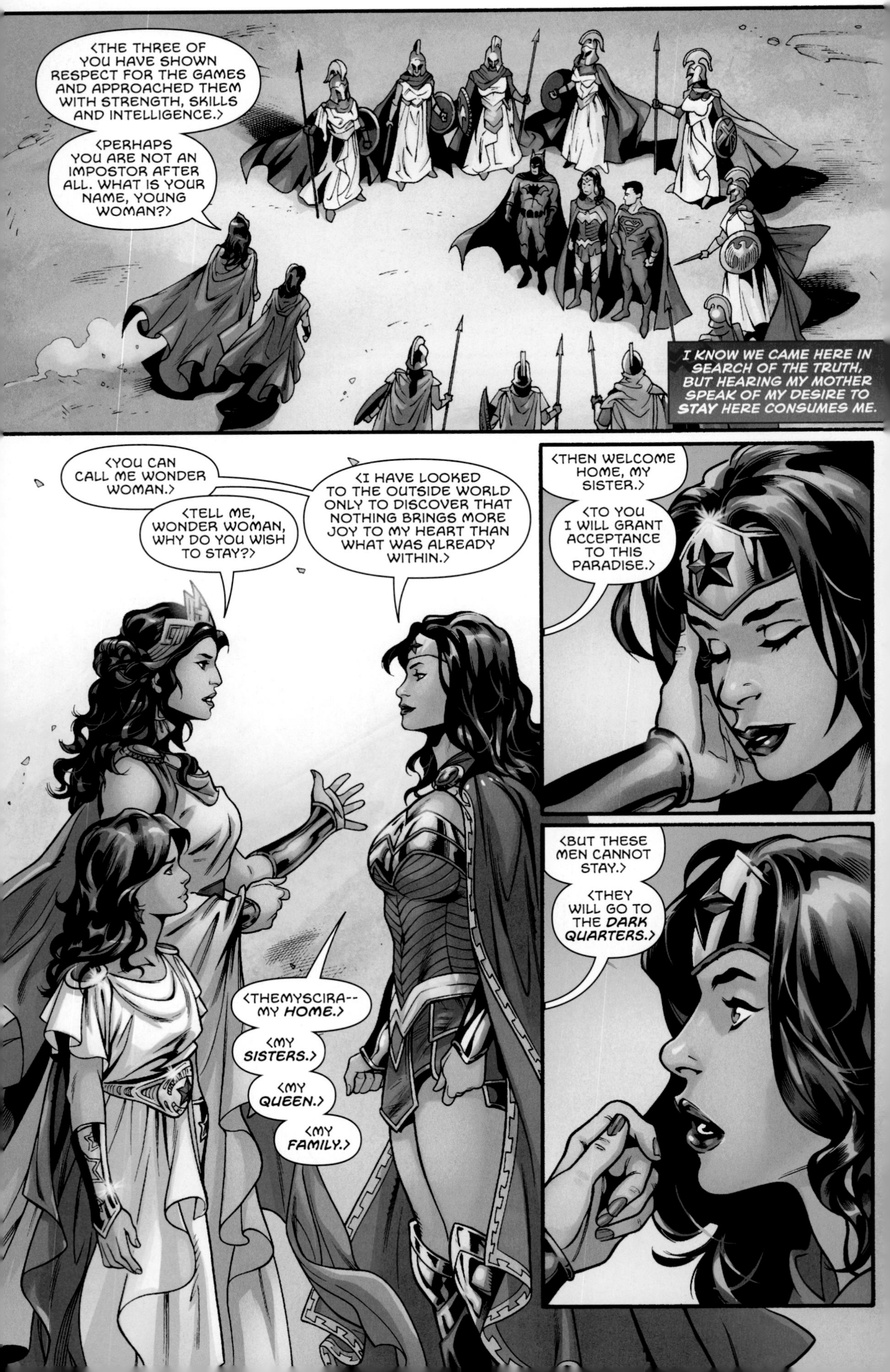
<THE THREE OF YOU HAVE SHOWN RESPECT FOR THE GAMES AND APPROACHED THEM WITH STRENGTH, SKILLS AND INTELLIGENCE.>
<PERHAPS YOU ARE NOT AN IMPOSTOR AFTER ALL. WHAT IS YOUR NAME, YOUNG WOMAN?>
I KNOW WE CAME HERE IN SEARCH OF THE TRUTH, BUT HEARING MY MOTHER SPEAK OF MY DESIRE TO STAY HERE CONSUMES ME.
<YOU CAN CALL ME WONDER WOMAN.>
<TELL ME, WONDER WOMAN, WHY DO YOU WISH TO STAY?>
<I HAVE LOOKED TO THE OUTSIDE WORLD ONLY TO DISCOVER THAT NOTHING BRINGS MORE JOY TO MY HEART THAN WHAT WAS ALREADY WITHIN.>
<THEMYSCIRA-- MY HOME.>
<MY SISTERS.>
<MY QUEEN.>
<MY FAMILY.>
<THEN WELCOME HOME, MY SISTER.>
<TO YOU I WILL GRANT ACCEPTANCE TO THIS PARADISE.>
<BUT THESE MEN CANNOT STAY.>
<THEY WILL GO TO THE DARK QUARTERS.>

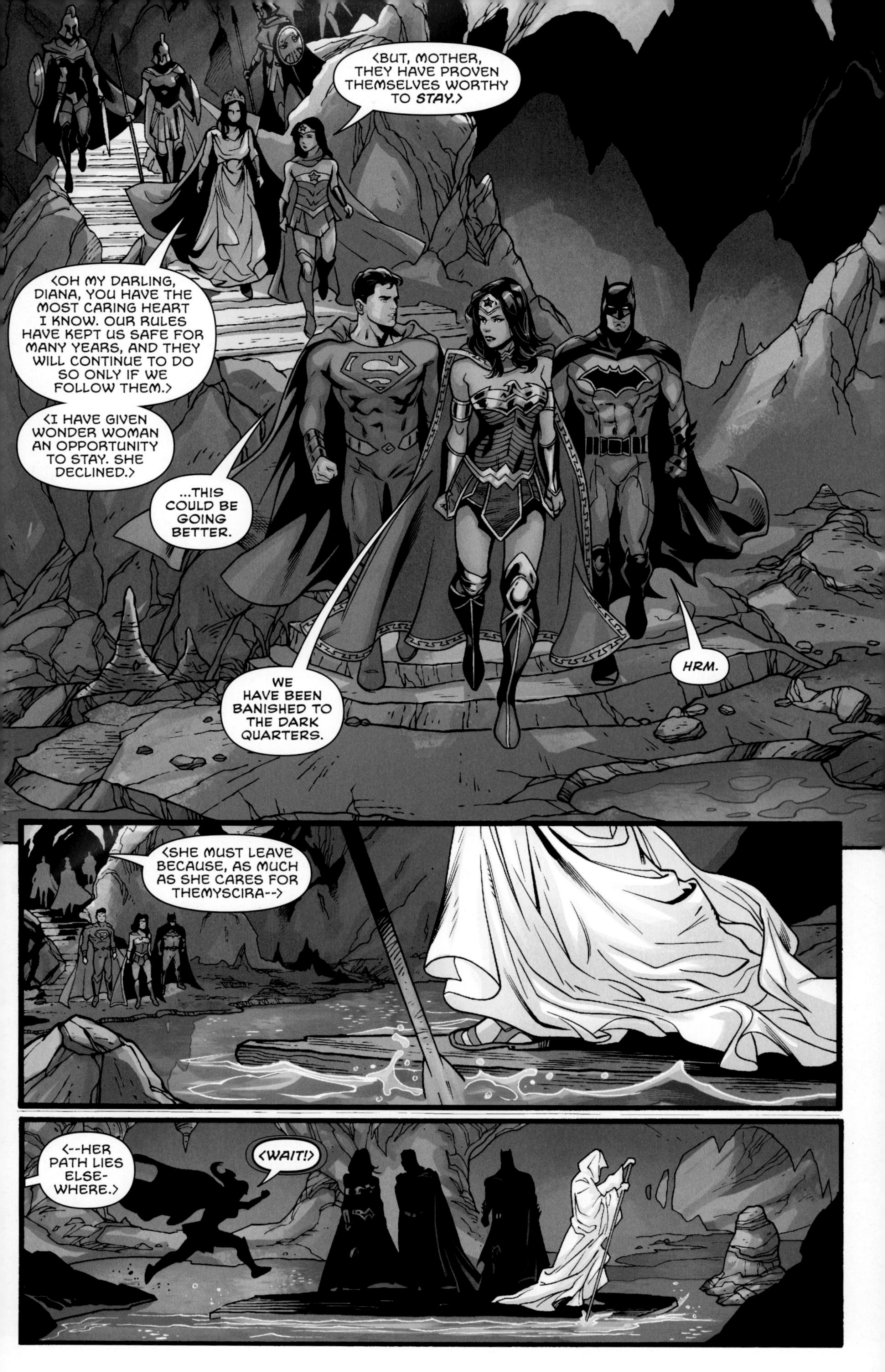

<BUT, MOTHER, THEY HAVE PROVEN THEMSELVES WORTHY TO STAY.>
<OH MY DARLING, DIANA, YOU HAVE THE MOST CARING HEART I KNOW. OUR RULES HAVE KEPT US SAFE FOR MANY YEARS, AND THEY WILL CONTINUE TO DO SO ONLY IF WE FOLLOW THEM.>
<I HAVE GIVEN WONDER WOMAN AN OPPORTUNITY TO STAY. SHE DECLINED.>
...THIS COULD BE GOING BETTER.
WE HAVE BEEN BANISHED TO THE DARK QUARTERS.
HRM.
<SHE MUST LEAVE BECAUSE, AS MUCH AS SHE CARES FOR THEMYSCIRA-->
<--HER PATH LIES ELSE-WHERE.>
<WAIT!>

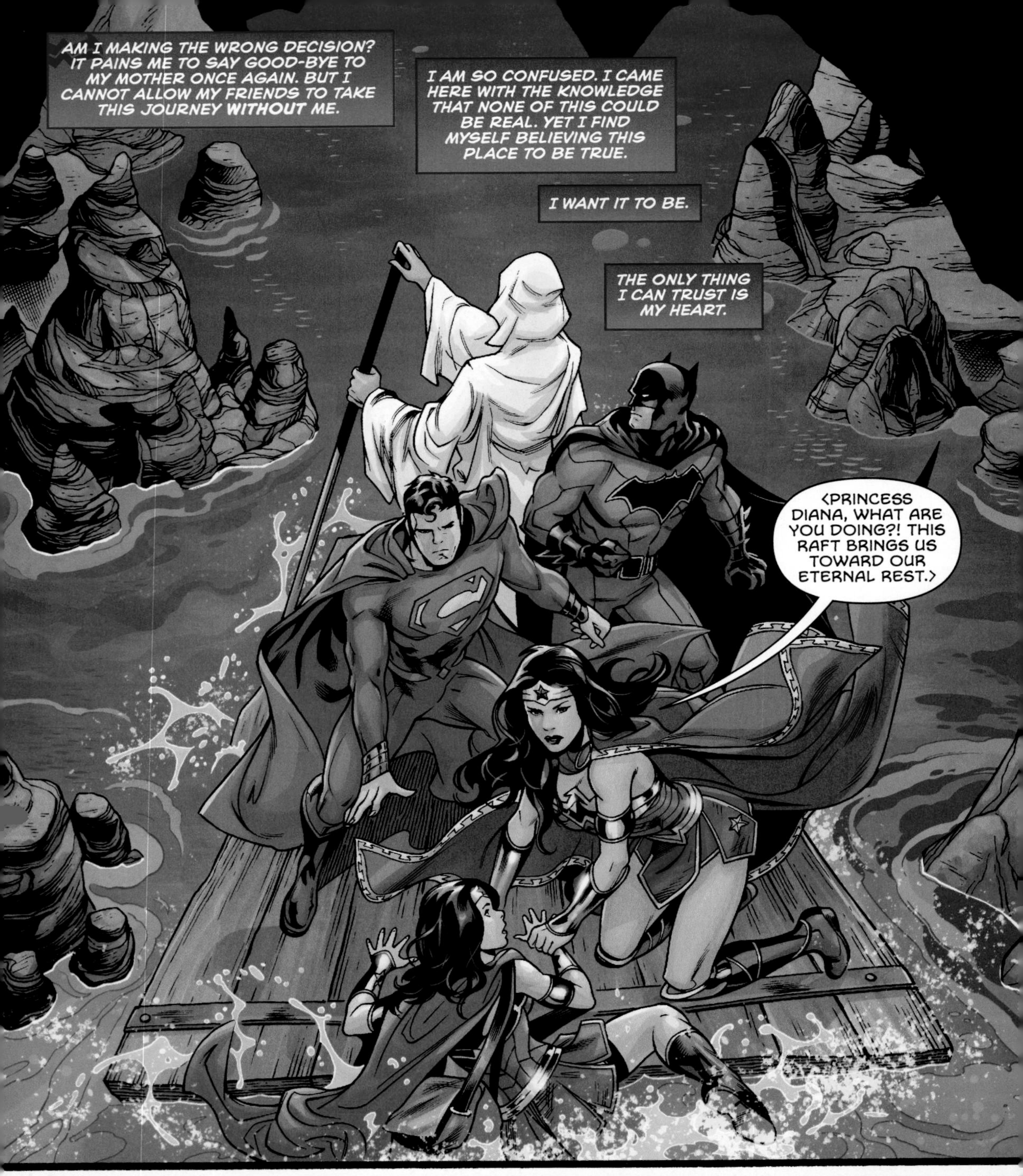
AM I MAKING THE WRONG DECISION? IT PAINS ME TO SAY GOOD-BYE TO MY MOTHER ONCE AGAIN. BUT I CANNOT ALLOW MY FRIENDS TO TAKE THIS JOURNEY WITHOUT ME.
I AM SO CONFUSED. I CAME HERE WITH THE KNOWLEDGE THAT NONE OF THIS COULD BE REAL. YET I FIND MYSELF BELIEVING THIS PLACE TO BE TRUE.
I WANT IT TO BE.
THE ONLY THING I CAN TRUST IS MY HEART.
<PRINCESS DIANA, WHAT ARE YOU DOING?! THIS RAFT BRINGS US TOWARD OUR ETERNAL REST.>

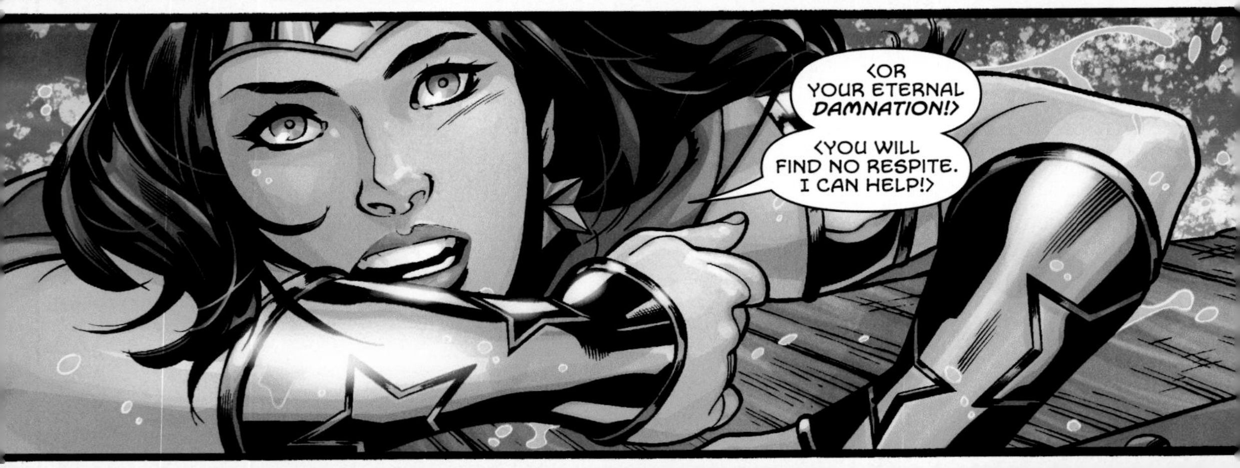
<OR YOUR ETERNAL *DAMNATION!*>
<YOU WILL FIND NO RESPITE. I CAN HELP!>

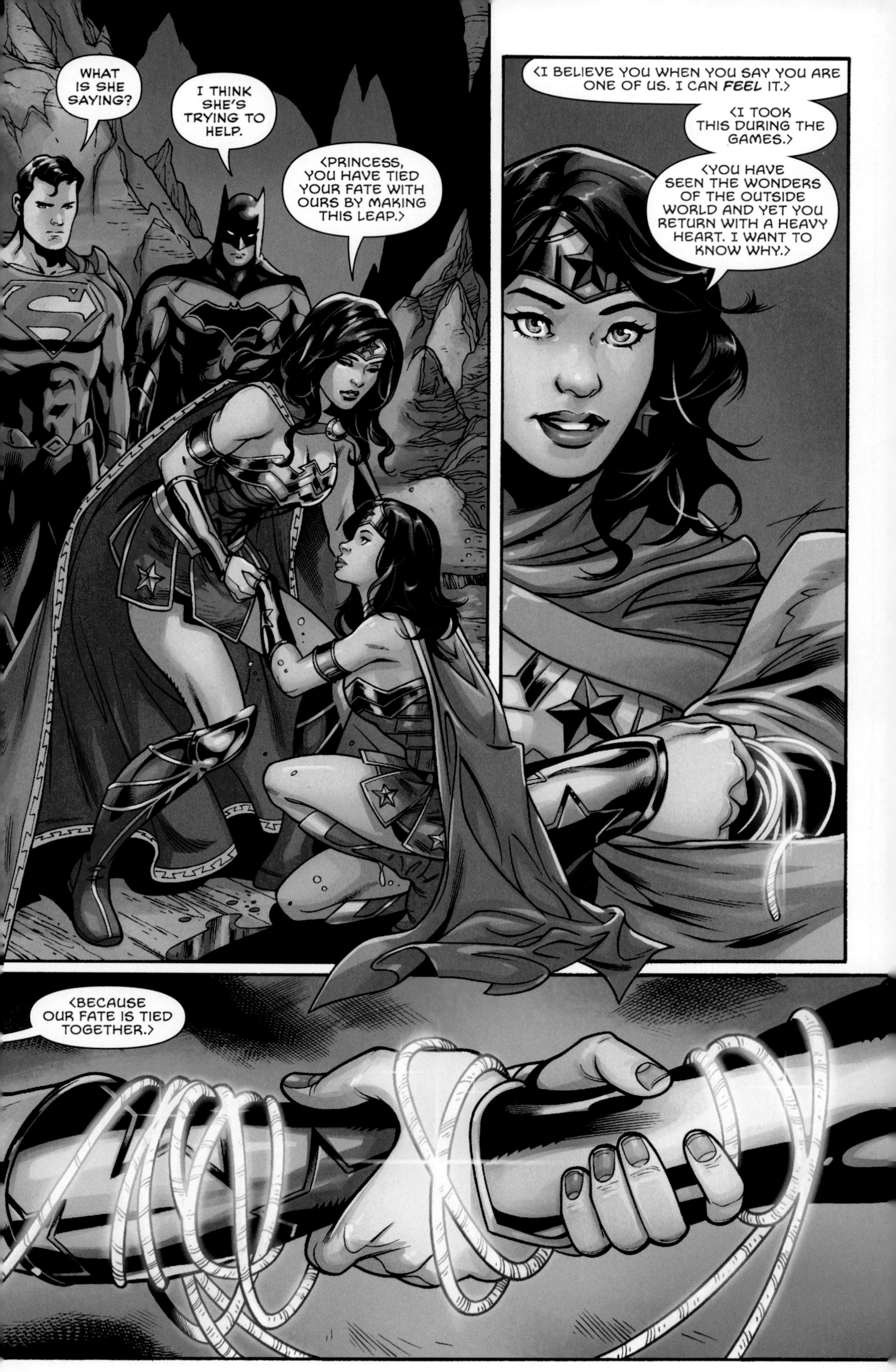
WHAT IS SHE SAYING?
I THINK SHE'S TRYING TO HELP.
<PRINCESS, YOU HAVE TIED YOUR FATE WITH OURS BY MAKING THIS LEAP.>
<I BELIEVE YOU WHEN YOU SAY YOU ARE ONE OF US. I CAN FEEL IT.>
<I TOOK THIS DURING THE GAMES.>
<YOU HAVE SEEN THE WONDERS OF THE OUTSIDE WORLD AND YET YOU RETURN WITH A HEAVY HEART. I WANT TO KNOW WHY.>
<BECAUSE OUR FATE IS TIED TOGETHER.>

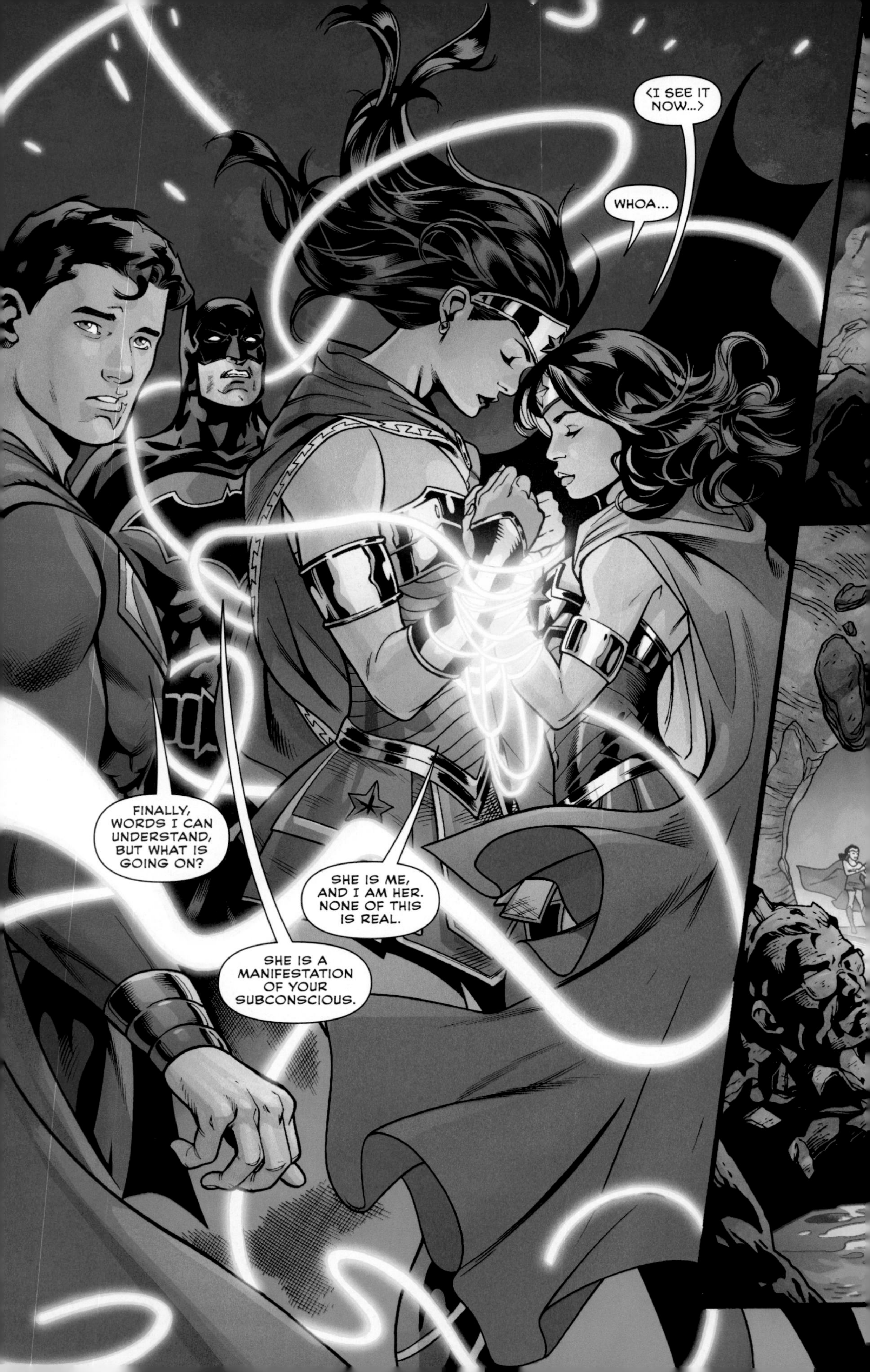

<I SEE IT NOW...>
WHOA...
FINALLY, WORDS I CAN UNDERSTAND, BUT WHAT IS GOING ON?
SHE IS ME, AND I AM HER. NONE OF THIS IS REAL.
SHE IS A MANIFESTATION OF YOUR SUBCONSCIOUS.

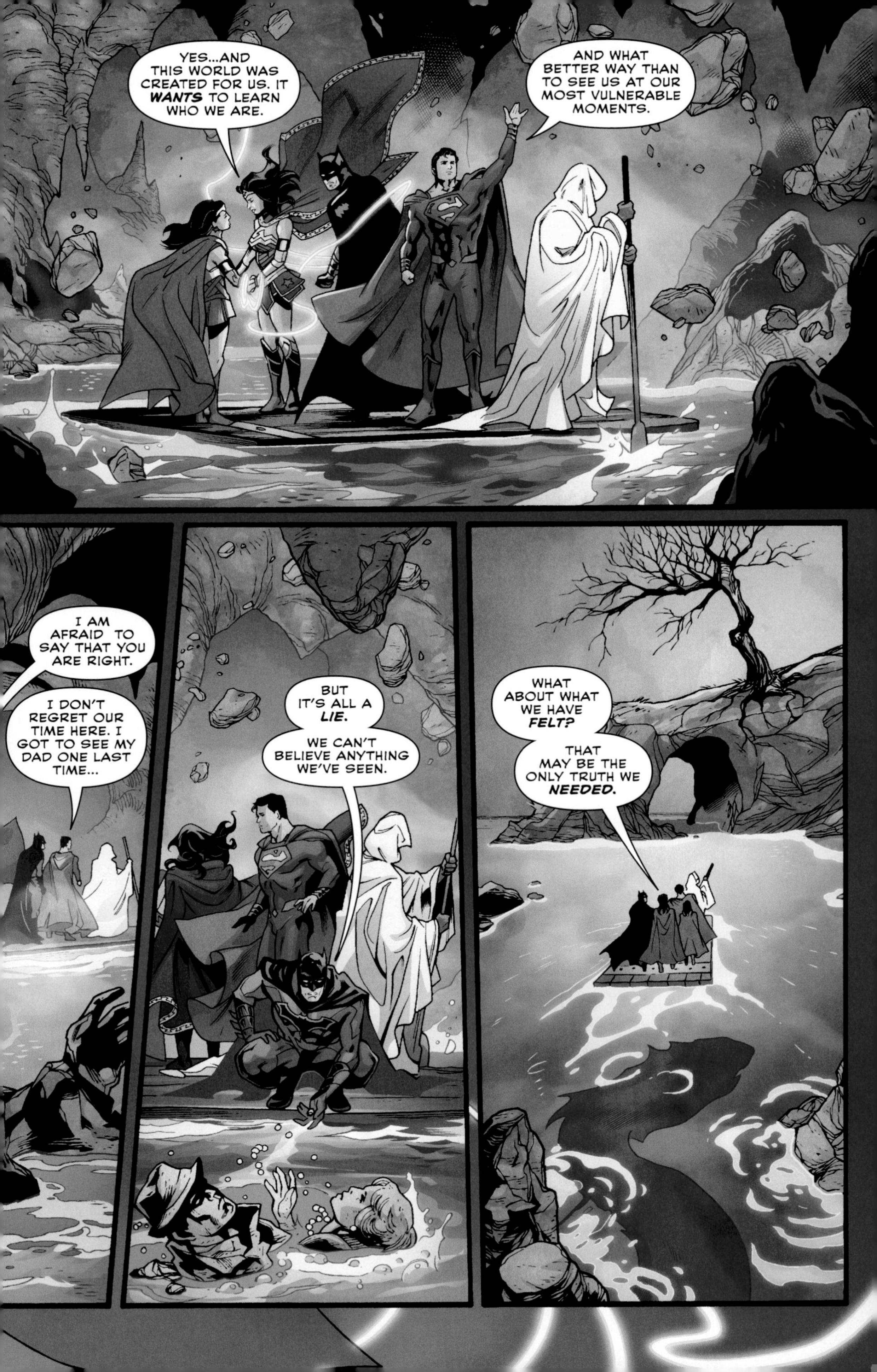
YES...AND THIS WORLD WAS CREATED FOR US. IT **WANTS** TO LEARN WHO WE ARE.
AND WHAT BETTER WAY THAN TO SEE US AT OUR MOST VULNERABLE MOMENTS.
I AM AFRAID TO SAY THAT YOU ARE RIGHT.
I DON'T REGRET OUR TIME HERE. I GOT TO SEE MY DAD ONE LAST TIME...
BUT IT'S ALL A **LIE.**
WE CAN'T BELIEVE ANYTHING WE'VE SEEN.
WHAT ABOUT WHAT WE HAVE **FELT?**
THAT MAY BE THE ONLY TRUTH WE **NEEDED.**

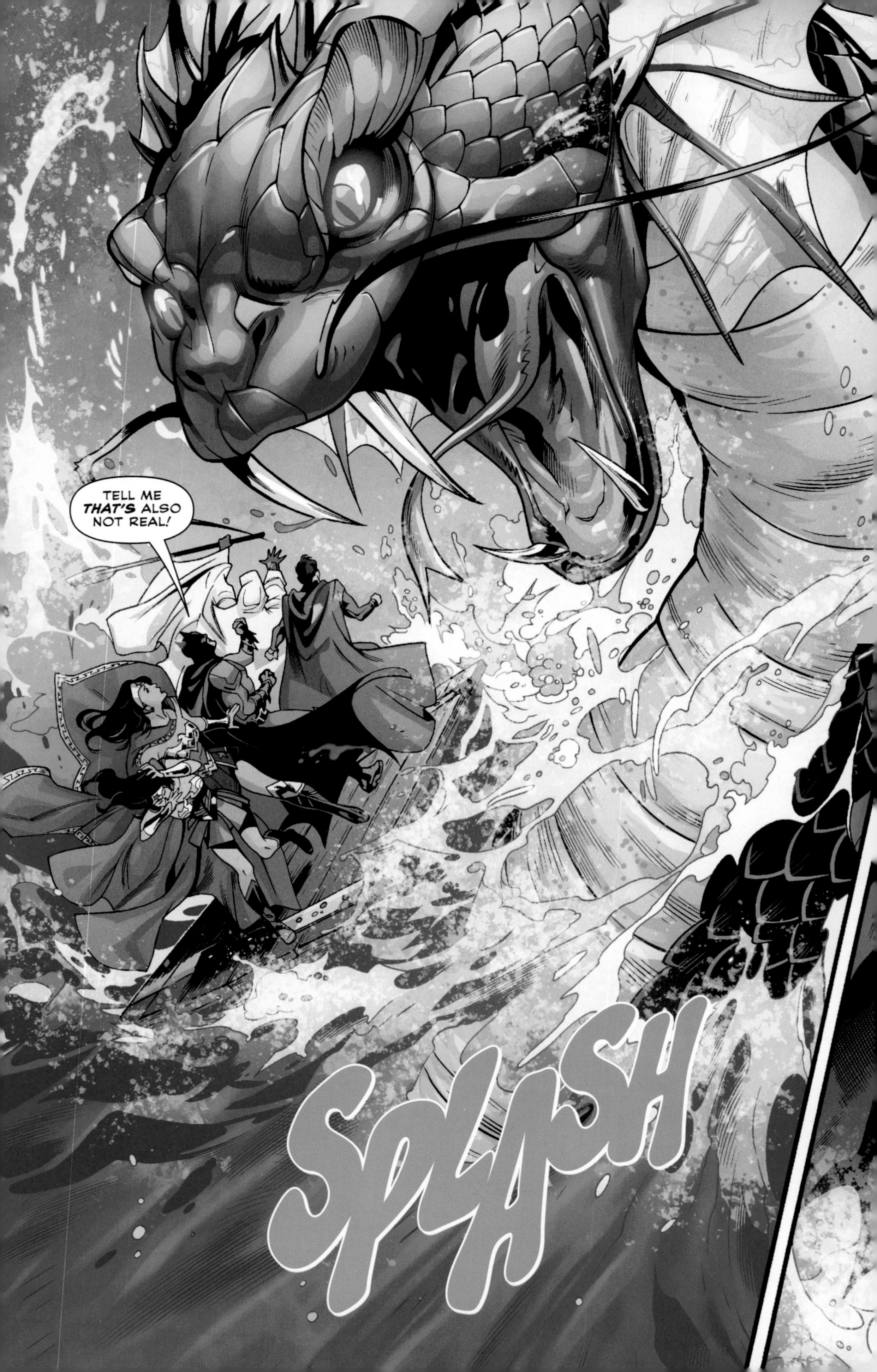
TELL ME THAT'S ALSO NOT REAL!
SPLASH

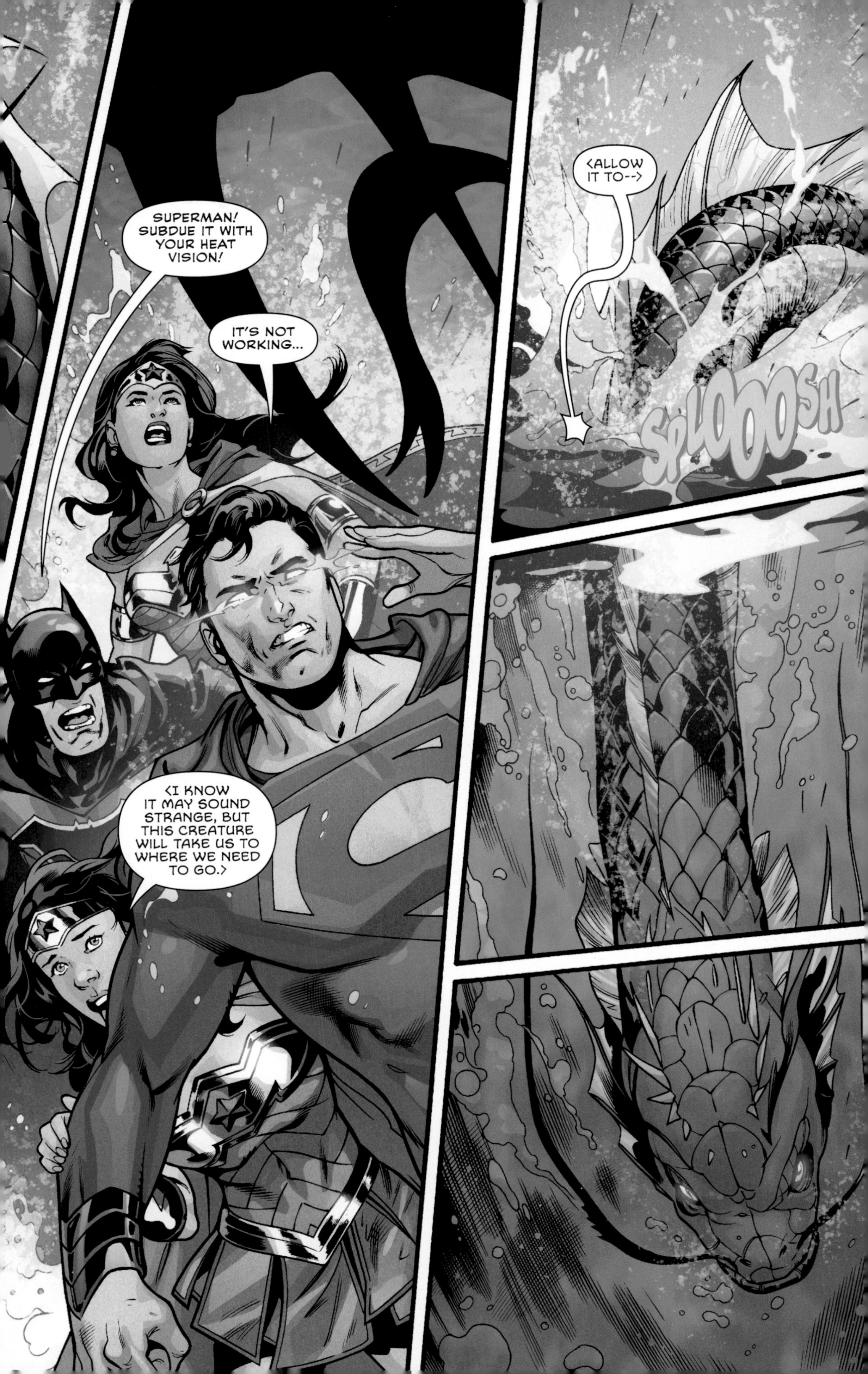
SUPERMAN! SUBDUE IT WITH YOUR HEAT VISION!
IT'S NOT WORKING...
<I KNOW IT MAY SOUND STRANGE, BUT THIS CREATURE WILL TAKE US TO WHERE WE NEED TO GO.>
<ALLOW IT TO-->
SPLOOOSH

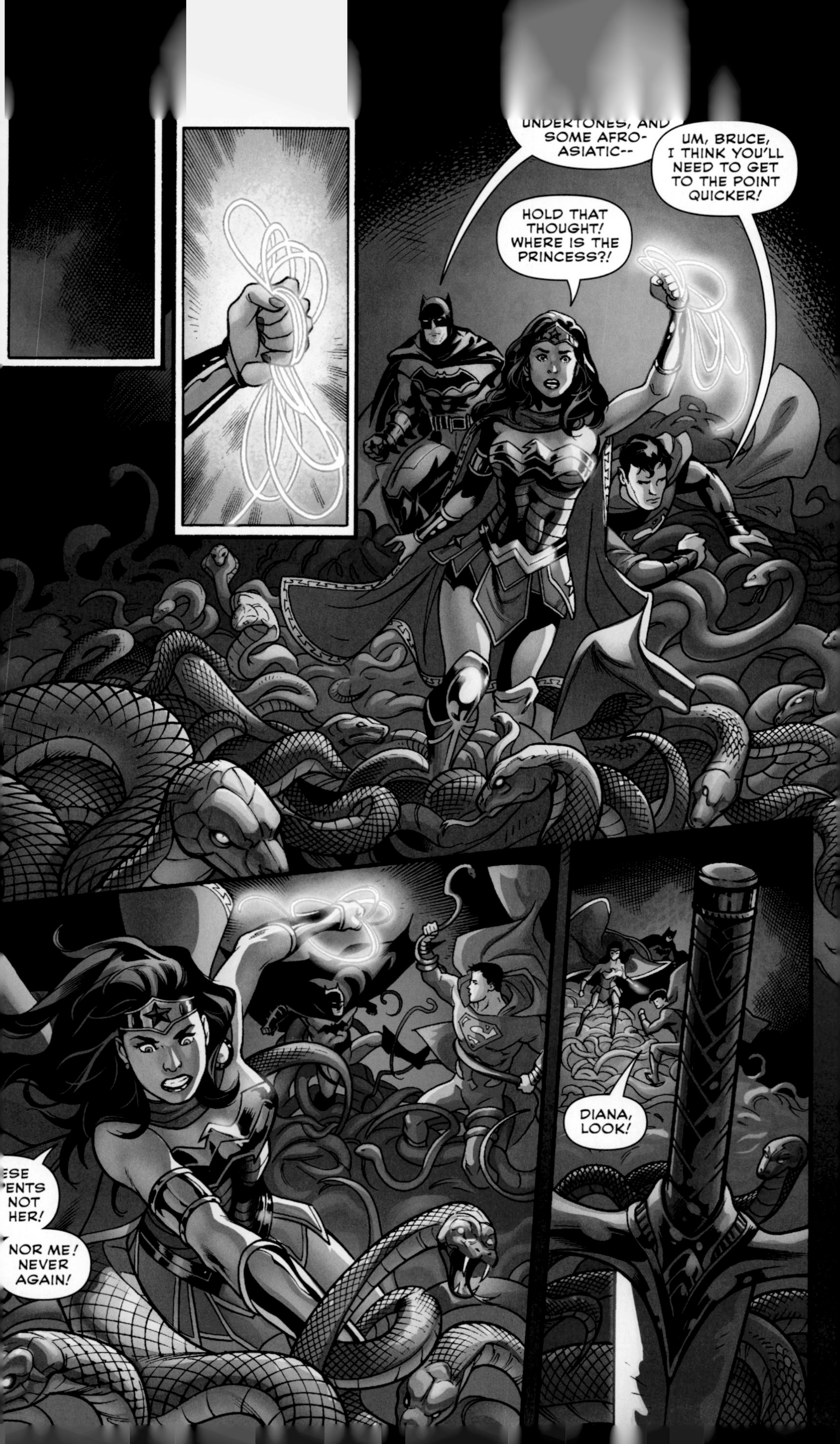
UNDERTONES, AND SOME AFRO-ASIATIC--
UM, BRUCE, I THINK YOU'LL NEED TO GET TO THE POINT QUICKER!
HOLD THAT THOUGHT! WHERE IS THE PRINCESS?!
ESE PENTS NOT HER!
NOR ME! NEVER AGAIN!
DIANA, LOOK!

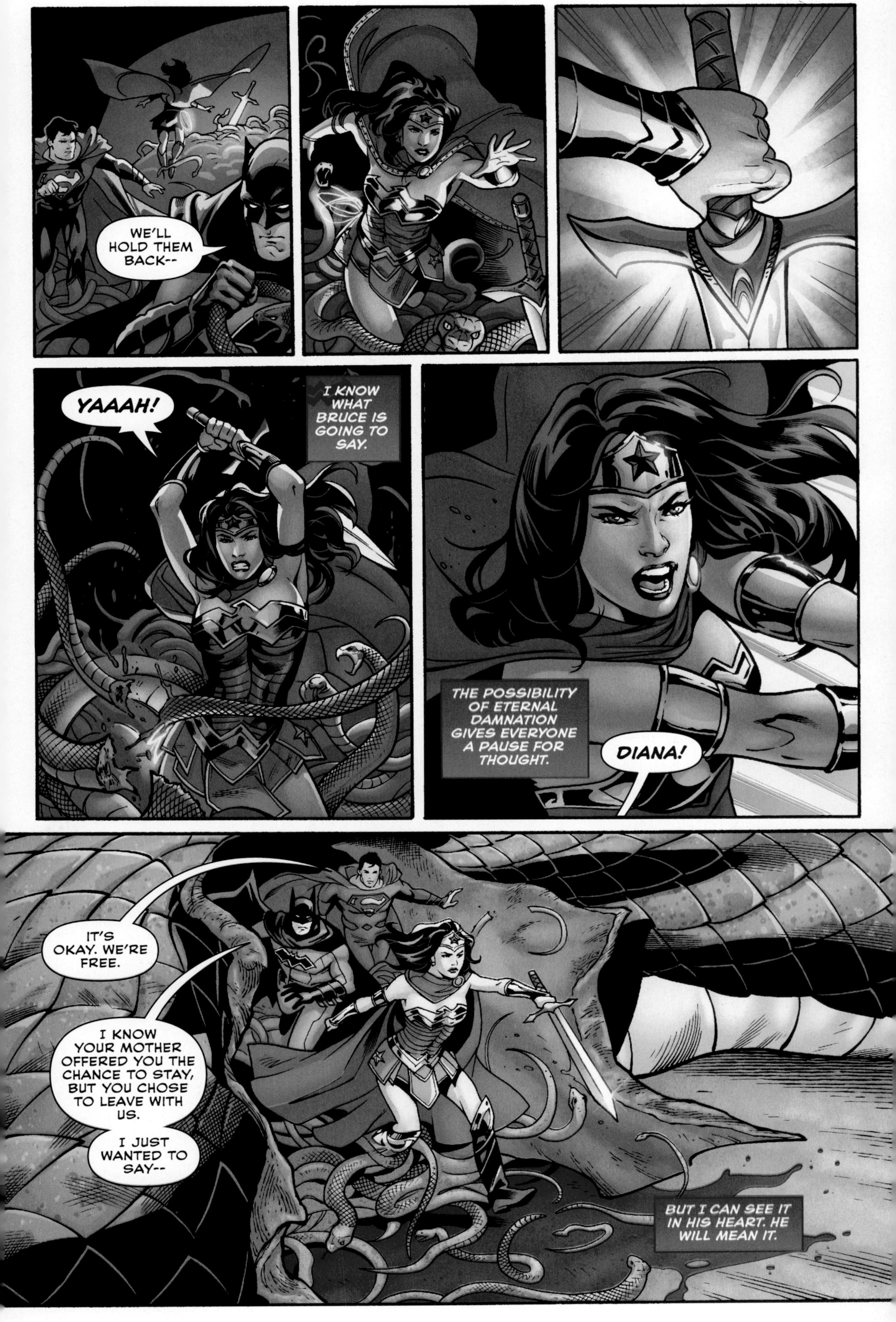
WE'LL HOLD THEM BACK--
YAAAH!
I KNOW WHAT BRUCE IS GOING TO SAY.
THE POSSIBILITY OF ETERNAL DAMNATION GIVES EVERYONE A PAUSE FOR THOUGHT.
DIANA!
IT'S OKAY. WE'RE FREE.
I KNOW YOUR MOTHER OFFERED YOU THE CHANCE TO STAY, BUT YOU CHOSE TO LEAVE WITH US.
I JUST WANTED TO SAY--
BUT I CAN SEE IT IN HIS HEART. HE WILL MEAN IT.

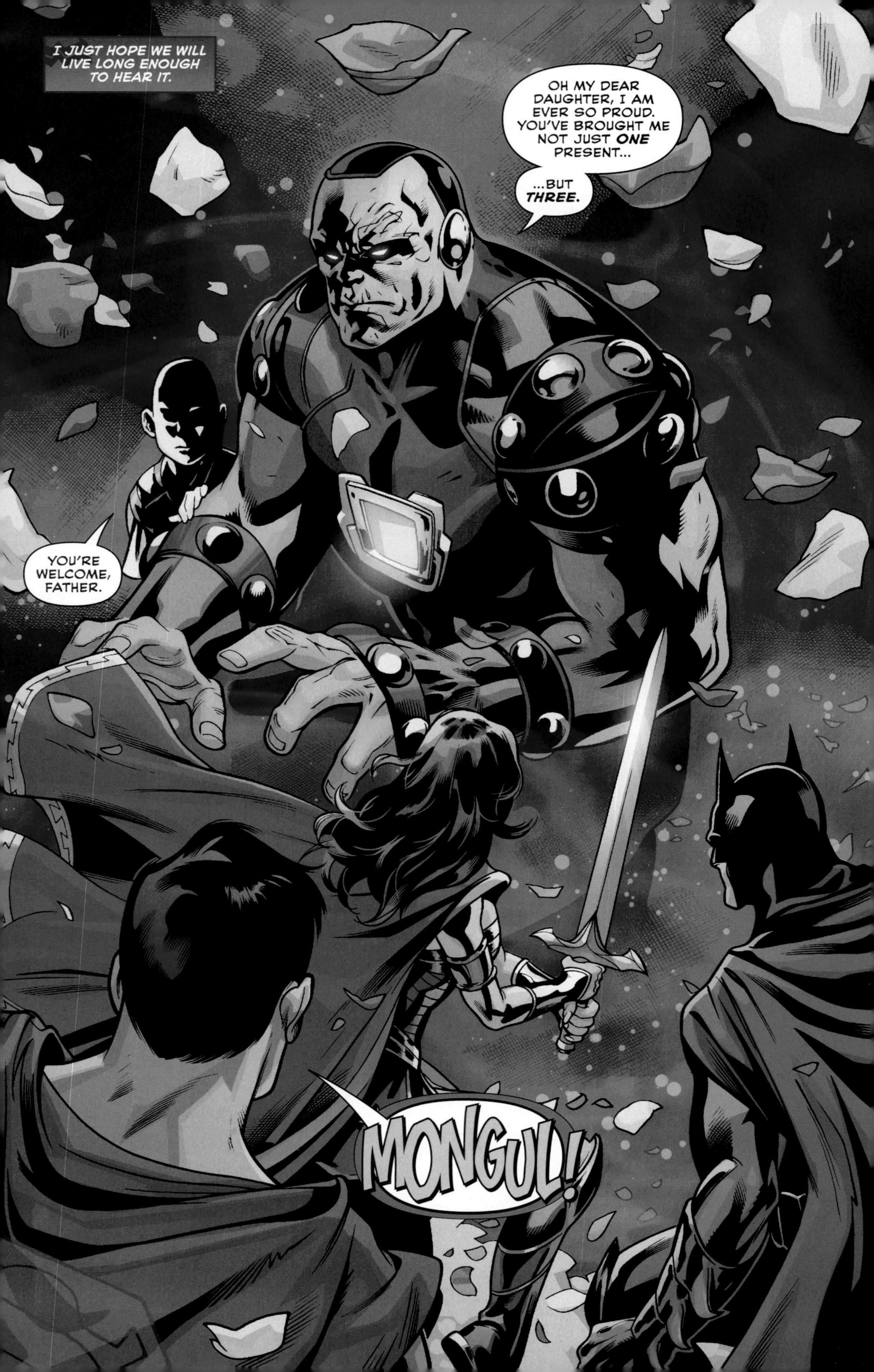
I JUST HOPE WE WILL LIVE LONG ENOUGH TO HEAR IT.
OH MY DEAR DAUGHTER, I AM EVER SO PROUD. YOU'VE BROUGHT ME NOT JUST ONE PRESENT...
...BUT THREE.
YOU'RE WELCOME, FATHER.
MONGUL!

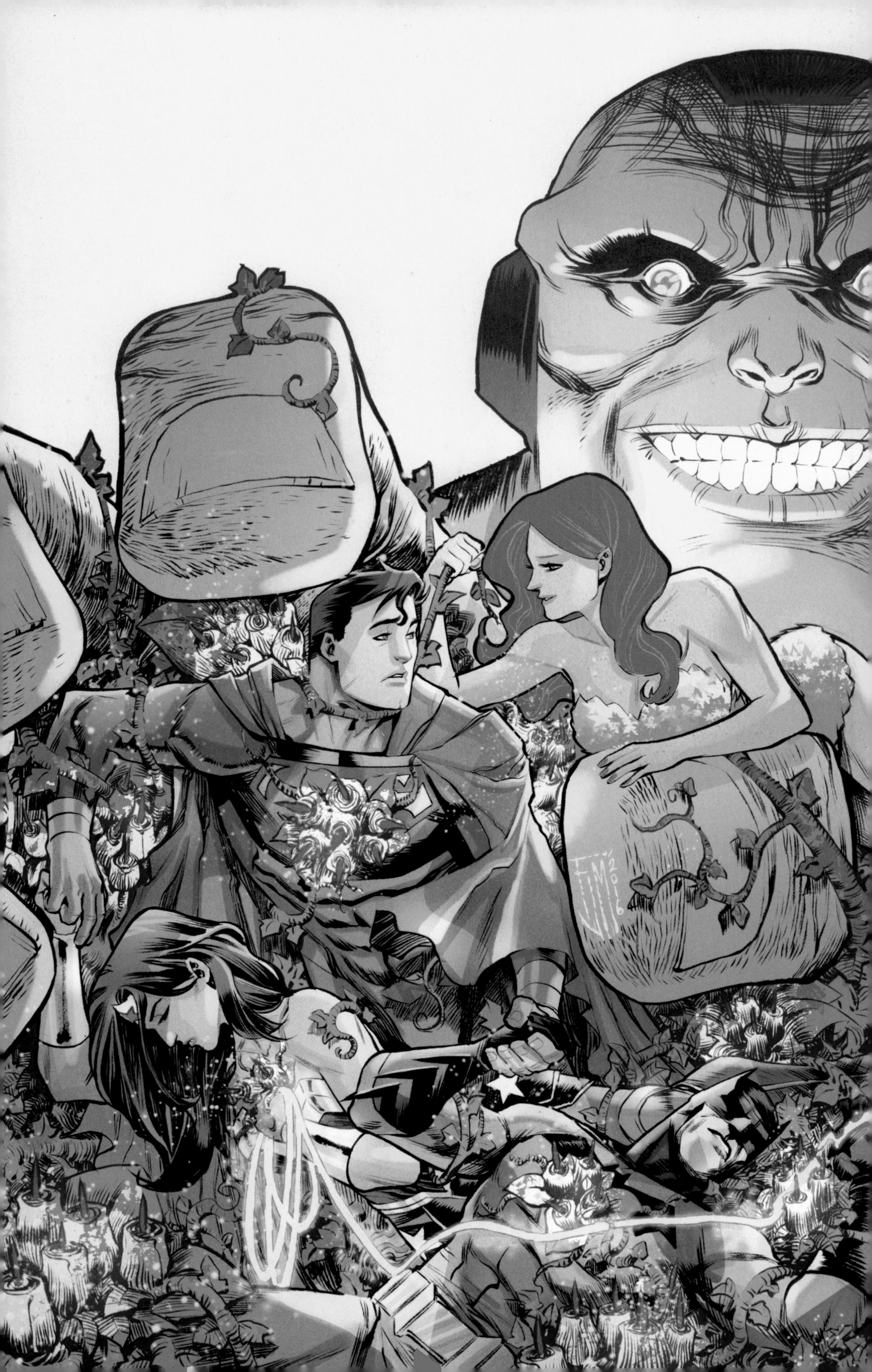

BETTER TOGETHER Part Five: DELIVER YOUR CHILDREN

FRANCIS MANAPUL artist

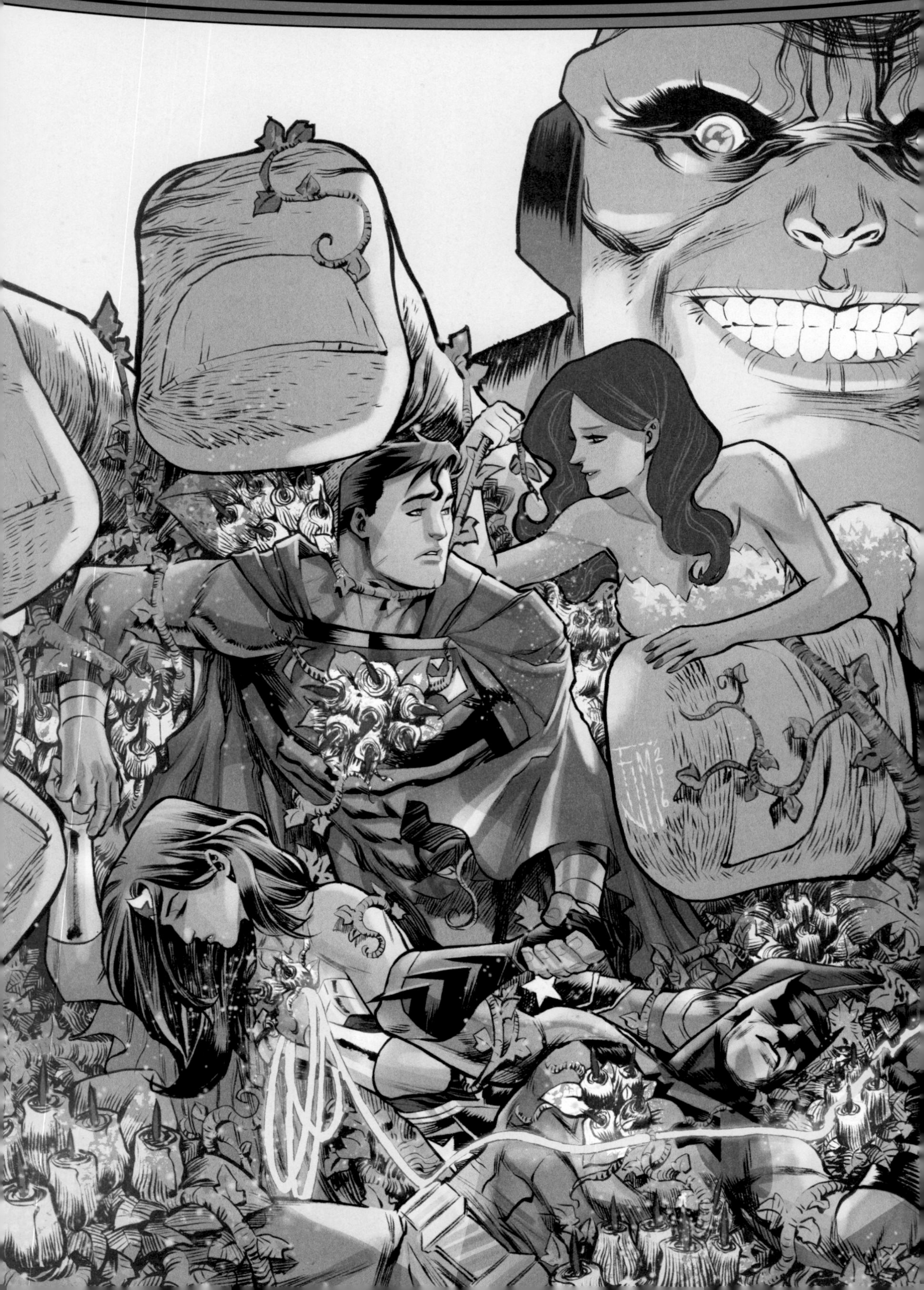

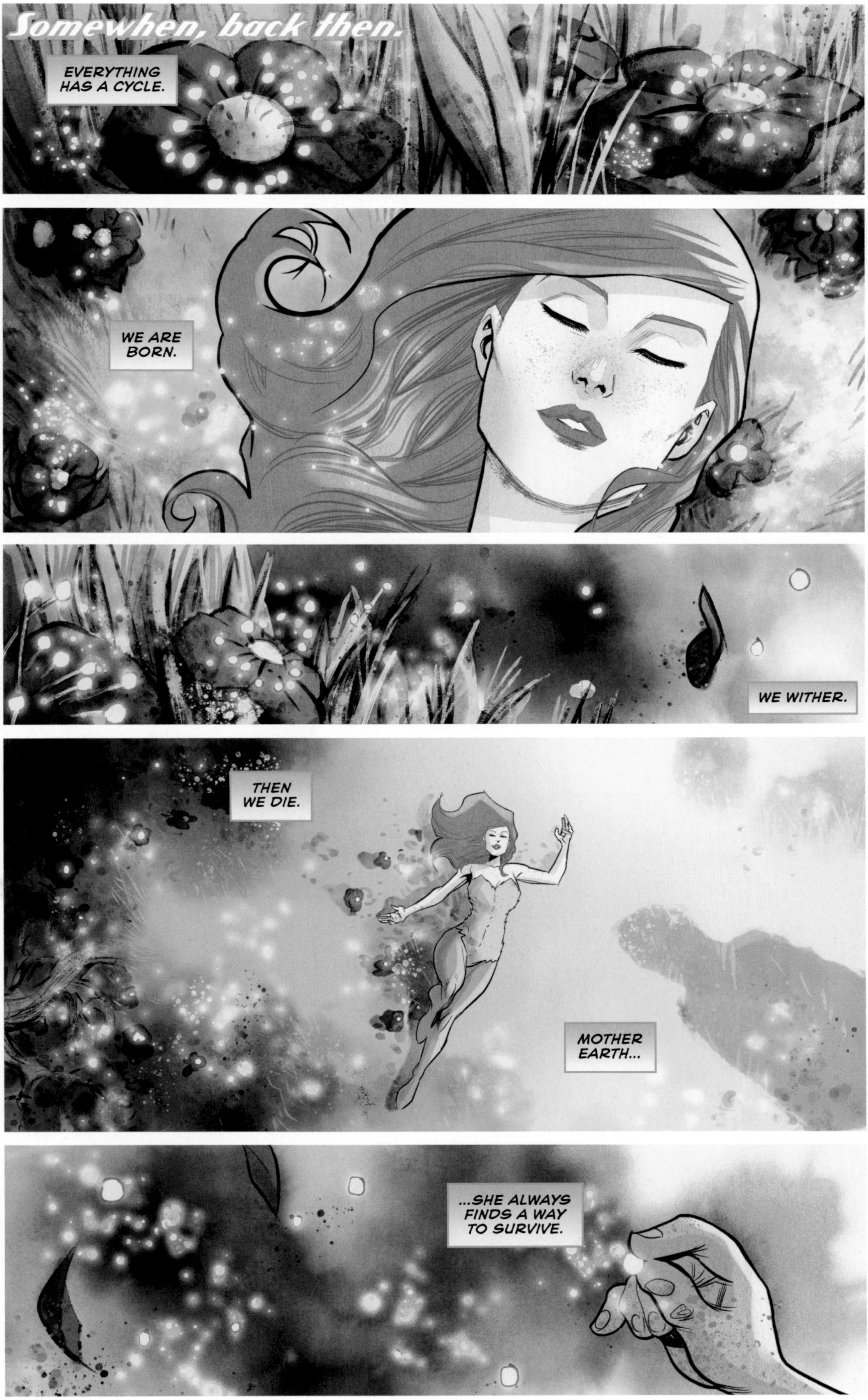
Somewhen, back then.
EVERYTHING HAS A CYCLE.
WE ARE BORN.
WE WITHER.
THEN WE DIE.
MOTHER EARTH...
...SHE ALWAYS FINDS A WAY TO SURVIVE.

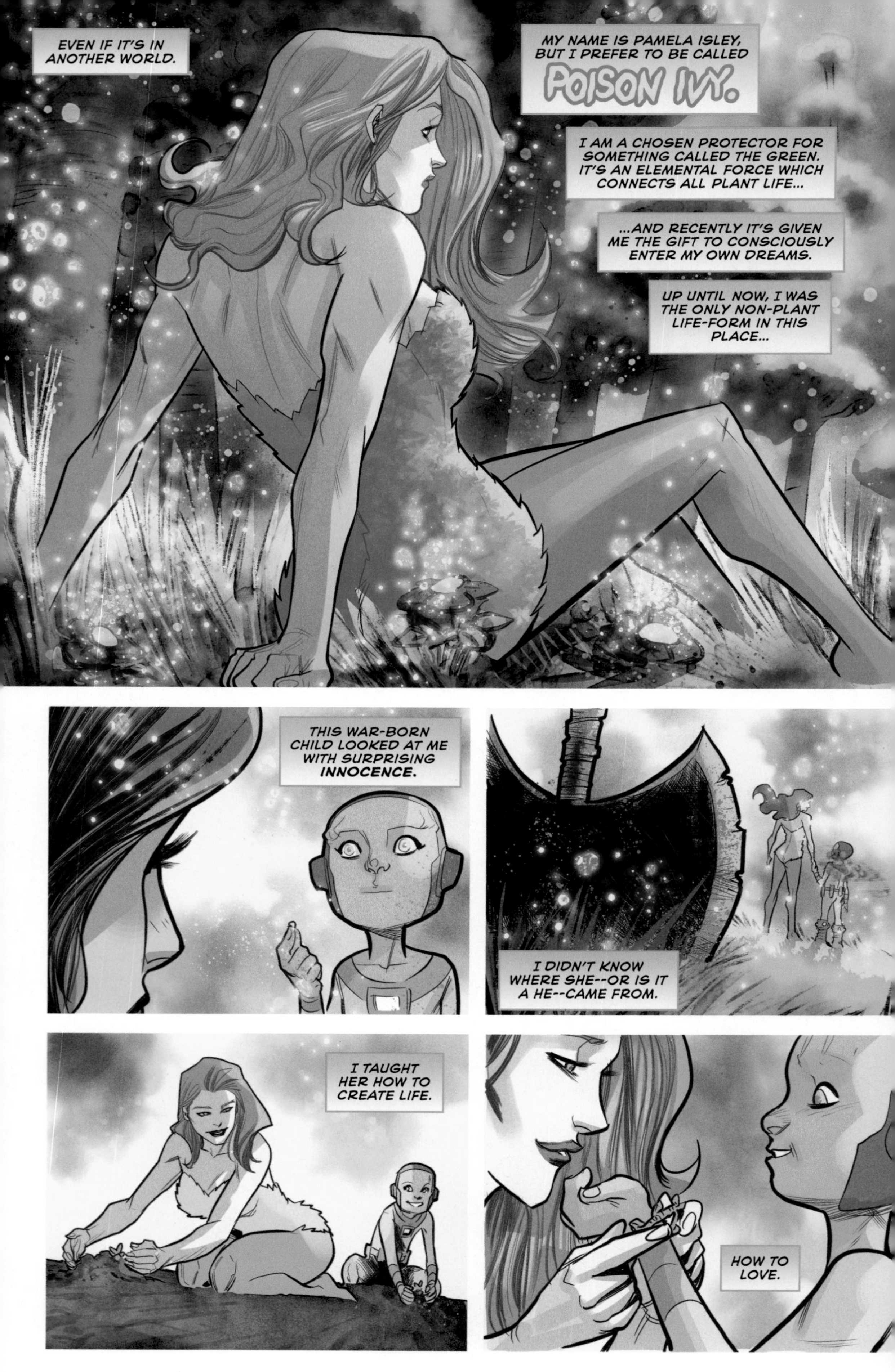
EVEN IF IT'S IN ANOTHER WORLD.
MY NAME IS PAMELA ISLEY, BUT I PREFER TO BE CALLED
POISON IVY.
I AM A CHOSEN PROTECTOR FOR SOMETHING CALLED THE GREEN. IT'S AN ELEMENTAL FORCE WHICH CONNECTS ALL PLANT LIFE...
...AND RECENTLY IT'S GIVEN ME THE GIFT TO CONSCIOUSLY ENTER MY OWN DREAMS.
UP UNTIL NOW, I WAS THE ONLY NON-PLANT LIFE-FORM IN THIS PLACE...
THIS WAR-BORN CHILD LOOKED AT ME WITH SURPRISING INNOCENCE.
I DIDN'T KNOW WHERE SHE--OR IS IT A HE--CAME FROM.
I TAUGHT HER HOW TO CREATE LIFE.
HOW TO LOVE.

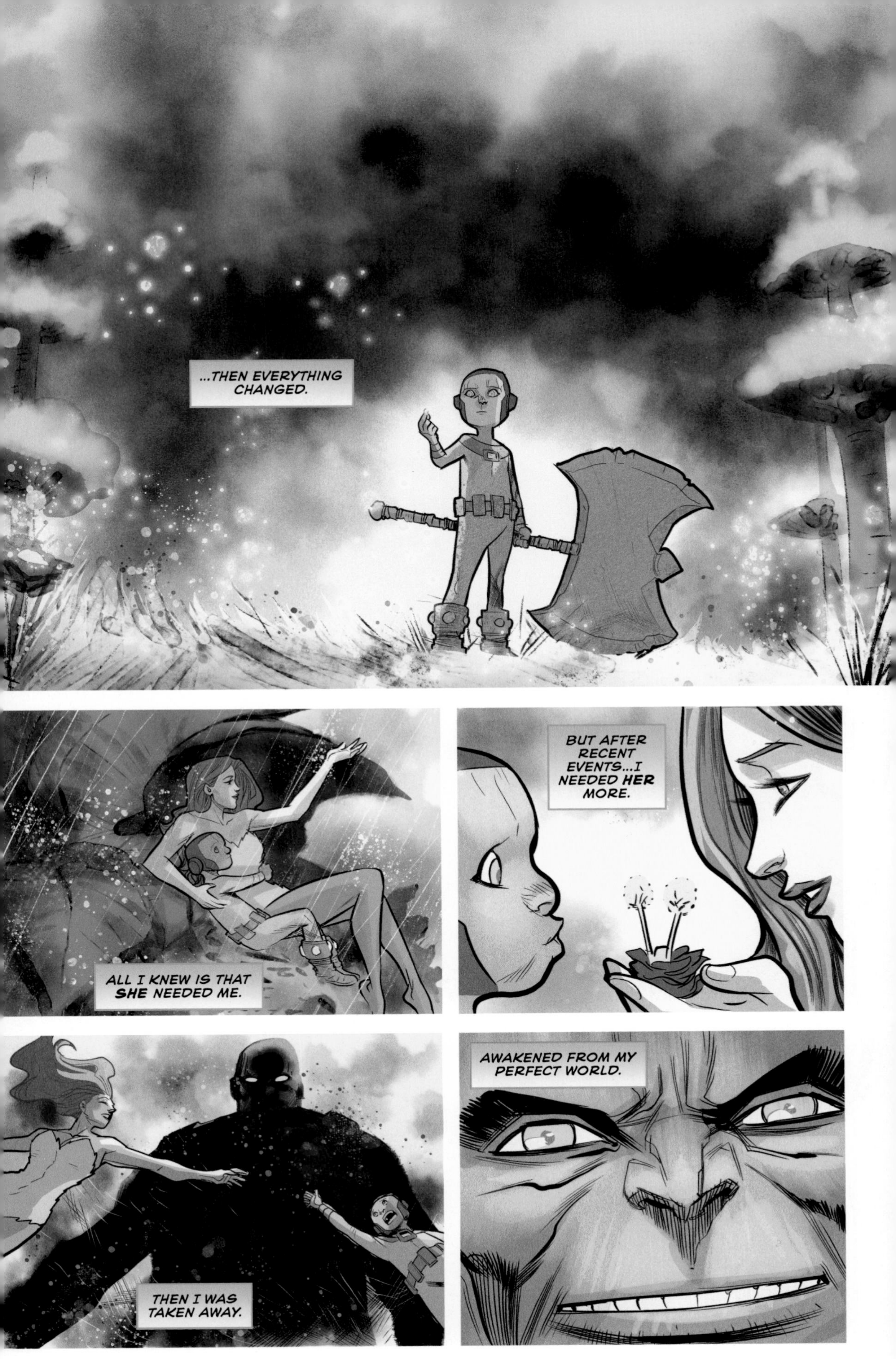
...THEN EVERYTHING CHANGED.
ALL I KNEW IS THAT SHE NEEDED ME.
BUT AFTER RECENT EVENTS...I NEEDED HER MORE.
THEN I WAS TAKEN AWAY.
AWAKENED FROM MY PERFECT WORLD.

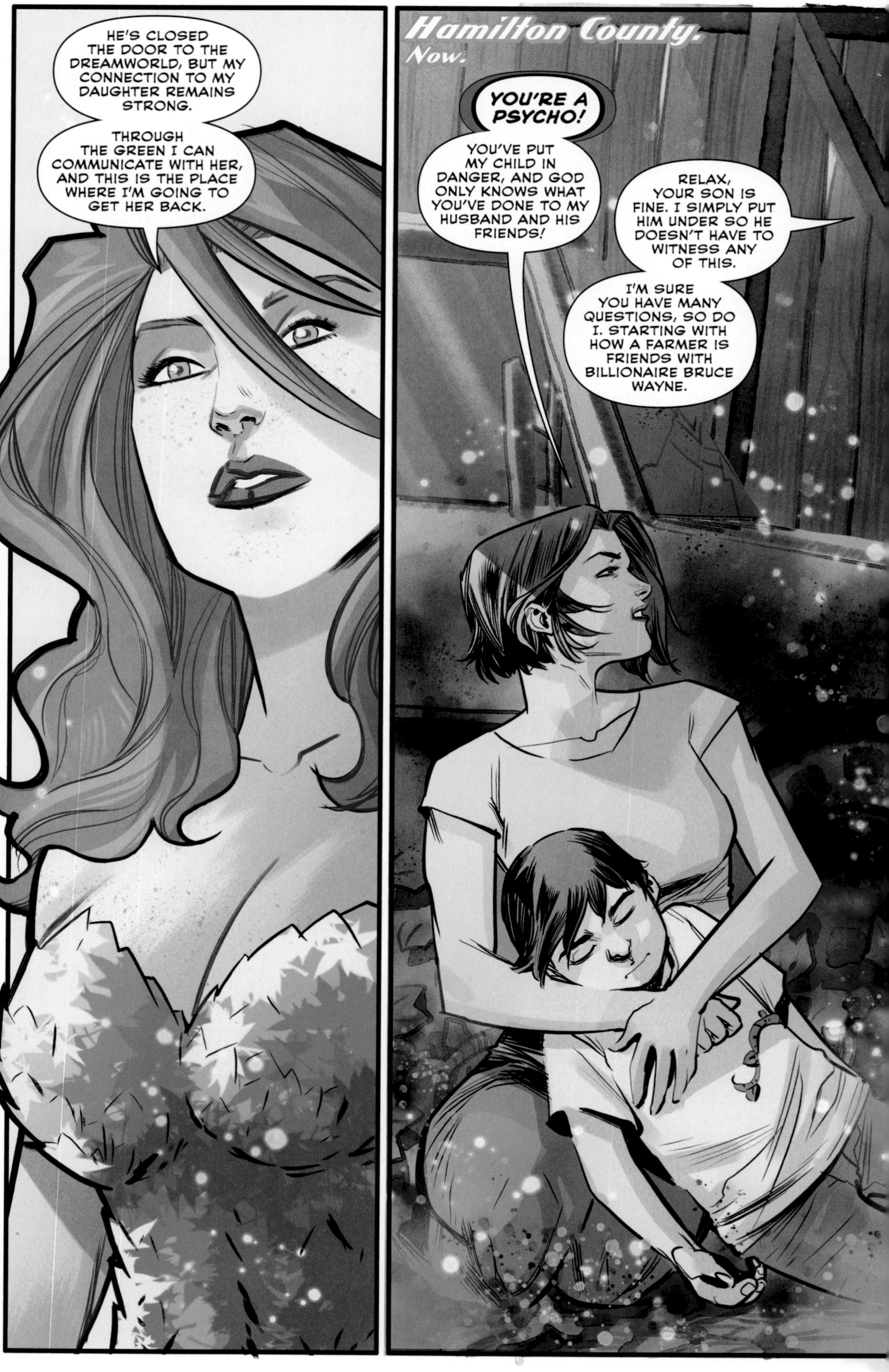
HE'S CLOSED THE DOOR TO THE DREAMWORLD, BUT MY CONNECTION TO MY DAUGHTER REMAINS STRONG.
THROUGH THE GREEN I CAN COMMUNICATE WITH HER, AND THIS IS THE PLACE WHERE I'M GOING TO GET HER BACK.
Hamilton County. Now.
YOU'RE A PSYCHO!
YOU'VE PUT MY CHILD IN DANGER, AND GOD ONLY KNOWS WHAT YOU'VE DONE TO MY HUSBAND AND HIS FRIENDS!
RELAX, YOUR SON IS FINE. I SIMPLY PUT HIM UNDER SO HE DOESN'T HAVE TO WITNESS ANY OF THIS.
I'M SURE YOU HAVE MANY QUESTIONS, SO DO I. STARTING WITH HOW A FARMER IS FRIENDS WITH BILLIONAIRE BRUCE WAYNE.

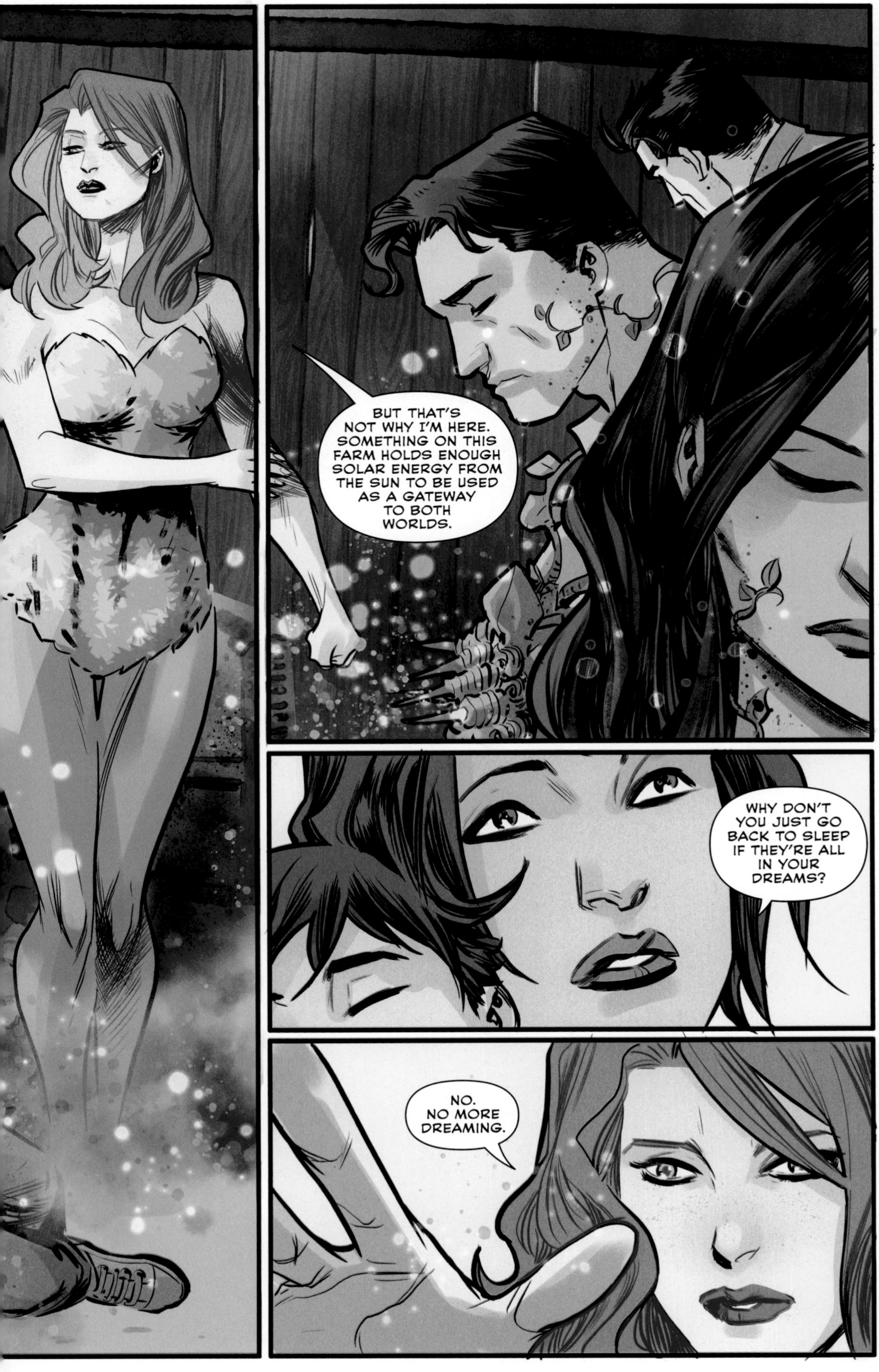
BUT THAT'S NOT WHY I'M HERE. SOMETHING ON THIS FARM HOLDS ENOUGH SOLAR ENERGY FROM THE SUN TO BE USED AS A GATEWAY TO BOTH WORLDS.
WHY DON'T YOU JUST GO BACK TO SLEEP IF THEY'RE ALL IN YOUR DREAMS?
NO. NO MORE DREAMING.

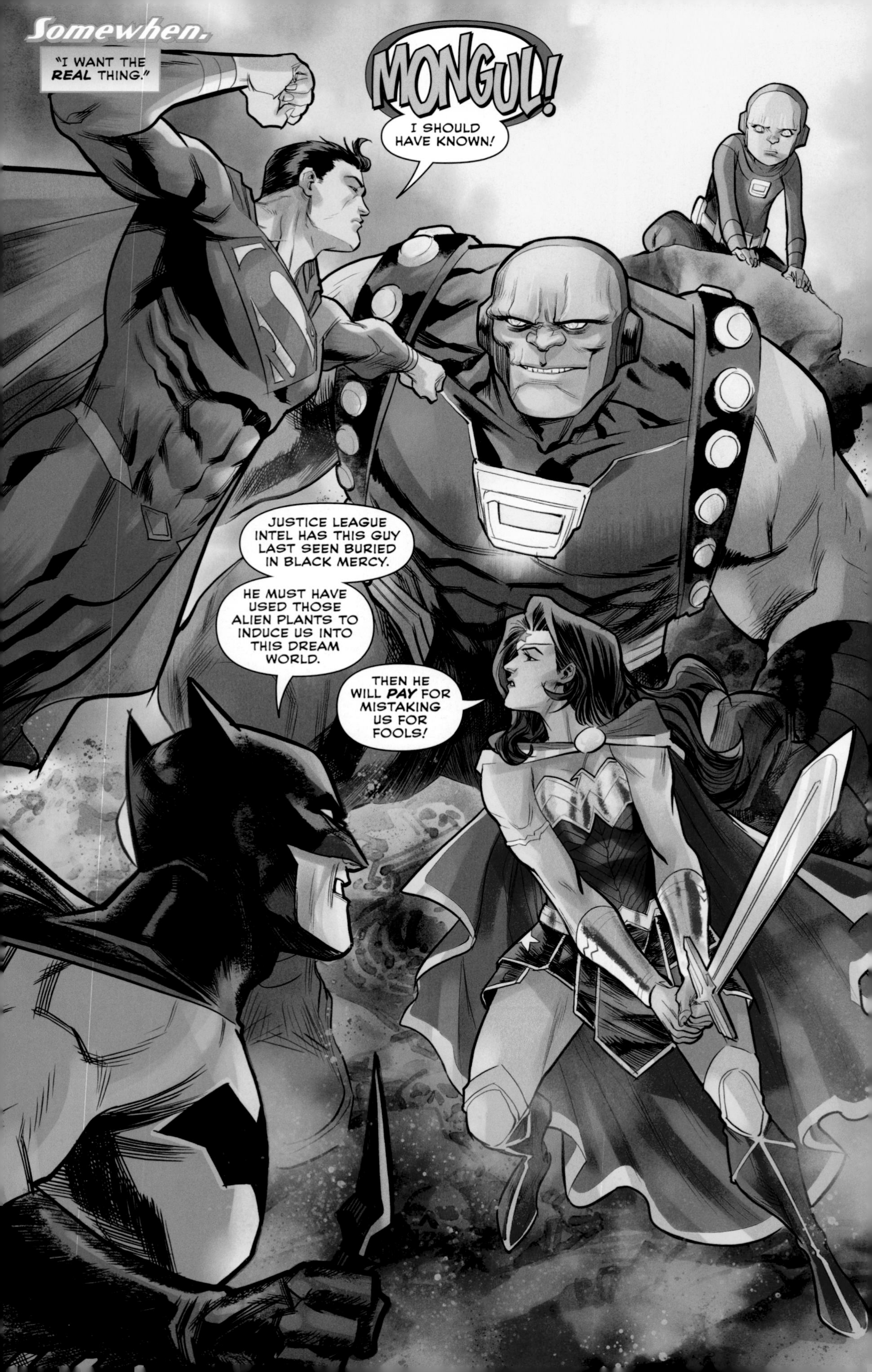
Somewhen.
"I WANT THE REAL THING."
MONGUL!
I SHOULD HAVE KNOWN!
JUSTICE LEAGUE INTEL HAS THIS GUY LAST SEEN BURIED IN BLACK MERCY.
HE MUST HAVE USED THOSE ALIEN PLANTS TO INDUCE US INTO THIS DREAM WORLD.
THEN HE WILL PAY FOR MISTAKING US FOR FOOLS!

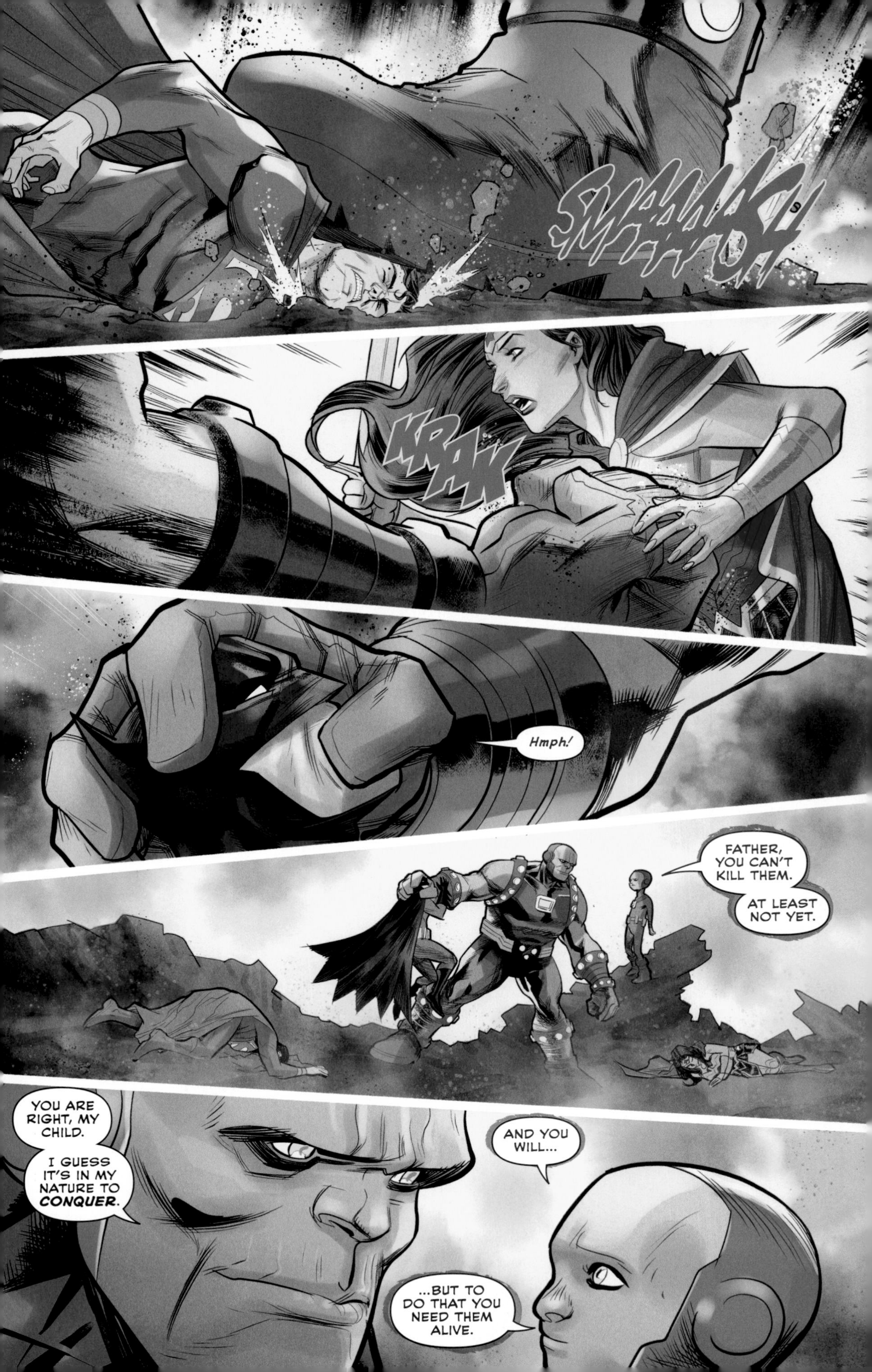
SMAAASH
KRAK
Hmph!
FATHER, YOU CAN'T KILL THEM.
AT LEAST NOT YET.
YOU ARE RIGHT, MY CHILD.
I GUESS IT'S IN MY NATURE TO CONQUER.
AND YOU WILL...
...BUT TO DO THAT YOU NEED THEM ALIVE.

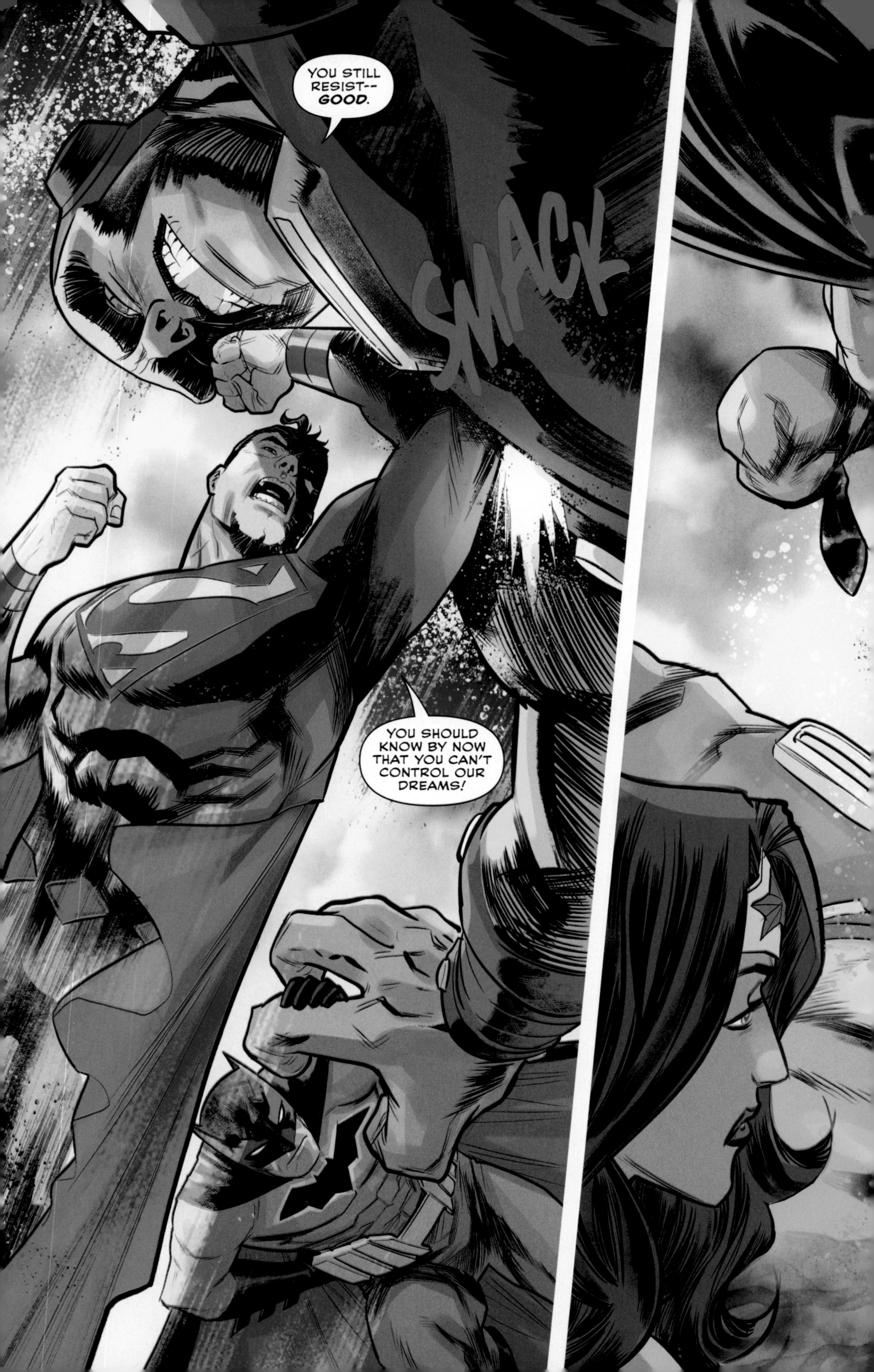
YOU STILL RESIST-- GOOD.
SMACK
YOU SHOULD KNOW BY NOW THAT YOU CAN'T CONTROL OUR DREAMS!

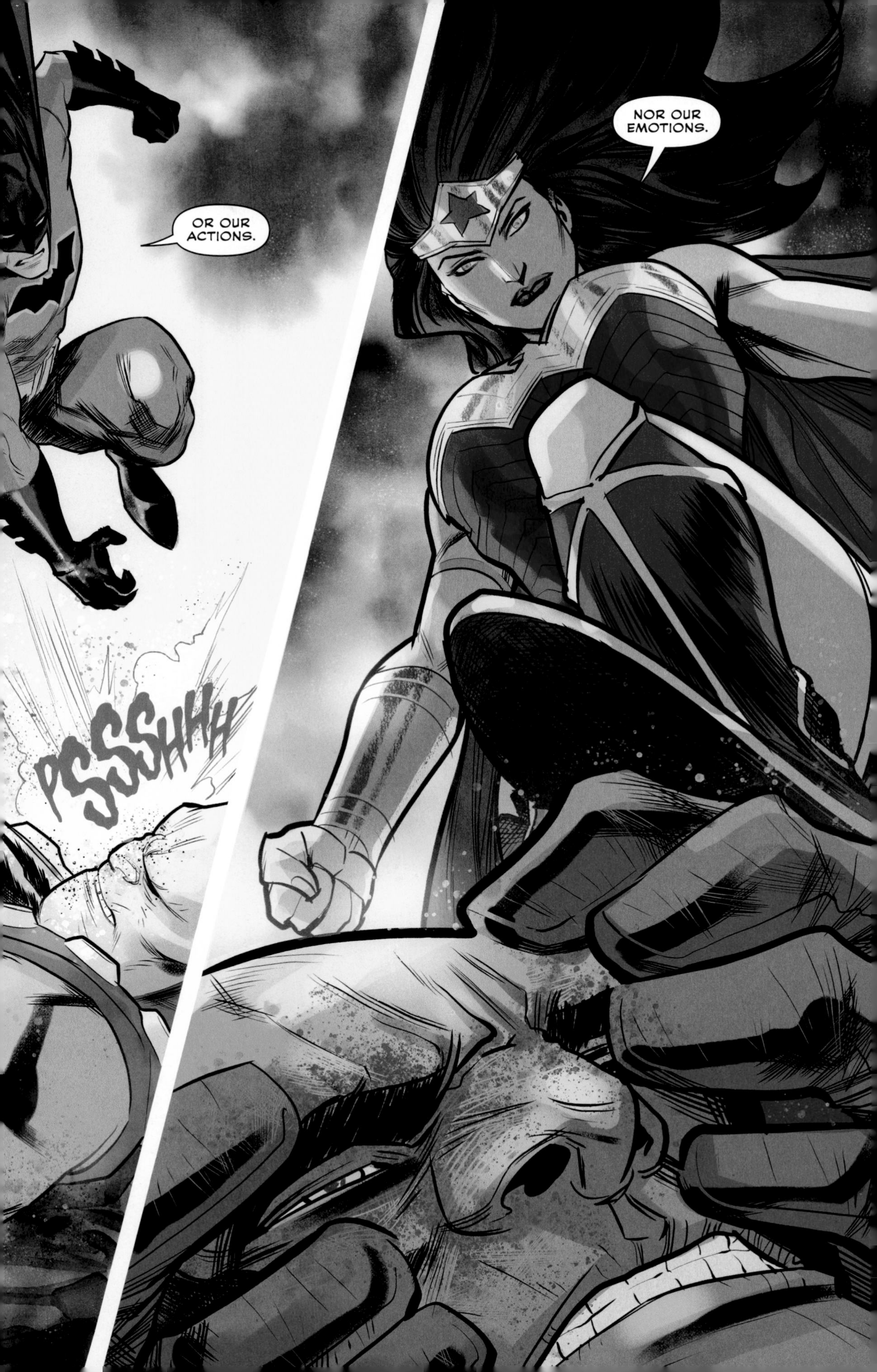
OR OUR ACTIONS.
NOR OUR EMOTIONS.
PSSSHHH

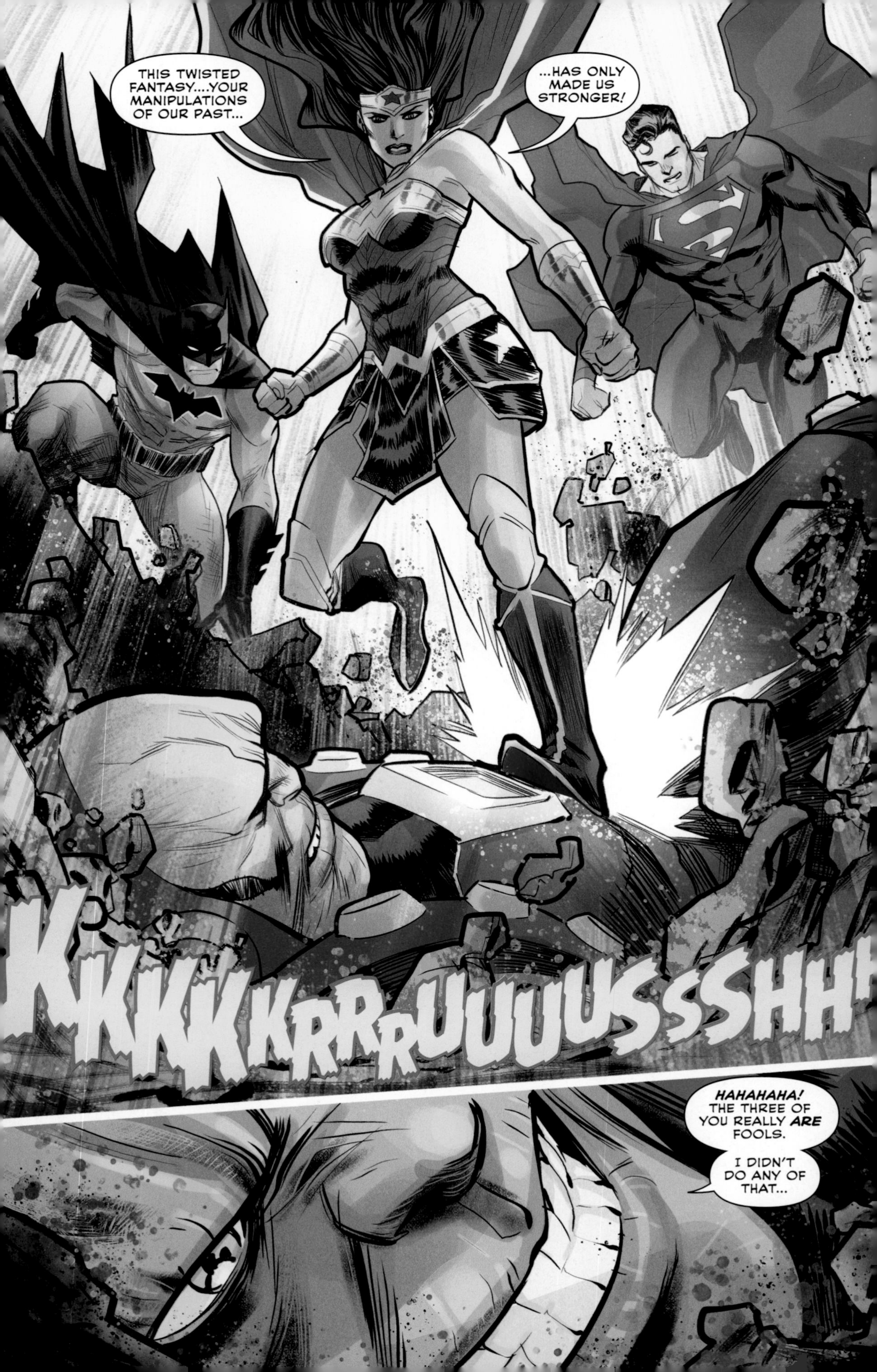
THIS TWISTED FANTASY....YOUR MANIPULATIONS OF OUR PAST...
...HAS ONLY MADE US STRONGER!
KKKKKRRRRUUUUSSSHH
HAHAHAHA! THE THREE OF YOU REALLY ARE FOOLS.
I DIDN'T DO ANY OF THAT...

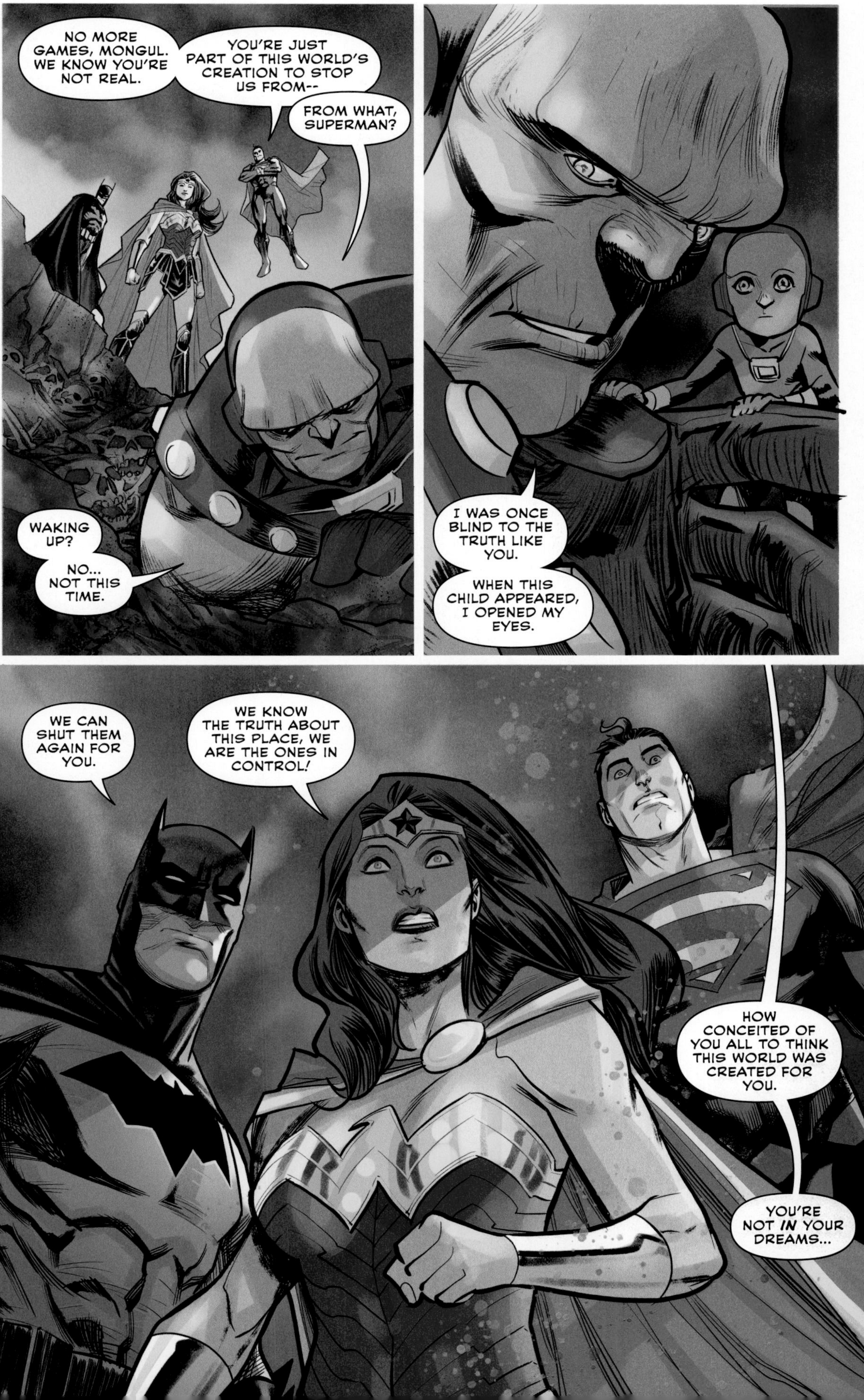
NO MORE GAMES, MONGUL. WE KNOW YOU'RE NOT REAL.
YOU'RE JUST PART OF THIS WORLD'S CREATION TO STOP US FROM--
FROM WHAT, SUPERMAN?
WAKING UP?
NO... NOT THIS TIME.
I WAS ONCE BLIND TO THE TRUTH LIKE YOU.
WHEN THIS CHILD APPEARED, I OPENED MY EYES.
WE CAN SHUT THEM AGAIN FOR YOU.
WE KNOW THE TRUTH ABOUT THIS PLACE, WE ARE THE ONES IN CONTROL!
HOW CONCEITED OF YOU ALL TO THINK THIS WORLD WAS CREATED FOR YOU.
YOU'RE NOT *IN* YOUR DREAMS...

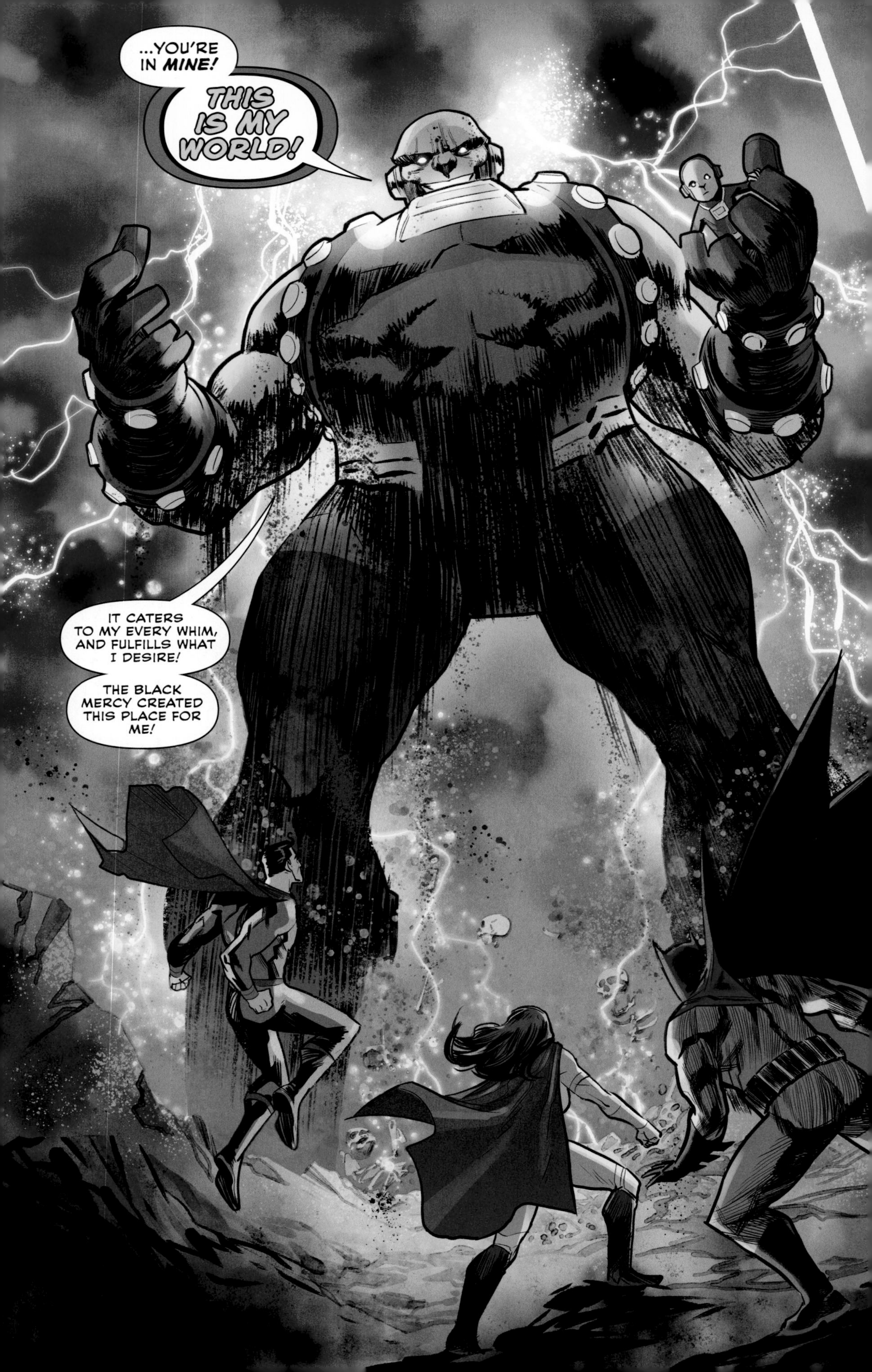
...YOU'RE IN MINE!
THIS IS MY WORLD!
IT CATERS TO MY EVERY WHIM, AND FULFILLS WHAT I DESIRE!
THE BLACK MERCY CREATED THIS PLACE FOR ME!

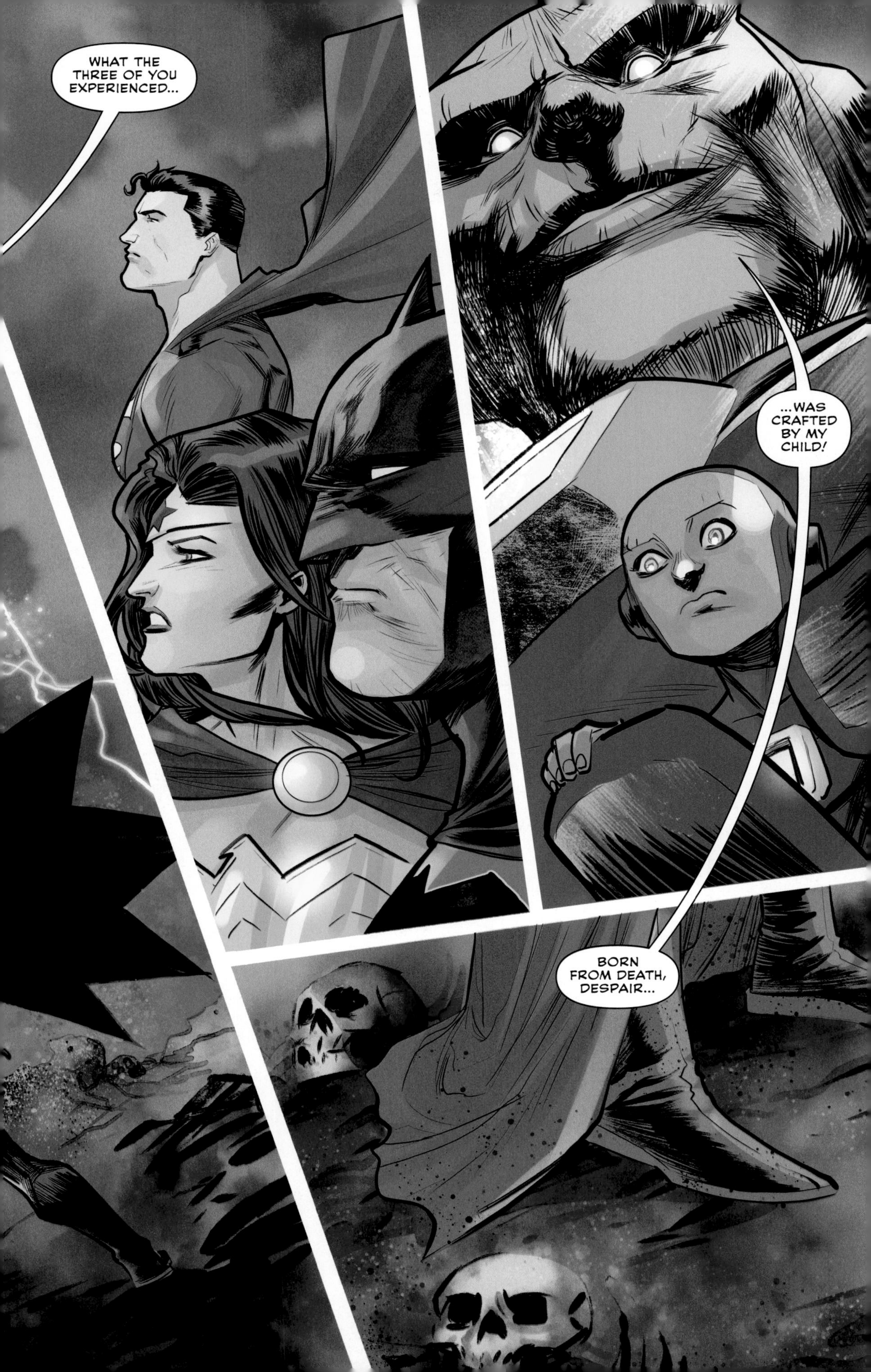
WHAT THE THREE OF YOU EXPERIENCED...
...WAS CRAFTED BY MY CHILD!
BORN FROM DEATH, DESPAIR...

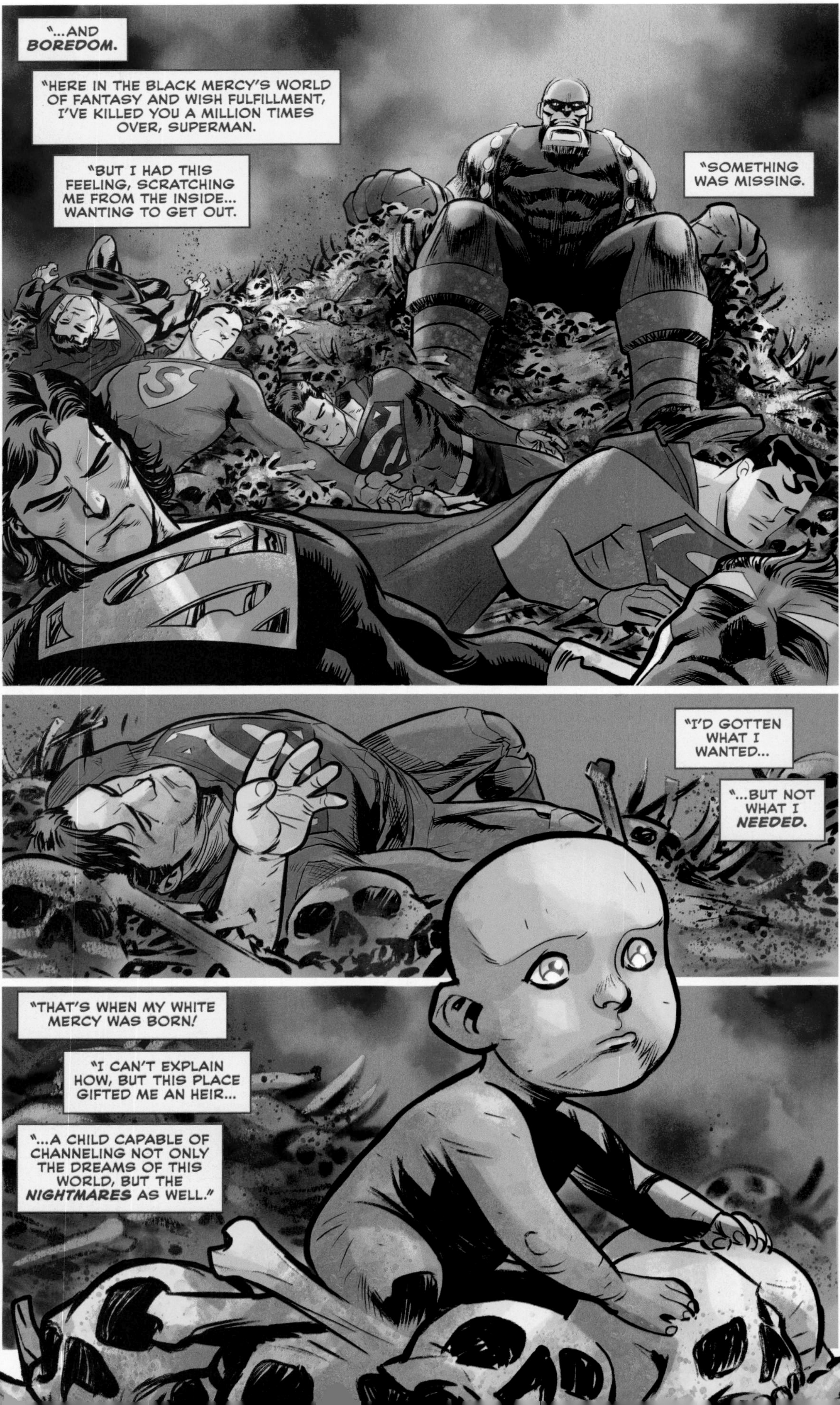
"...AND *BOREDOM*.
"HERE IN THE BLACK MERCY'S WORLD OF FANTASY AND WISH FULFILLMENT, I'VE KILLED YOU A MILLION TIMES OVER, SUPERMAN.
"BUT I HAD THIS FEELING, SCRATCHING ME FROM THE INSIDE... WANTING TO GET OUT.
"SOMETHING WAS MISSING.
"I'D GOTTEN WHAT I WANTED...
"...BUT NOT WHAT I *NEEDED*.
"THAT'S WHEN MY WHITE MERCY WAS BORN!
"I CAN'T EXPLAIN HOW, BUT THIS PLACE GIFTED ME AN HEIR...
"...A CHILD CAPABLE OF CHANNELING NOT ONLY THE DREAMS OF THIS WORLD, BUT THE *NIGHTMARES* AS WELL."

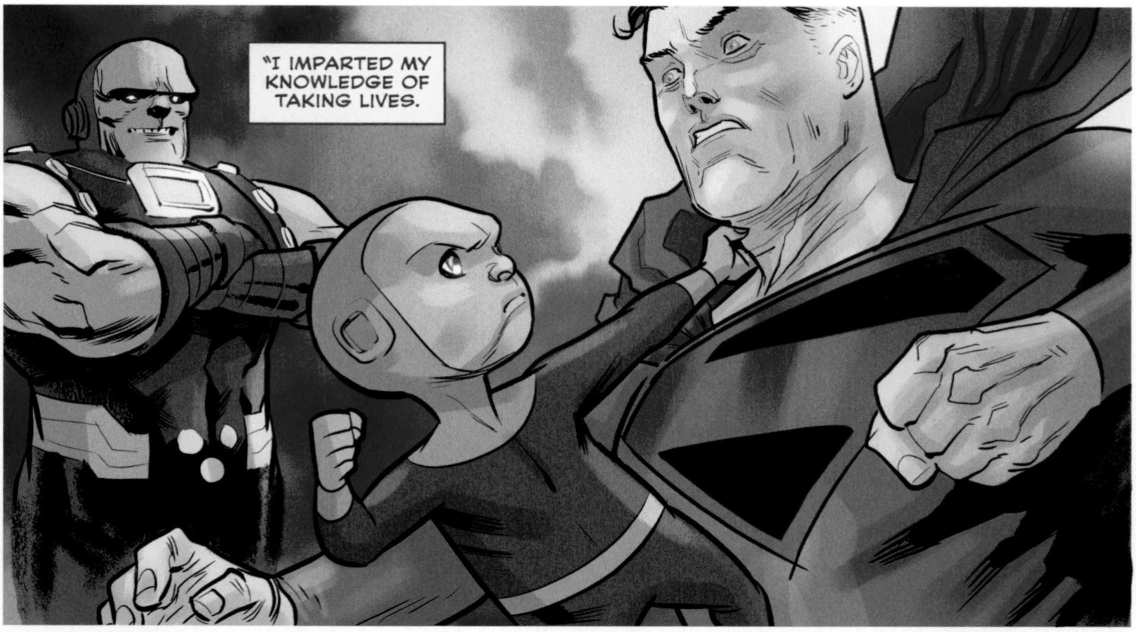
"I IMPARTED MY KNOWLEDGE OF TAKING LIVES.

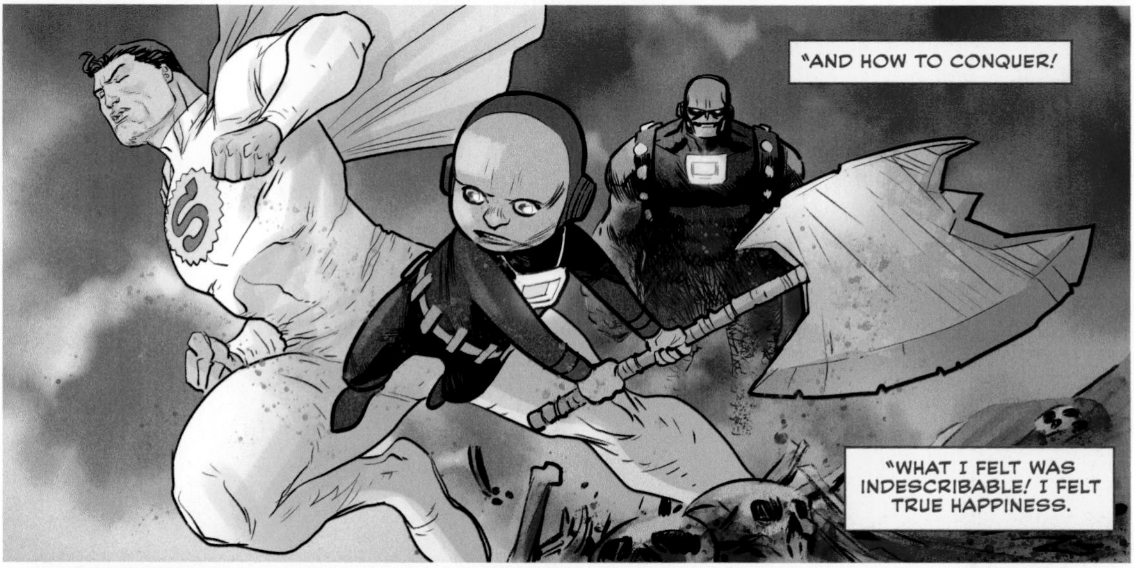
"AND HOW TO CONQUER!
"WHAT I FELT WAS INDESCRIBABLE! I FELT TRUE HAPPINESS.

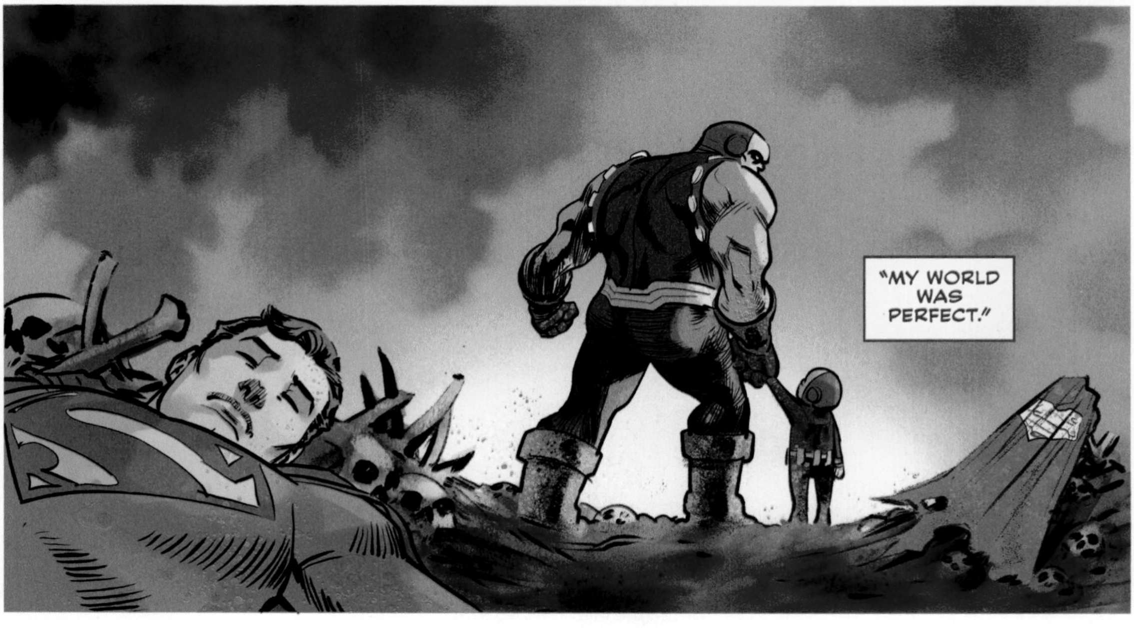
"MY WORLD WAS PERFECT."

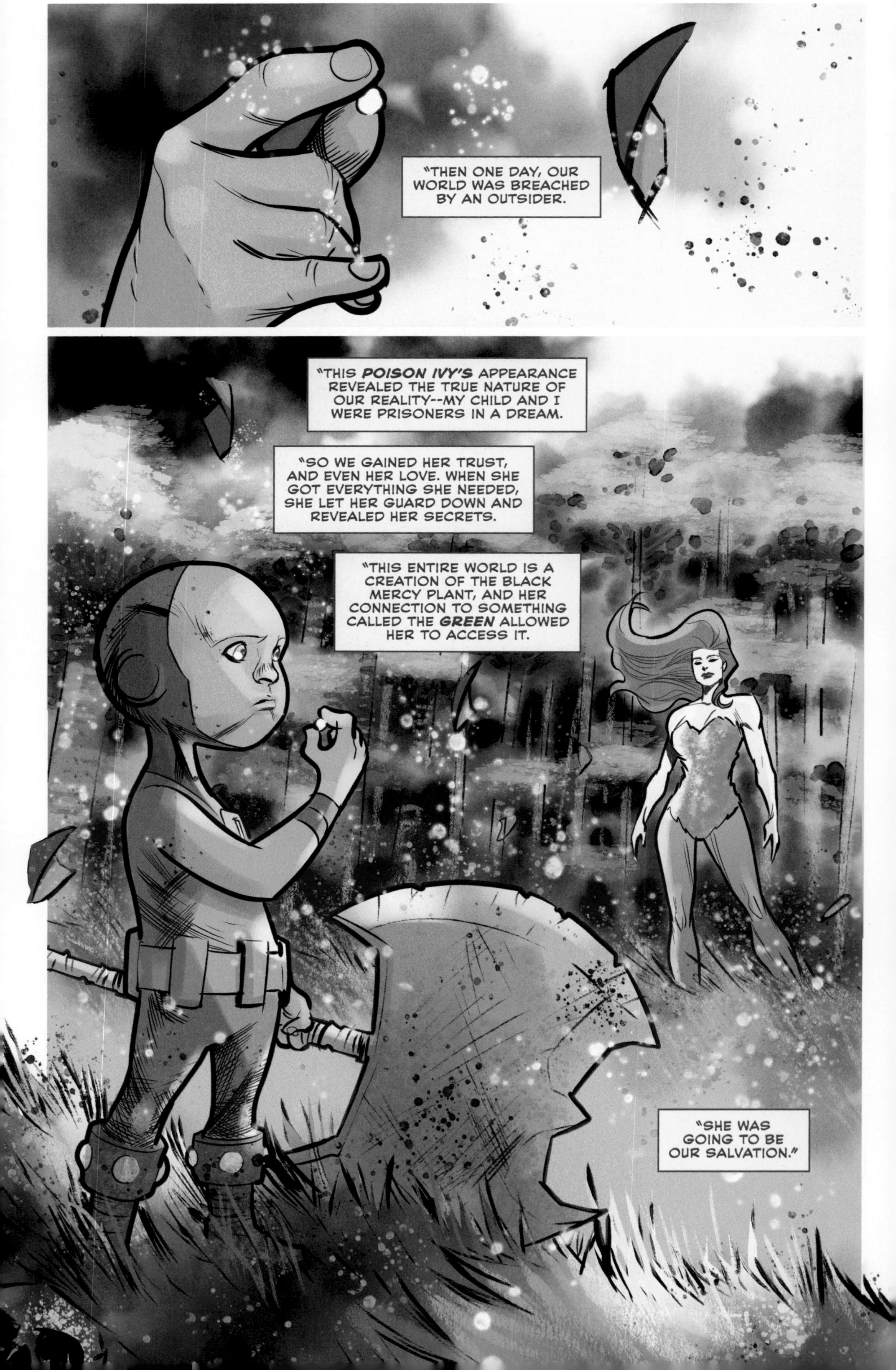
"THEN ONE DAY, OUR WORLD WAS BREACHED BY AN OUTSIDER.
"THIS POISON IVY'S APPEARANCE REVEALED THE TRUE NATURE OF OUR REALITY--MY CHILD AND I WERE PRISONERS IN A DREAM.
"SO WE GAINED HER TRUST, AND EVEN HER LOVE. WHEN SHE GOT EVERYTHING SHE NEEDED, SHE LET HER GUARD DOWN AND REVEALED HER SECRETS.
"THIS ENTIRE WORLD IS A CREATION OF THE BLACK MERCY PLANT, AND HER CONNECTION TO SOMETHING CALLED THE GREEN ALLOWED HER TO ACCESS IT.
"SHE WAS GOING TO BE OUR SALVATION."

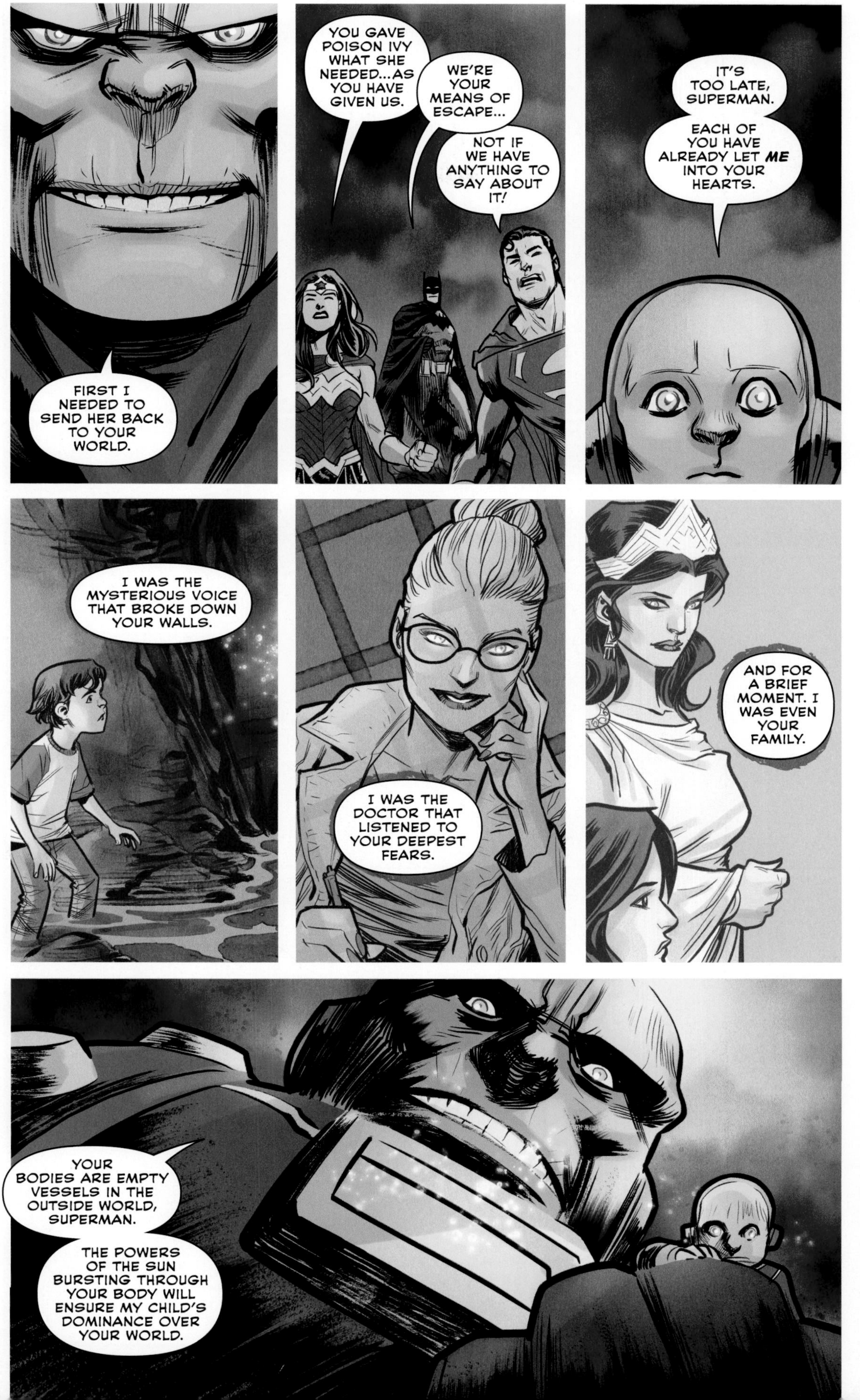
FIRST I NEEDED TO SEND HER BACK TO YOUR WORLD.
YOU GAVE POISON IVY WHAT SHE NEEDED...AS YOU HAVE GIVEN US.
WE'RE YOUR MEANS OF ESCAPE...
NOT IF WE HAVE ANYTHING TO SAY ABOUT IT!
IT'S TOO LATE, SUPERMAN.
EACH OF YOU HAVE ALREADY LET ME INTO YOUR HEARTS.
I WAS THE MYSTERIOUS VOICE THAT BROKE DOWN YOUR WALLS.
I WAS THE DOCTOR THAT LISTENED TO YOUR DEEPEST FEARS.
AND FOR A BRIEF MOMENT. I WAS EVEN YOUR FAMILY.
YOUR BODIES ARE EMPTY VESSELS IN THE OUTSIDE WORLD, SUPERMAN.
THE POWERS OF THE SUN BURSTING THROUGH YOUR BODY WILL ENSURE MY CHILD'S DOMINANCE OVER YOUR WORLD.

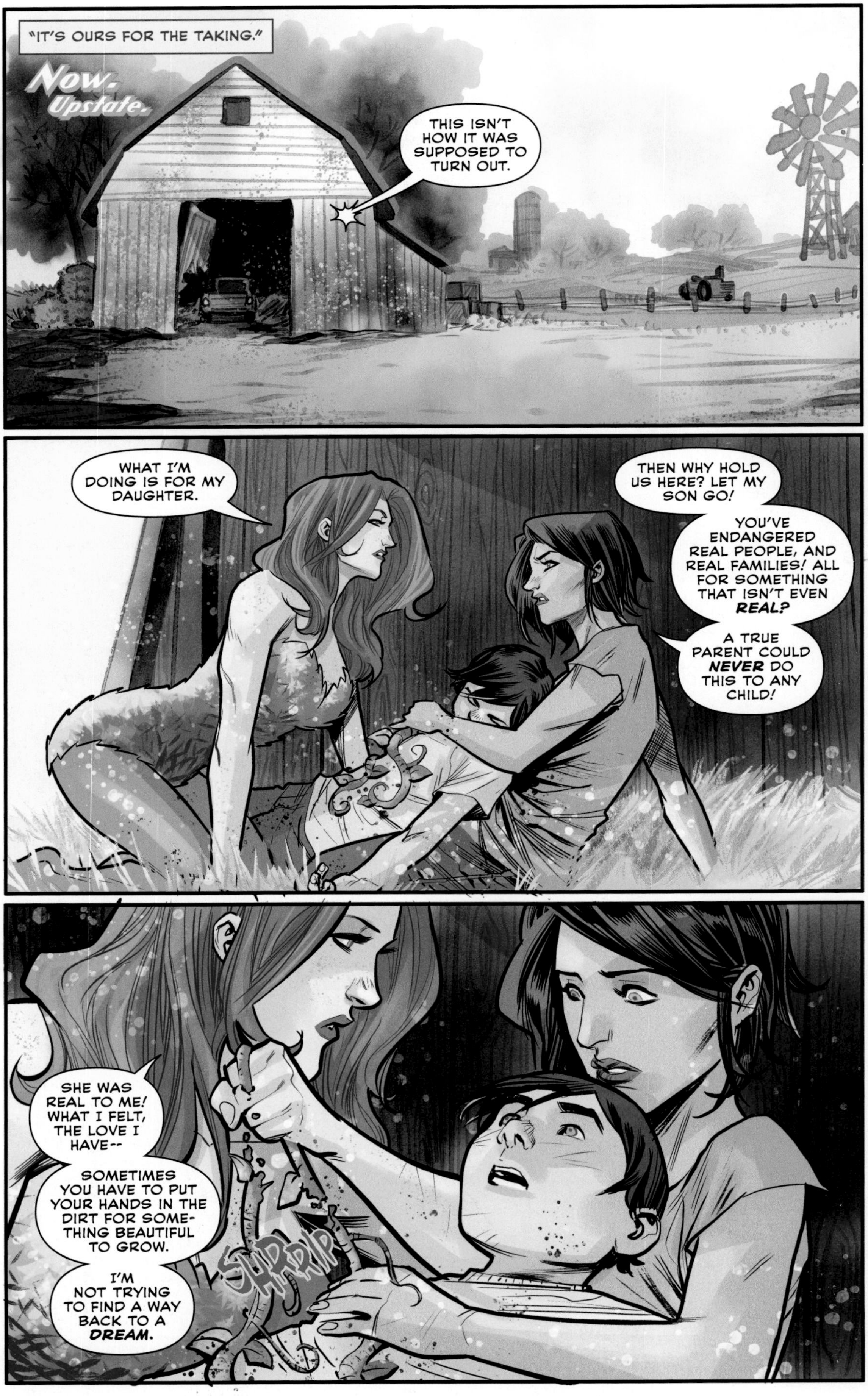
"IT'S OURS FOR THE TAKING."
Now. Upstate.
THIS ISN'T HOW IT WAS SUPPOSED TO TURN OUT.
WHAT I'M DOING IS FOR MY DAUGHTER.
THEN WHY HOLD US HERE? LET MY SON GO!
YOU'VE ENDANGERED REAL PEOPLE, AND REAL FAMILIES! ALL FOR SOMETHING THAT ISN'T EVEN **REAL?**
A TRUE PARENT COULD **NEVER** DO THIS TO ANY CHILD!
SHE WAS REAL TO ME! WHAT I FELT, THE LOVE I HAVE--
SOMETIMES YOU HAVE TO PUT YOUR HANDS IN THE DIRT FOR SOMETHING BEAUTIFUL TO GROW.
I'M NOT TRYING TO FIND A WAY BACK TO A ***DREAM.***
SHRRIP

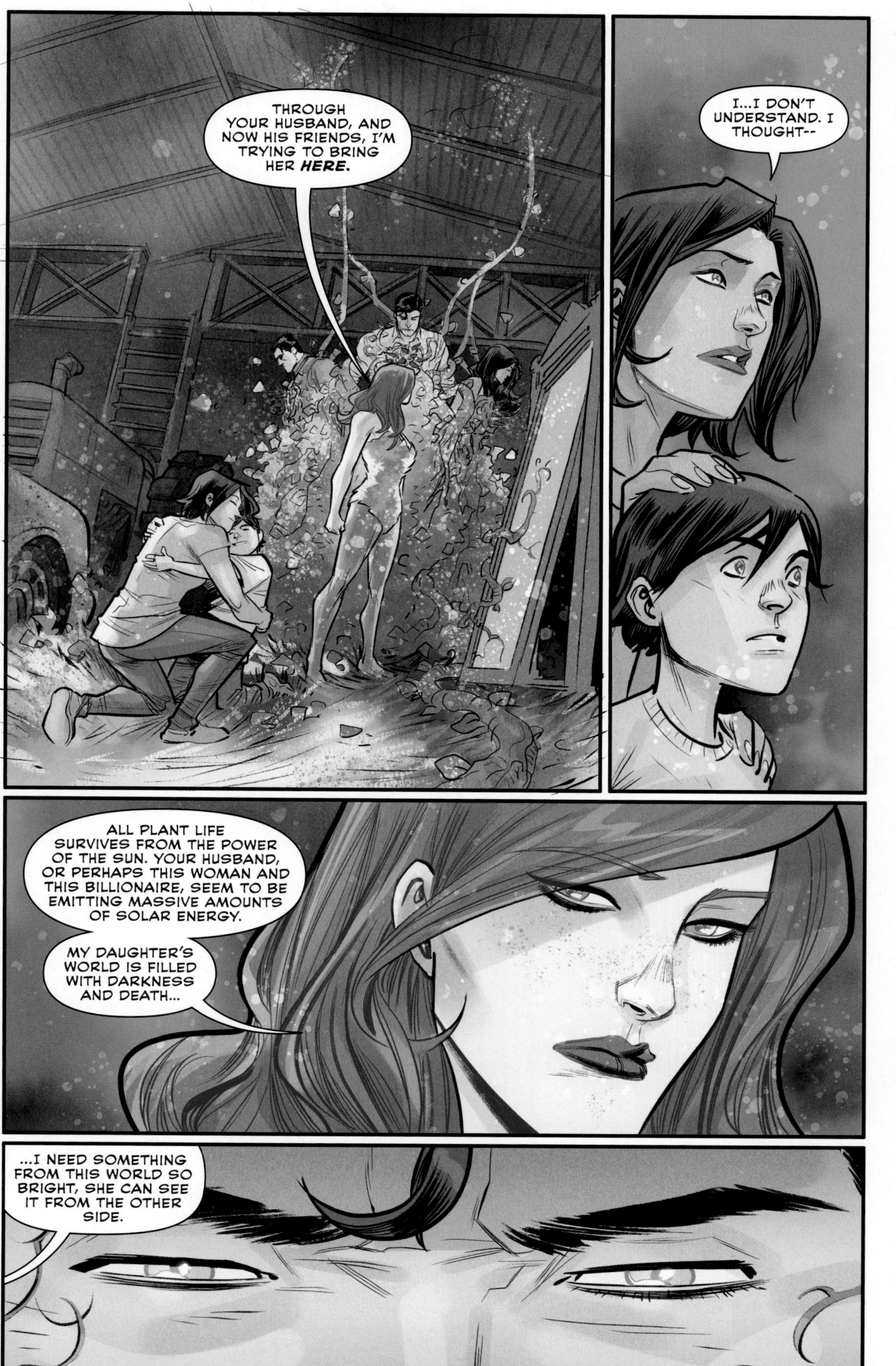
THROUGH YOUR HUSBAND, AND NOW HIS FRIENDS, I'M TRYING TO BRING HER *HERE*.
I...I DON'T UNDERSTAND. I THOUGHT--
ALL PLANT LIFE SURVIVES FROM THE POWER OF THE SUN. YOUR HUSBAND, OR PERHAPS THIS WOMAN AND THIS BILLIONAIRE, SEEM TO BE EMITTING MASSIVE AMOUNTS OF SOLAR ENERGY.
MY DAUGHTER'S WORLD IS FILLED WITH DARKNESS AND DEATH...
...I NEED SOMETHING FROM THIS WORLD SO BRIGHT, SHE CAN SEE IT FROM THE OTHER SIDE.

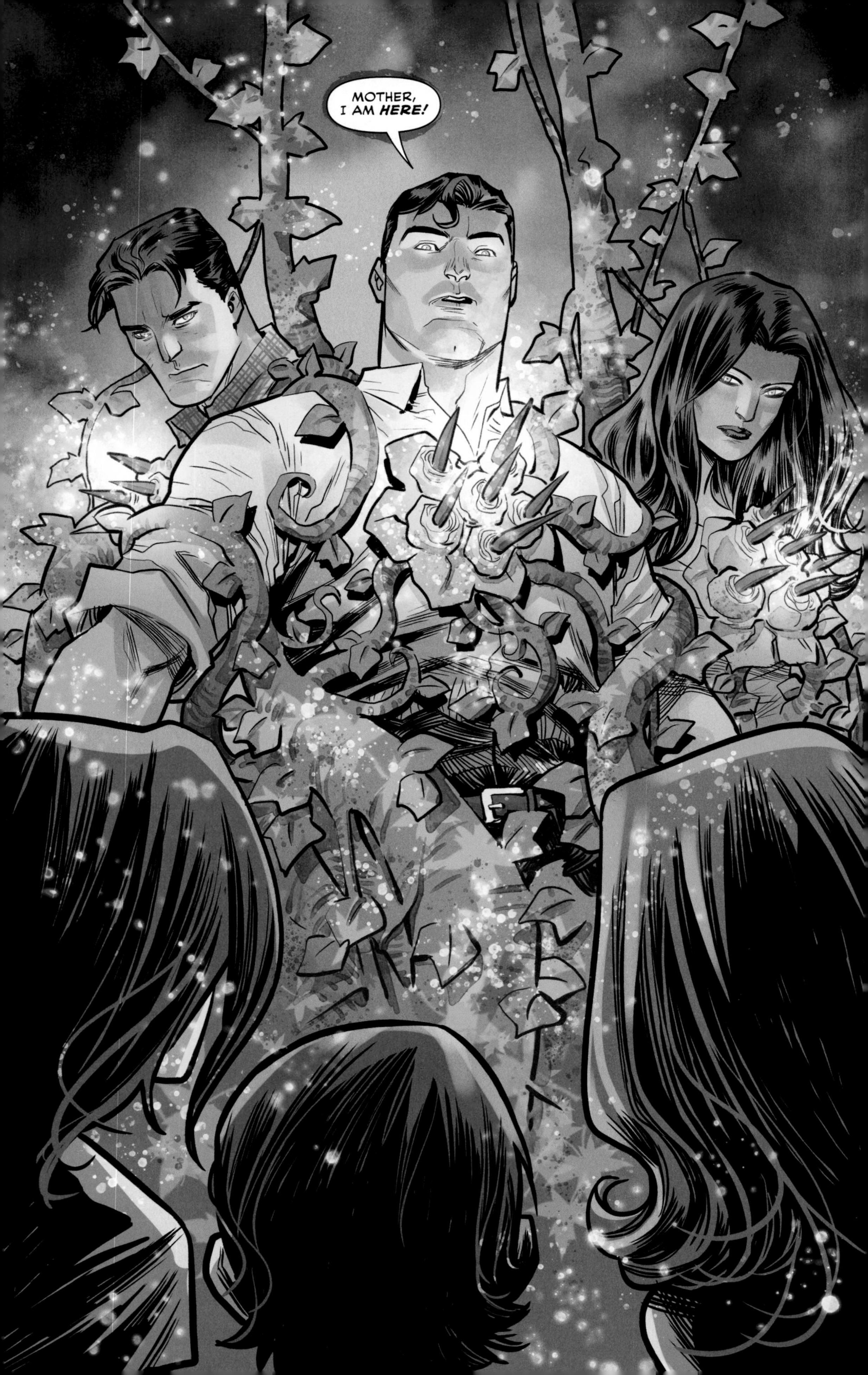
MOTHER, I AM HERE!

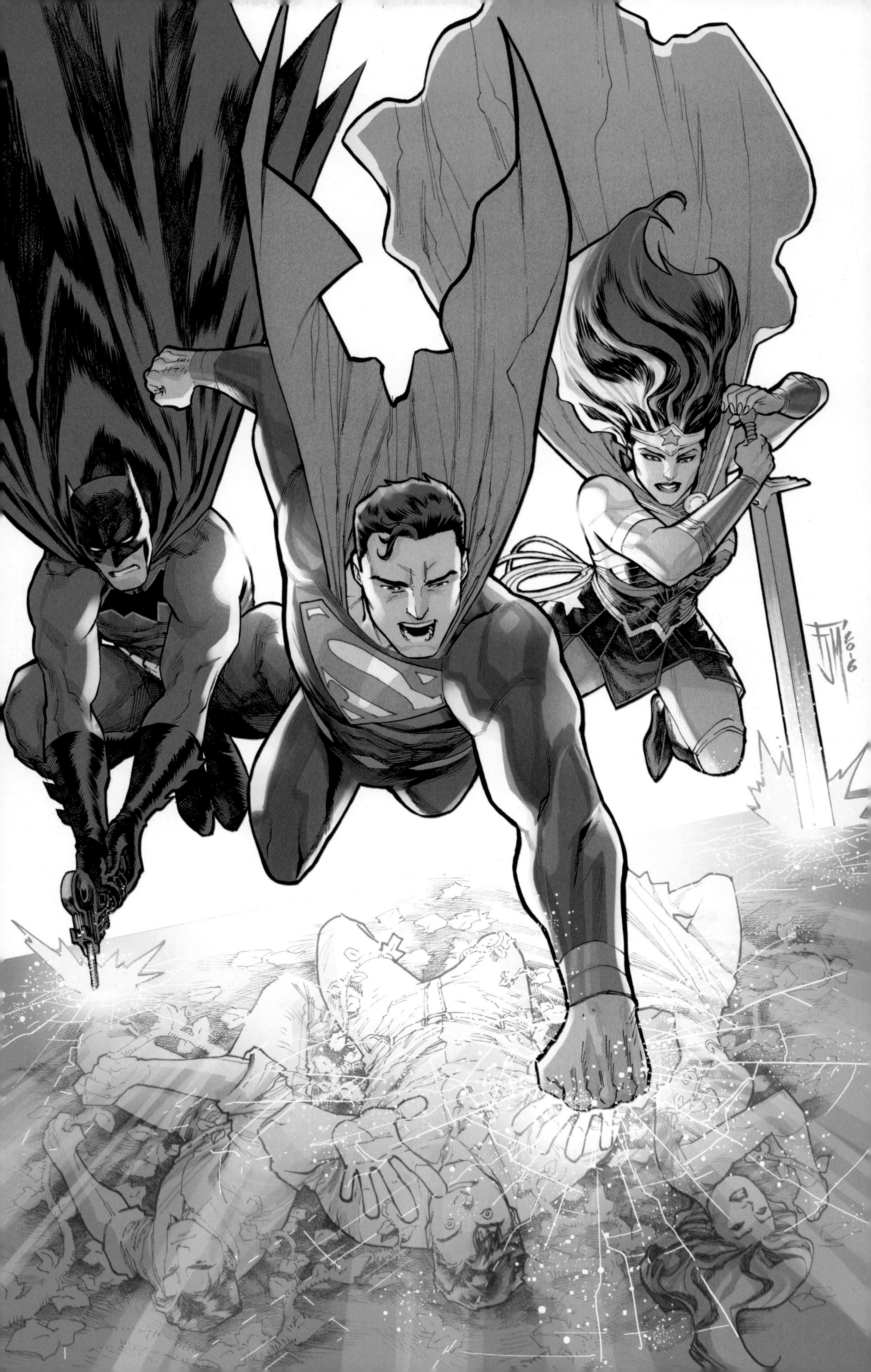

BETTER TOGETHER Finale: AT THE MERCY

EMANUELA LUPACCHINO penciller * RAY McCARTHY, MATT SANTORELLI inkers * HI-FI colorist

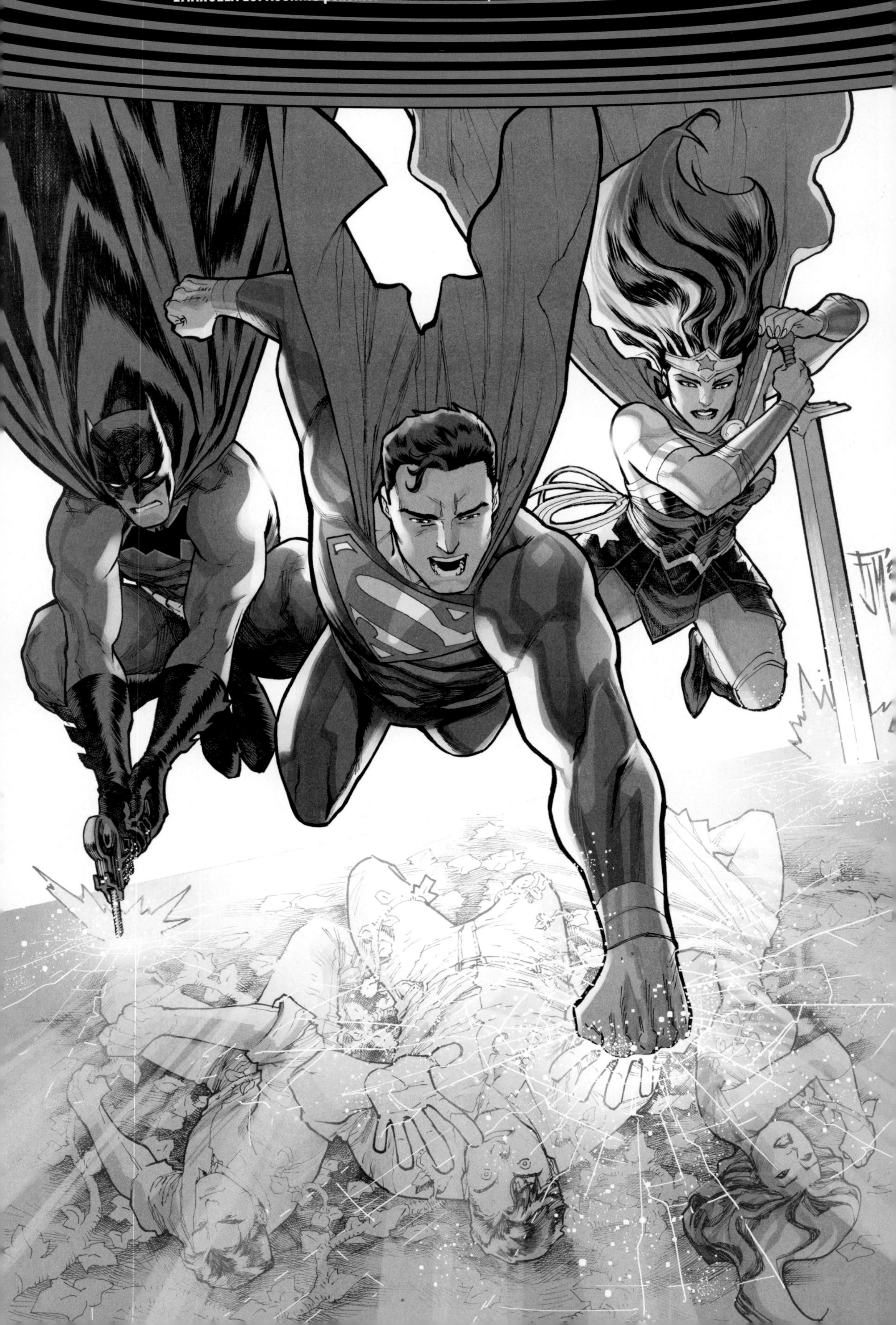

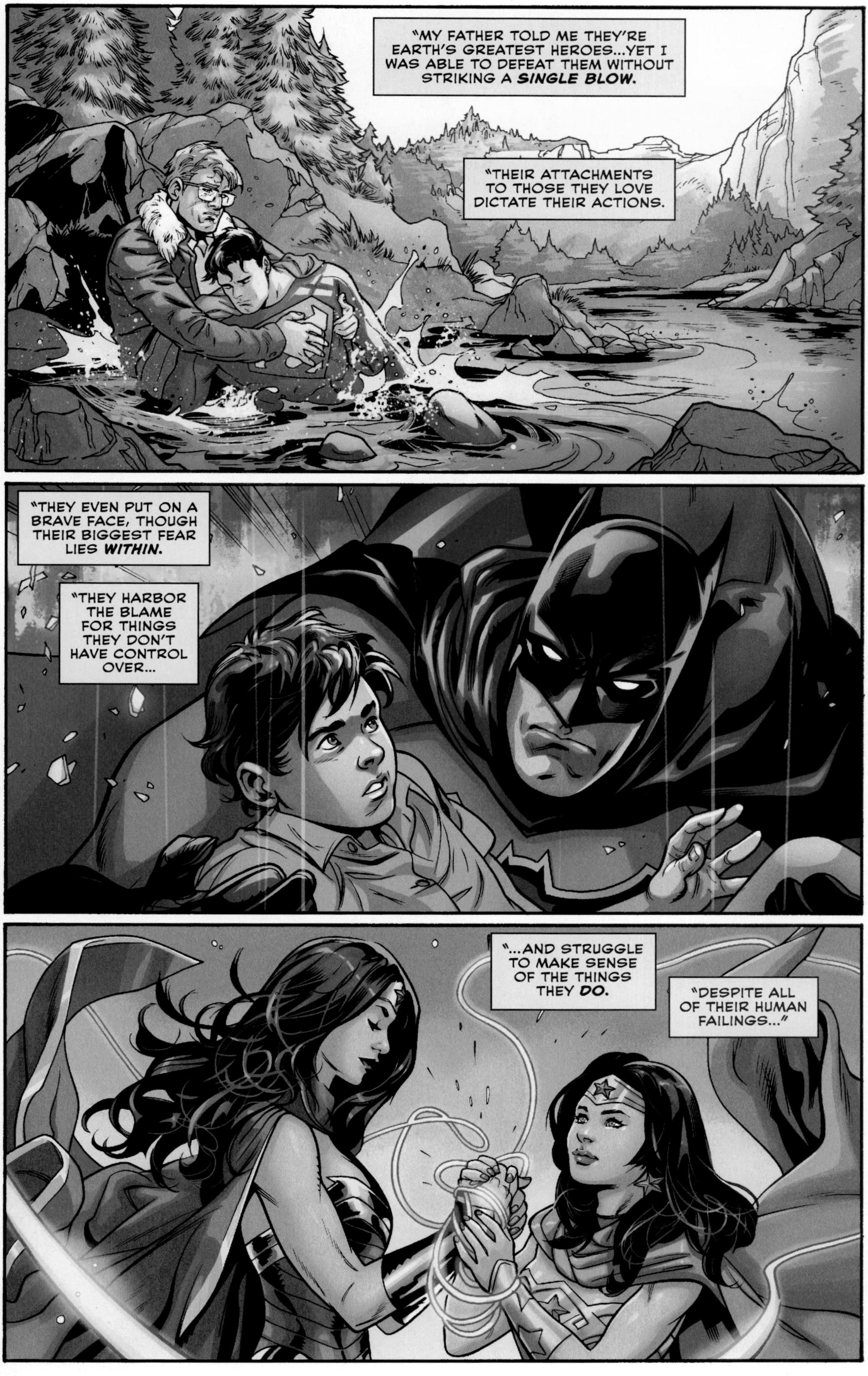
"MY FATHER TOLD ME THEY'RE EARTH'S GREATEST HEROES...YET I WAS ABLE TO DEFEAT THEM WITHOUT STRIKING A *SINGLE BLOW*.
"THEIR ATTACHMENTS TO THOSE THEY LOVE DICTATE THEIR ACTIONS.
"THEY EVEN PUT ON A BRAVE FACE, THOUGH THEIR BIGGEST FEAR LIES *WITHIN*.
"THEY HARBOR THE BLAME FOR THINGS THEY DON'T HAVE CONTROL OVER...
"...AND STRUGGLE TO MAKE SENSE OF THE THINGS THEY *DO*.
"DESPITE ALL OF THEIR HUMAN FAILINGS..."

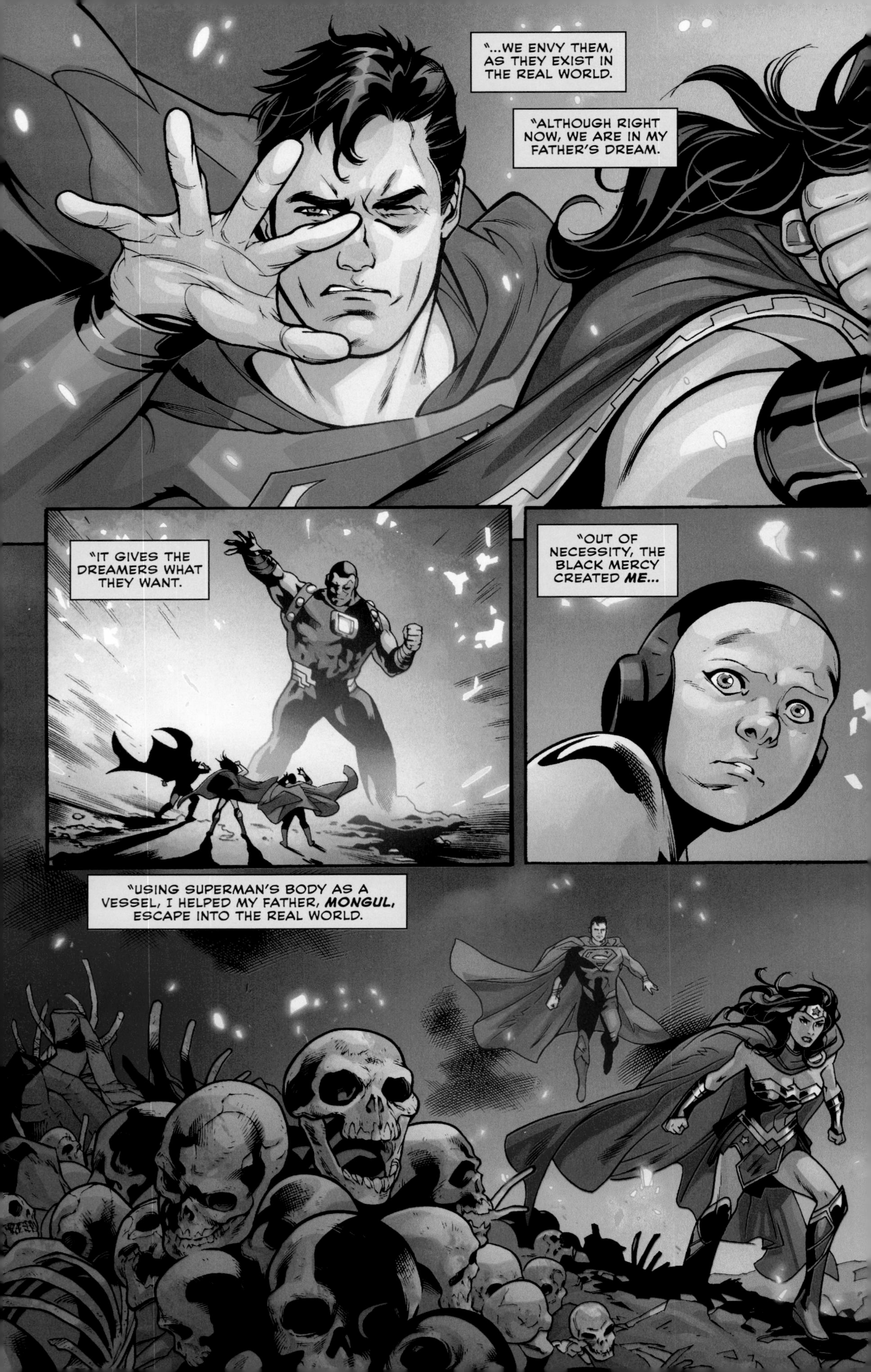
"...WE ENVY THEM, AS THEY EXIST IN THE REAL WORLD.
"ALTHOUGH RIGHT NOW, WE ARE IN MY FATHER'S DREAM.
"IT GIVES THE DREAMERS WHAT THEY WANT.
"OUT OF NECESSITY, THE BLACK MERCY CREATED *ME*...
"USING SUPERMAN'S BODY AS A VESSEL, I HELPED MY FATHER, *MONGUL*, ESCAPE INTO THE REAL WORLD.

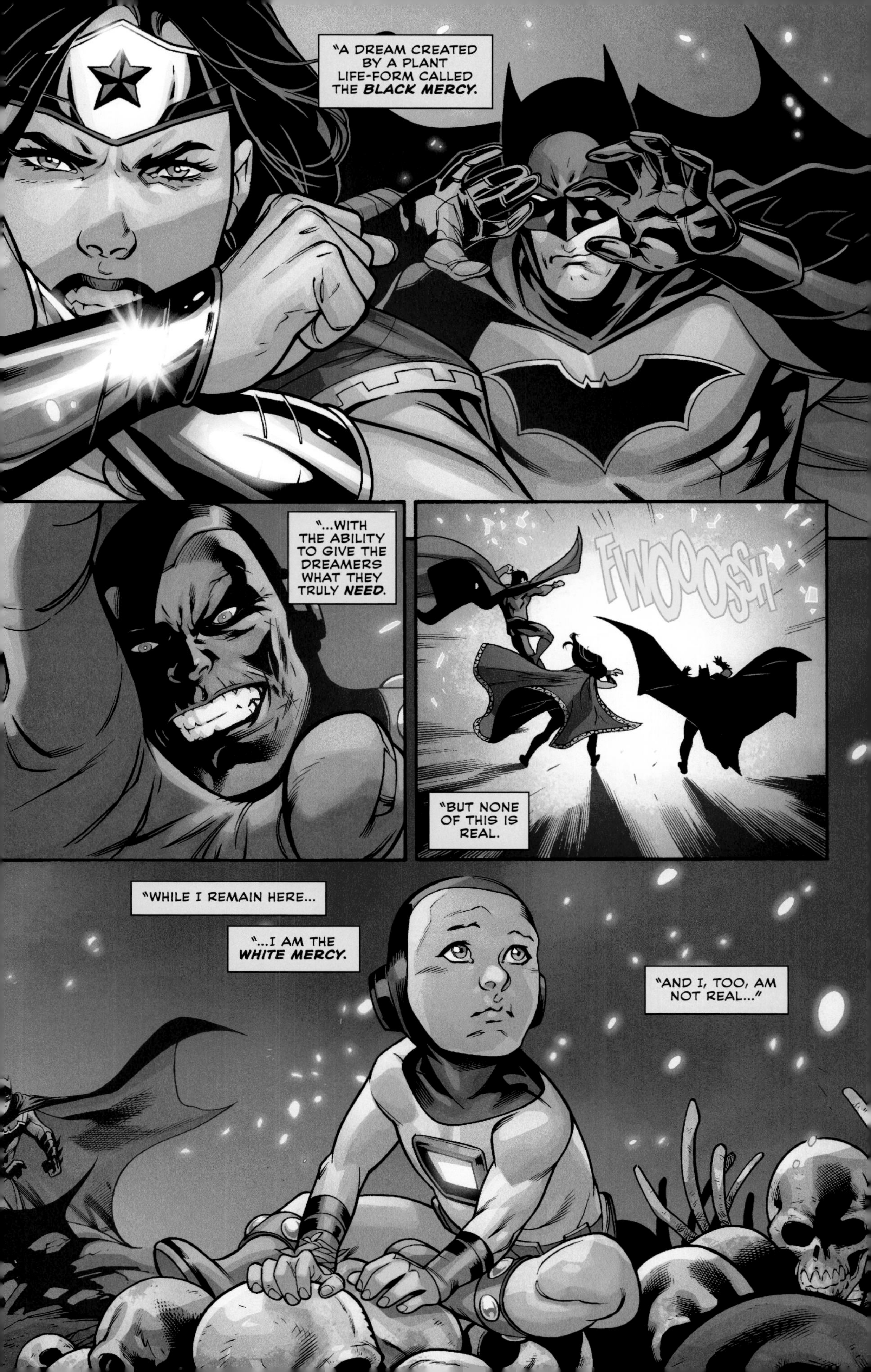
"A DREAM CREATED BY A PLANT LIFE-FORM CALLED THE ***BLACK MERCY***.
"...WITH THE ABILITY TO GIVE THE DREAMERS WHAT THEY TRULY ***NEED***.
FWOOOOSH
"BUT NONE OF THIS IS REAL.
"WHILE I REMAIN HERE...
"...I AM THE ***WHITE MERCY***.
"AND I, TOO, AM NOT REAL..."

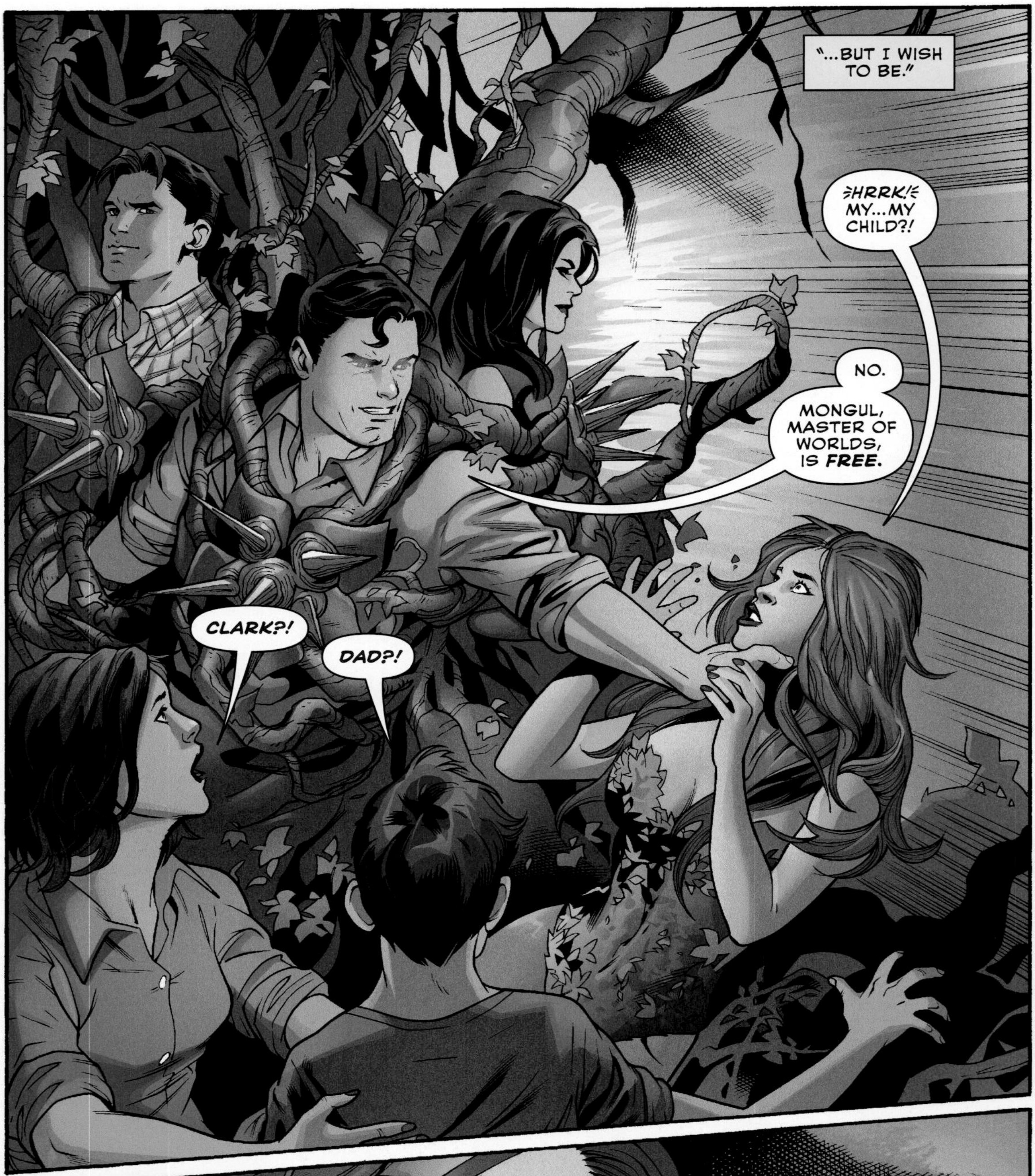
"...BUT I WISH TO BE."
HRRK! MY...MY CHILD?!
NO.
MONGUL, MASTER OF WORLDS, IS FREE.
CLARK?!
DAD?!

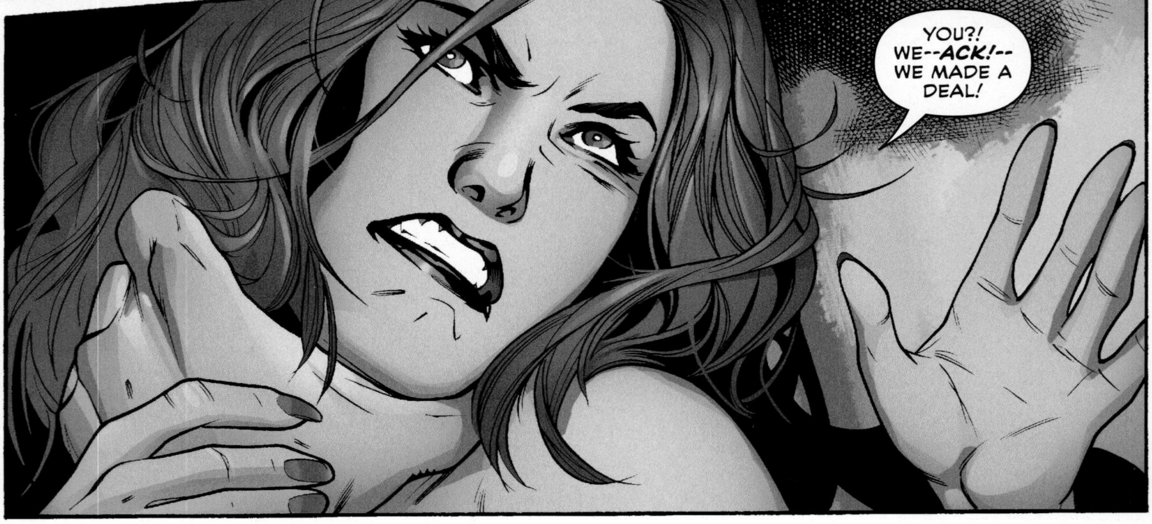
YOU?! WE--ACK!--WE MADE A DEAL!

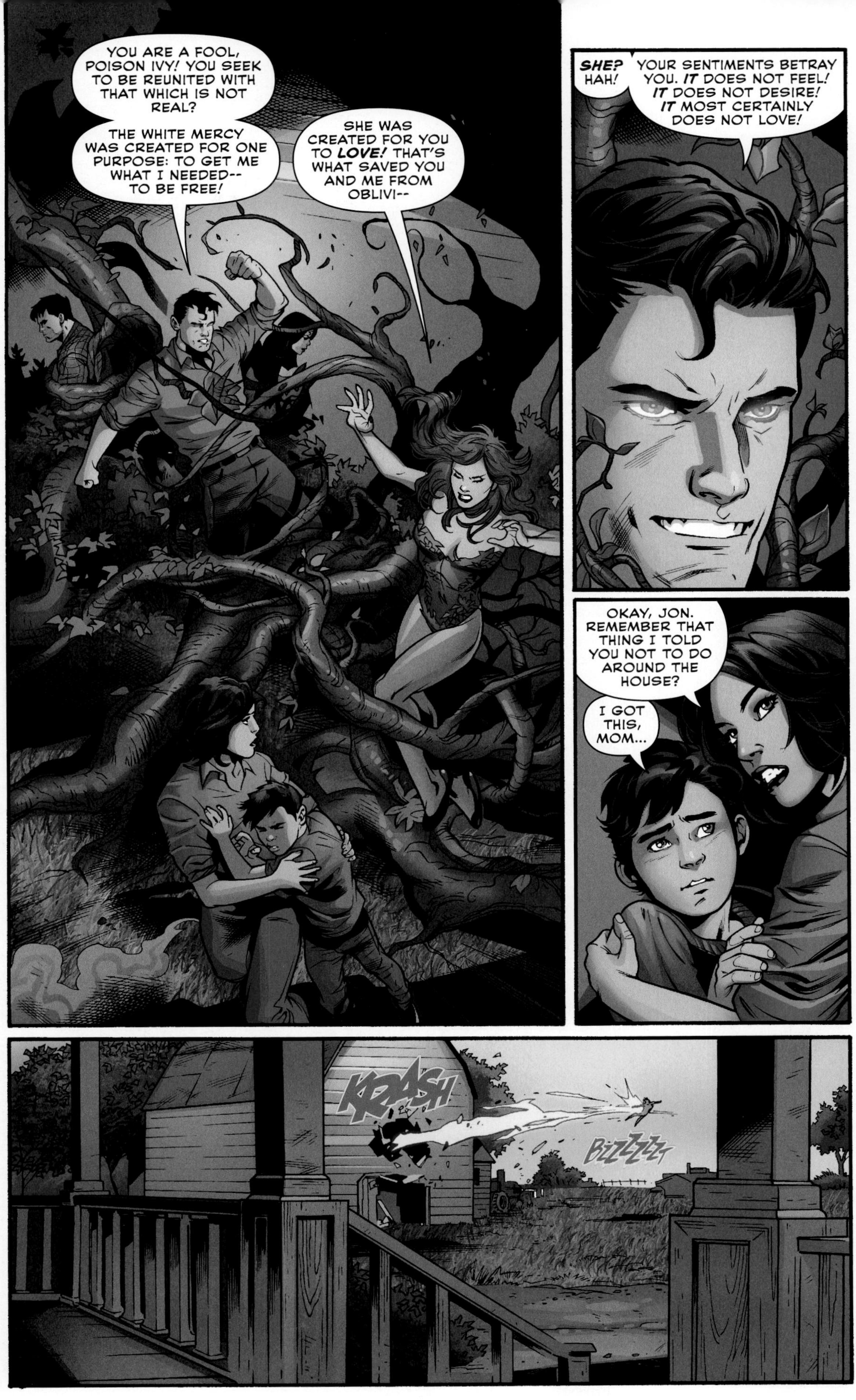
YOU ARE A FOOL, POISON IVY! YOU SEEK TO BE REUNITED WITH THAT WHICH IS NOT REAL?
THE WHITE MERCY WAS CREATED FOR ONE PURPOSE: TO GET ME WHAT I NEEDED-- TO BE FREE!
SHE WAS CREATED FOR YOU TO LOVE! THAT'S WHAT SAVED YOU AND ME FROM OBLIVI--
SHE? HAH!
YOUR SENTIMENTS BETRAY YOU. IT DOES NOT FEEL! IT DOES NOT DESIRE! IT MOST CERTAINLY DOES NOT LOVE!
OKAY, JON. REMEMBER THAT THING I TOLD YOU NOT TO DO AROUND THE HOUSE?
I GOT THIS, MOM...
KRASH
BZZZZZZT

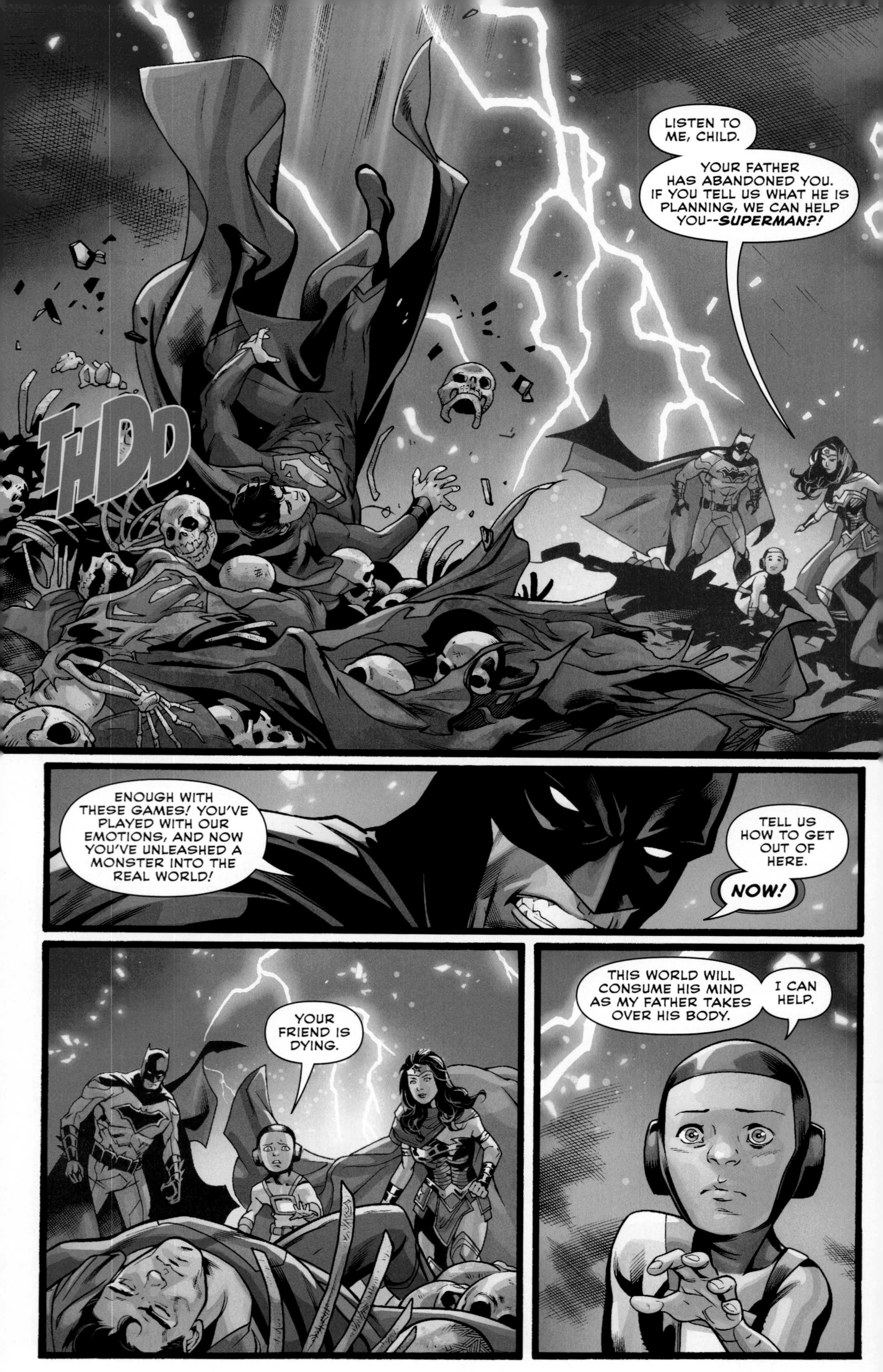
LISTEN TO ME, CHILD.
YOUR FATHER HAS ABANDONED YOU. IF YOU TELL US WHAT HE IS PLANNING, WE CAN HELP YOU--SUPERMAN?!
THDD
ENOUGH WITH THESE GAMES! YOU'VE PLAYED WITH OUR EMOTIONS, AND NOW YOU'VE UNLEASHED A MONSTER INTO THE REAL WORLD!
TELL US HOW TO GET OUT OF HERE.
NOW!
YOUR FRIEND IS DYING.
THIS WORLD WILL CONSUME HIS MIND AS MY FATHER TAKES OVER HIS BODY.
I CAN HELP.

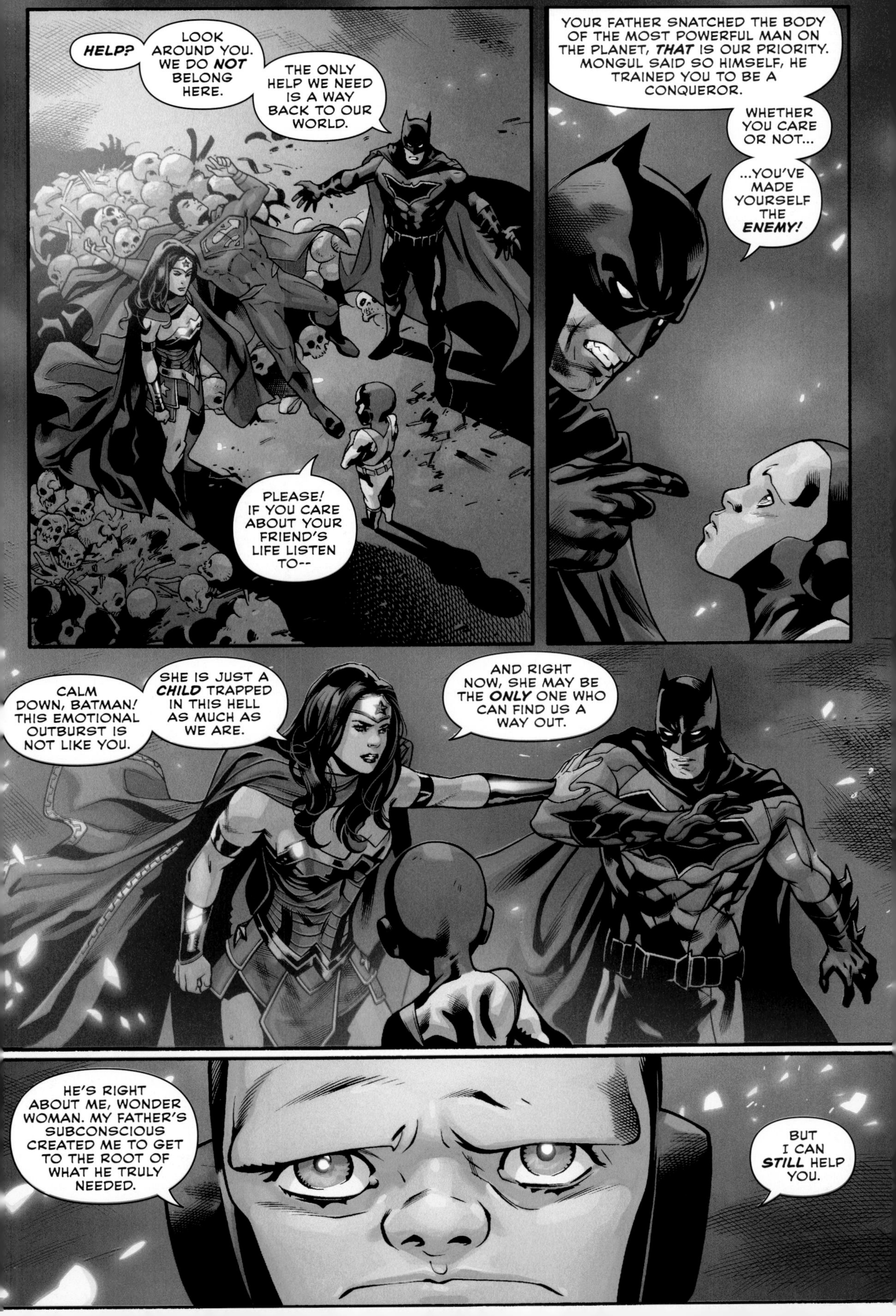
HELP?
LOOK AROUND YOU. WE DO NOT BELONG HERE.
THE ONLY HELP WE NEED IS A WAY BACK TO OUR WORLD.
PLEASE! IF YOU CARE ABOUT YOUR FRIEND'S LIFE LISTEN TO--
YOUR FATHER SNATCHED THE BODY OF THE MOST POWERFUL MAN ON THE PLANET, THAT IS OUR PRIORITY. MONGUL SAID SO HIMSELF, HE TRAINED YOU TO BE A CONQUEROR.
WHETHER YOU CARE OR NOT...
...YOU'VE MADE YOURSELF THE ENEMY!
CALM DOWN, BATMAN! THIS EMOTIONAL OUTBURST IS NOT LIKE YOU.
SHE IS JUST A CHILD TRAPPED IN THIS HELL AS MUCH AS WE ARE.
AND RIGHT NOW, SHE MAY BE THE ONLY ONE WHO CAN FIND US A WAY OUT.
HE'S RIGHT ABOUT ME, WONDER WOMAN. MY FATHER'S SUBCONSCIOUS CREATED ME TO GET TO THE ROOT OF WHAT HE TRULY NEEDED.
BUT I CAN STILL HELP YOU.

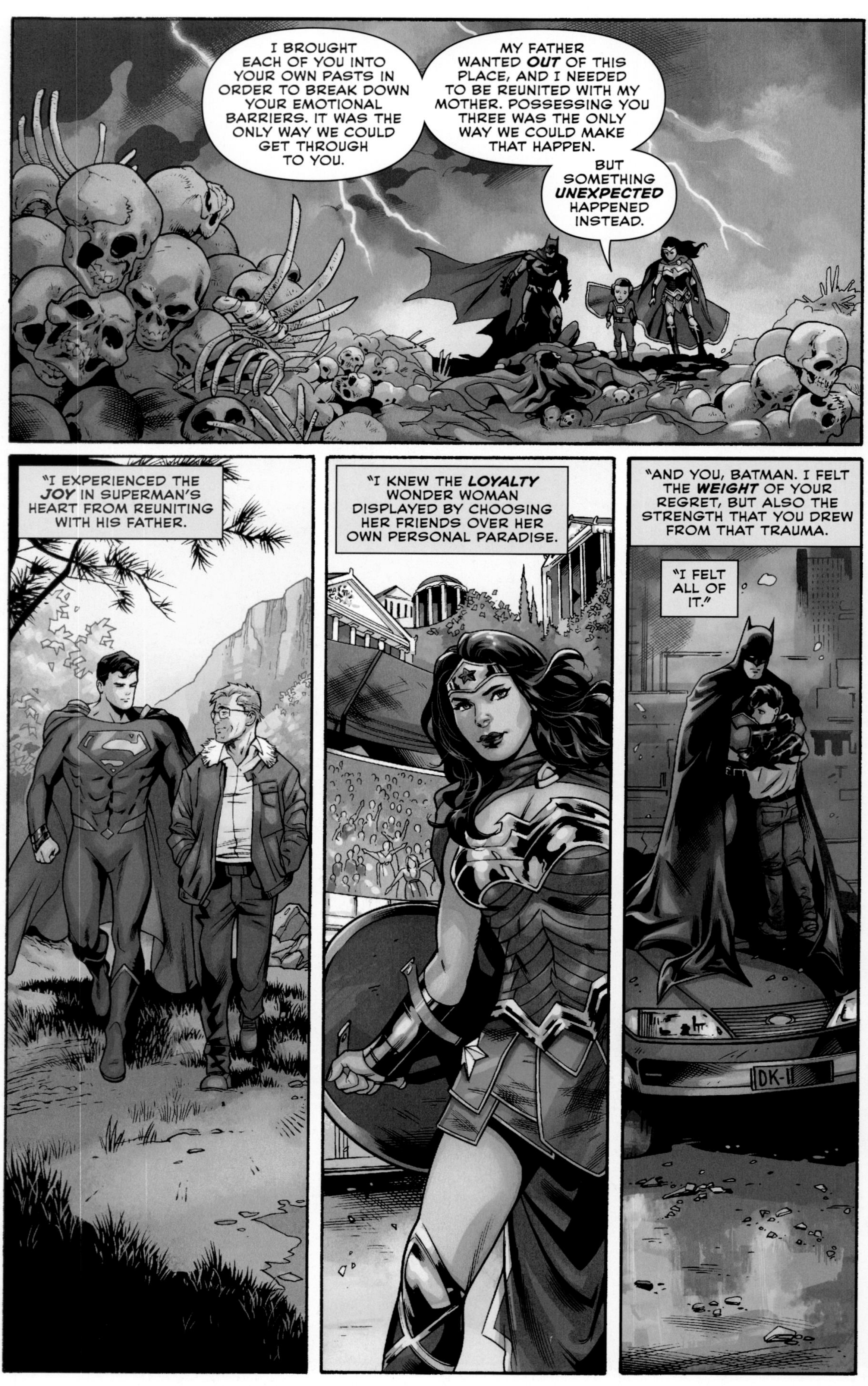
I BROUGHT EACH OF YOU INTO YOUR OWN PASTS IN ORDER TO BREAK DOWN YOUR EMOTIONAL BARRIERS. IT WAS THE ONLY WAY WE COULD GET THROUGH TO YOU.
MY FATHER WANTED *OUT* OF THIS PLACE, AND I NEEDED TO BE REUNITED WITH MY MOTHER. POSSESSING YOU THREE WAS THE ONLY WAY WE COULD MAKE THAT HAPPEN.
BUT SOMETHING *UNEXPECTED* HAPPENED INSTEAD.
"I EXPERIENCED THE *JOY* IN SUPERMAN'S HEART FROM REUNITING WITH HIS FATHER.
"I KNEW THE *LOYALTY* WONDER WOMAN DISPLAYED BY CHOOSING HER FRIENDS OVER HER OWN PERSONAL PARADISE.
"AND YOU, BATMAN. I FELT THE *WEIGHT* OF YOUR REGRET, BUT ALSO THE STRENGTH THAT YOU DREW FROM THAT TRAUMA.
"I FELT ALL OF IT."
DK-I

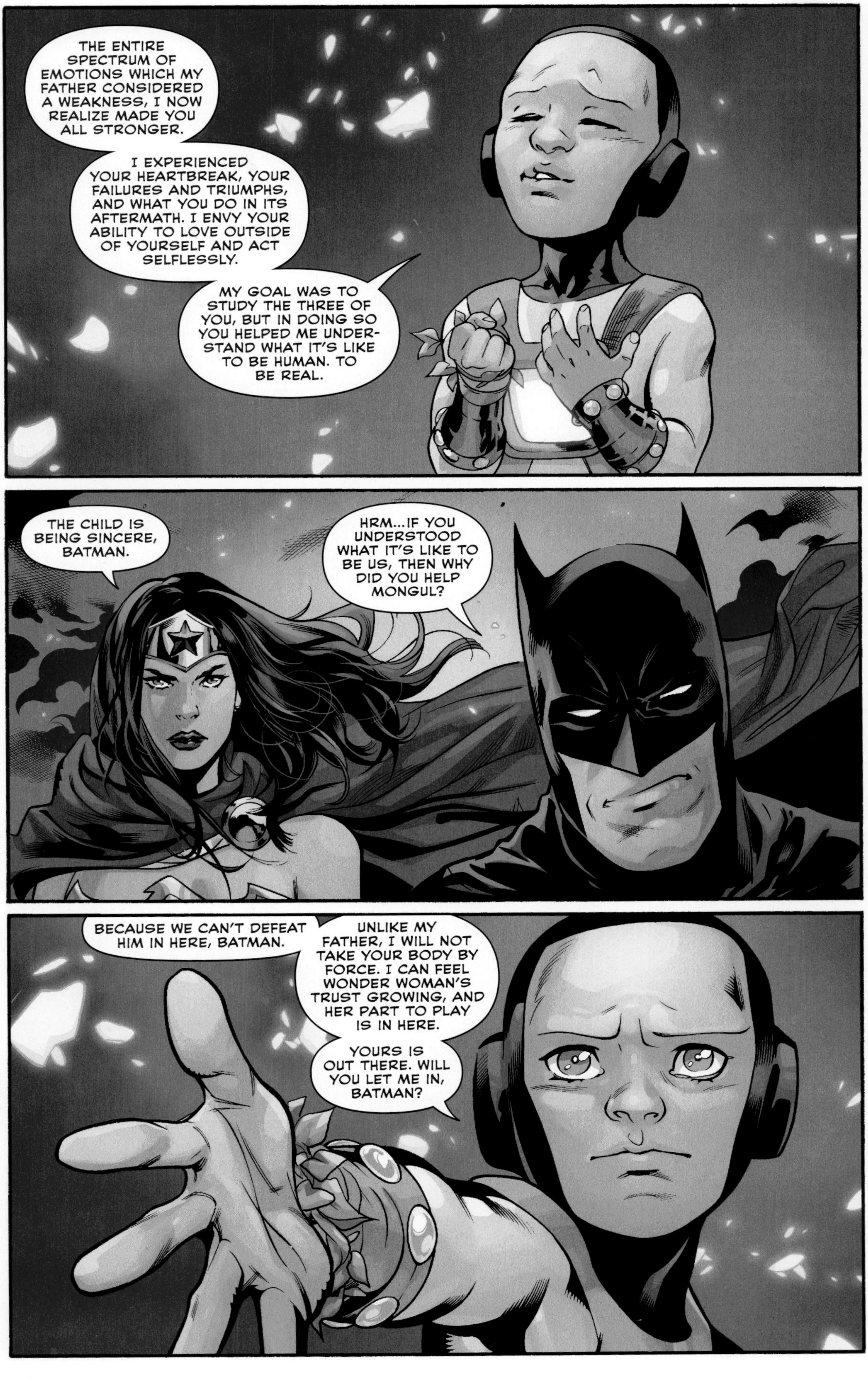
THE ENTIRE SPECTRUM OF EMOTIONS WHICH MY FATHER CONSIDERED A WEAKNESS, I NOW REALIZE MADE YOU ALL STRONGER.
I EXPERIENCED YOUR HEARTBREAK, YOUR FAILURES AND TRIUMPHS, AND WHAT YOU DO IN ITS AFTERMATH. I ENVY YOUR ABILITY TO LOVE OUTSIDE OF YOURSELF AND ACT SELFLESSLY.
MY GOAL WAS TO STUDY THE THREE OF YOU, BUT IN DOING SO YOU HELPED ME UNDERSTAND WHAT IT'S LIKE TO BE HUMAN. TO BE REAL.
THE CHILD IS BEING SINCERE, BATMAN.
HRM...IF YOU UNDERSTOOD WHAT IT'S LIKE TO BE US, THEN WHY DID YOU HELP MONGUL?
BECAUSE WE CAN'T DEFEAT HIM IN HERE, BATMAN.
UNLIKE MY FATHER, I WILL NOT TAKE YOUR BODY BY FORCE. I CAN FEEL WONDER WOMAN'S TRUST GROWING, AND HER PART TO PLAY IS IN HERE.
YOURS IS OUT THERE. WILL YOU LET ME IN, BATMAN?

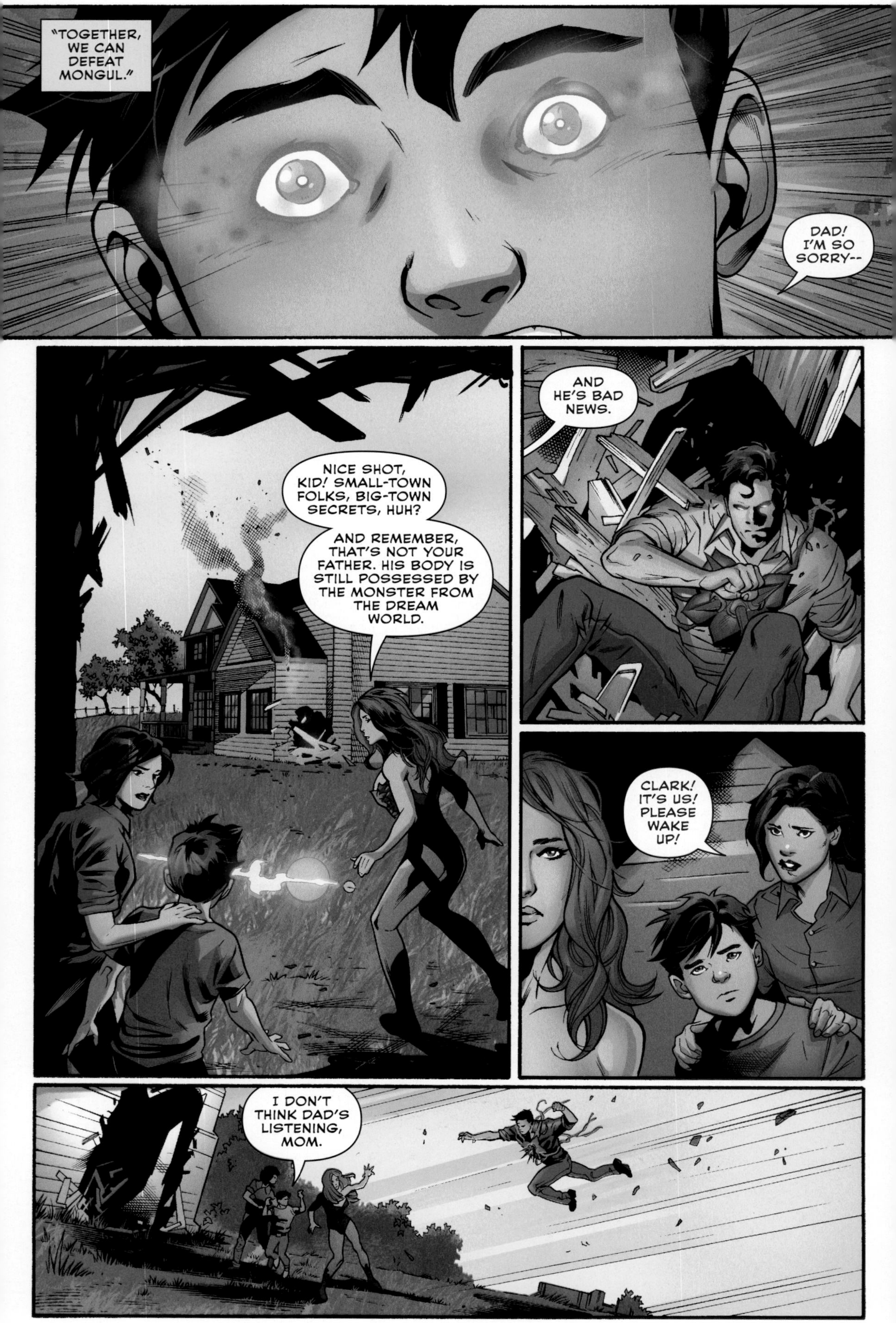
"TOGETHER, WE CAN DEFEAT MONGUL."
DAD! I'M SO SORRY--
NICE SHOT, KID! SMALL-TOWN FOLKS, BIG-TOWN SECRETS, HUH?
AND REMEMBER, THAT'S NOT YOUR FATHER. HIS BODY IS STILL POSSESSED BY THE MONSTER FROM THE DREAM WORLD.
AND HE'S BAD NEWS.
CLARK! IT'S US! PLEASE WAKE UP!
I DON'T THINK DAD'S LISTENING, MOM.

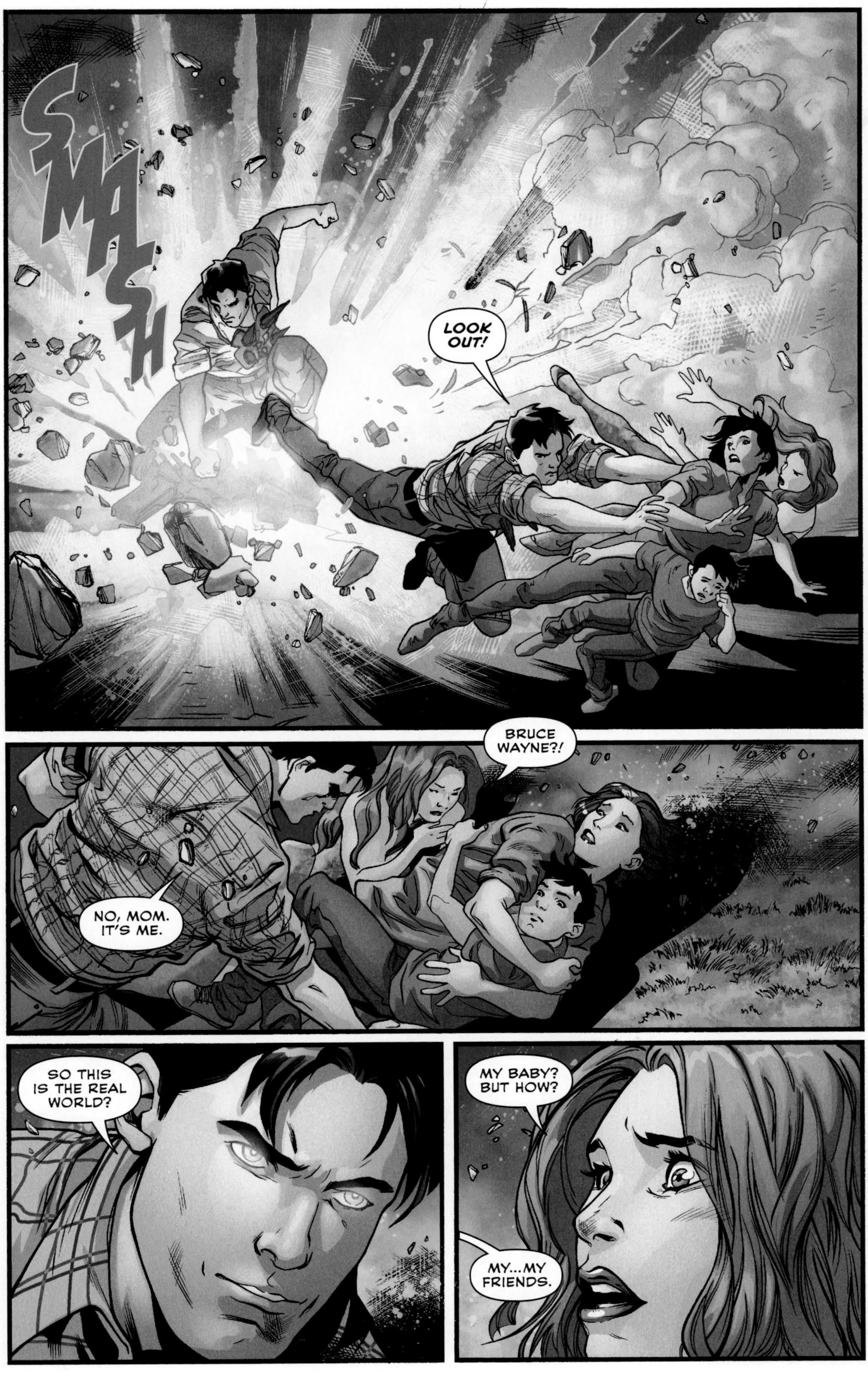
SMASH
LOOK OUT!
BRUCE WAYNE?!
NO, MOM. IT'S ME.
SO THIS IS THE REAL WORLD?
MY BABY? BUT HOW?
MY...MY FRIENDS.

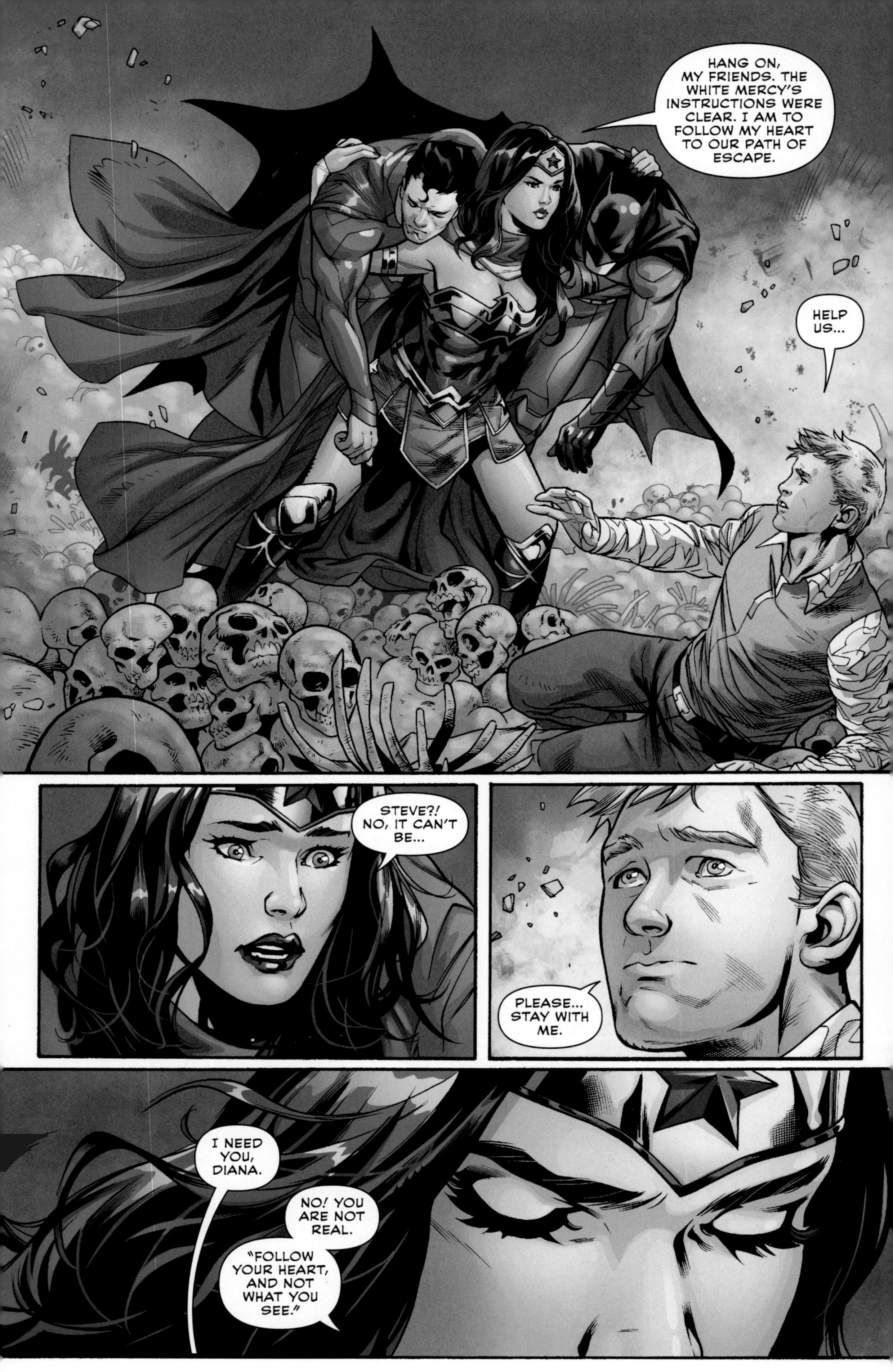
HANG ON, MY FRIENDS. THE WHITE MERCY'S INSTRUCTIONS WERE CLEAR. I AM TO FOLLOW MY HEART TO OUR PATH OF ESCAPE.
HELP US...
STEVE?! NO, IT CAN'T BE...
PLEASE... STAY WITH ME.
I NEED YOU, DIANA.
NO! YOU ARE NOT REAL.
"FOLLOW YOUR HEART, AND NOT WHAT YOU SEE."

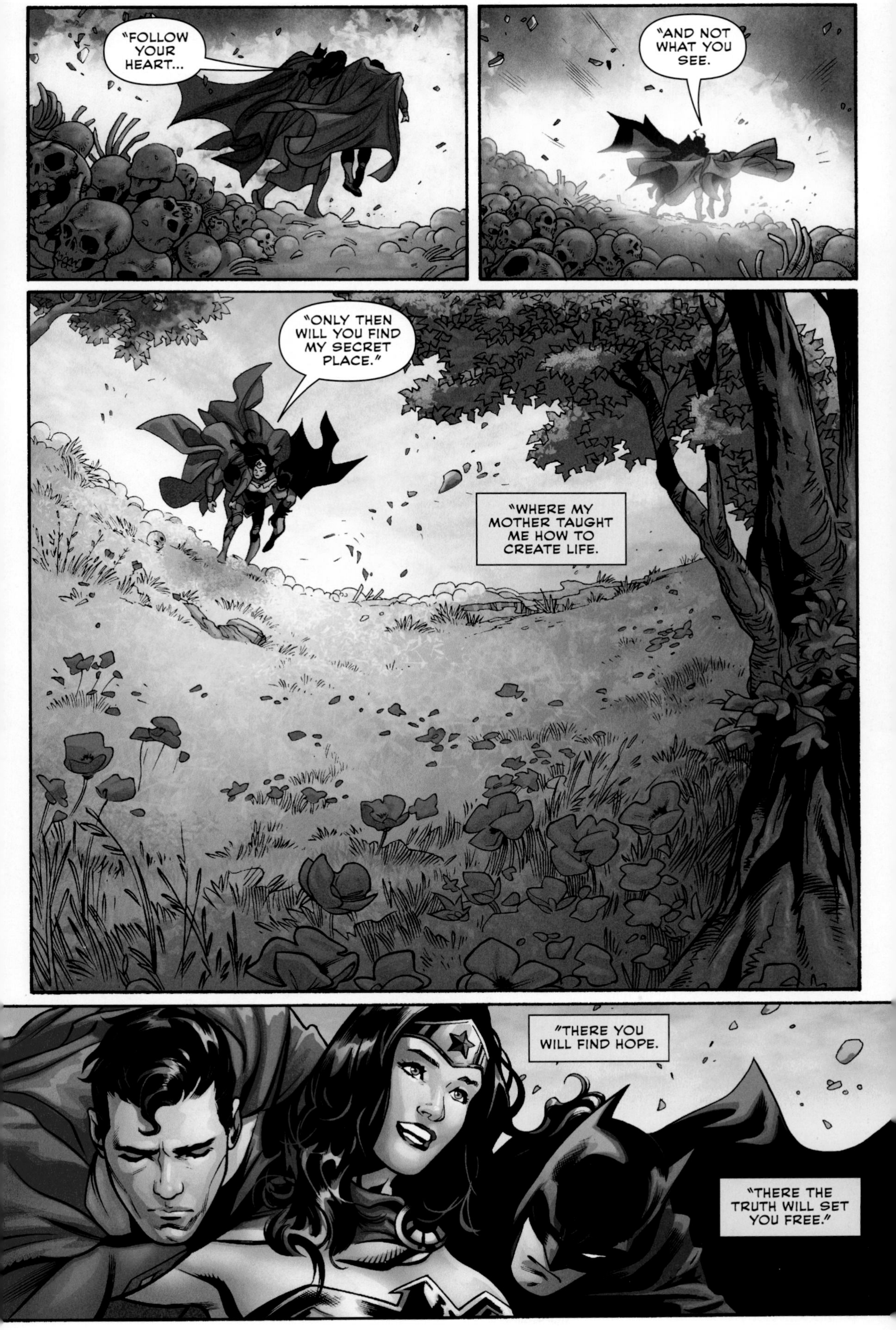
"FOLLOW YOUR HEART...
"AND NOT WHAT YOU SEE.
"ONLY THEN WILL YOU FIND MY SECRET PLACE."
"WHERE MY MOTHER TAUGHT ME HOW TO CREATE LIFE.
"THERE YOU WILL FIND HOPE.
"THERE THE TRUTH WILL SET YOU FREE."

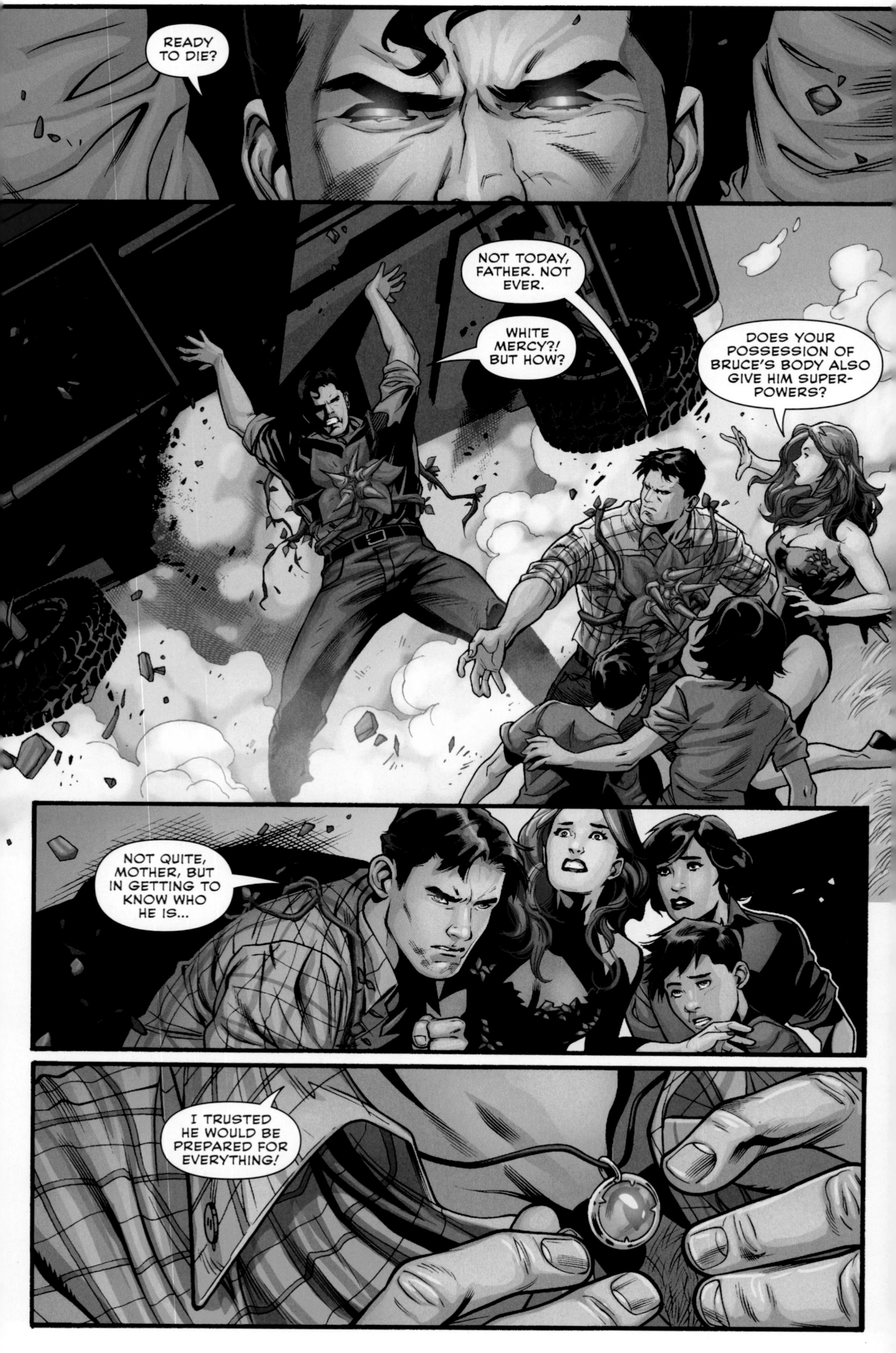
READY TO DIE?
NOT TODAY, FATHER. NOT EVER.
WHITE MERCY?! BUT HOW?
DOES YOUR POSSESSION OF BRUCE'S BODY ALSO GIVE HIM SUPER-POWERS?
NOT QUITE, MOTHER, BUT IN GETTING TO KNOW WHO HE IS...
I TRUSTED HE WOULD BE PREPARED FOR EVERYTHING!

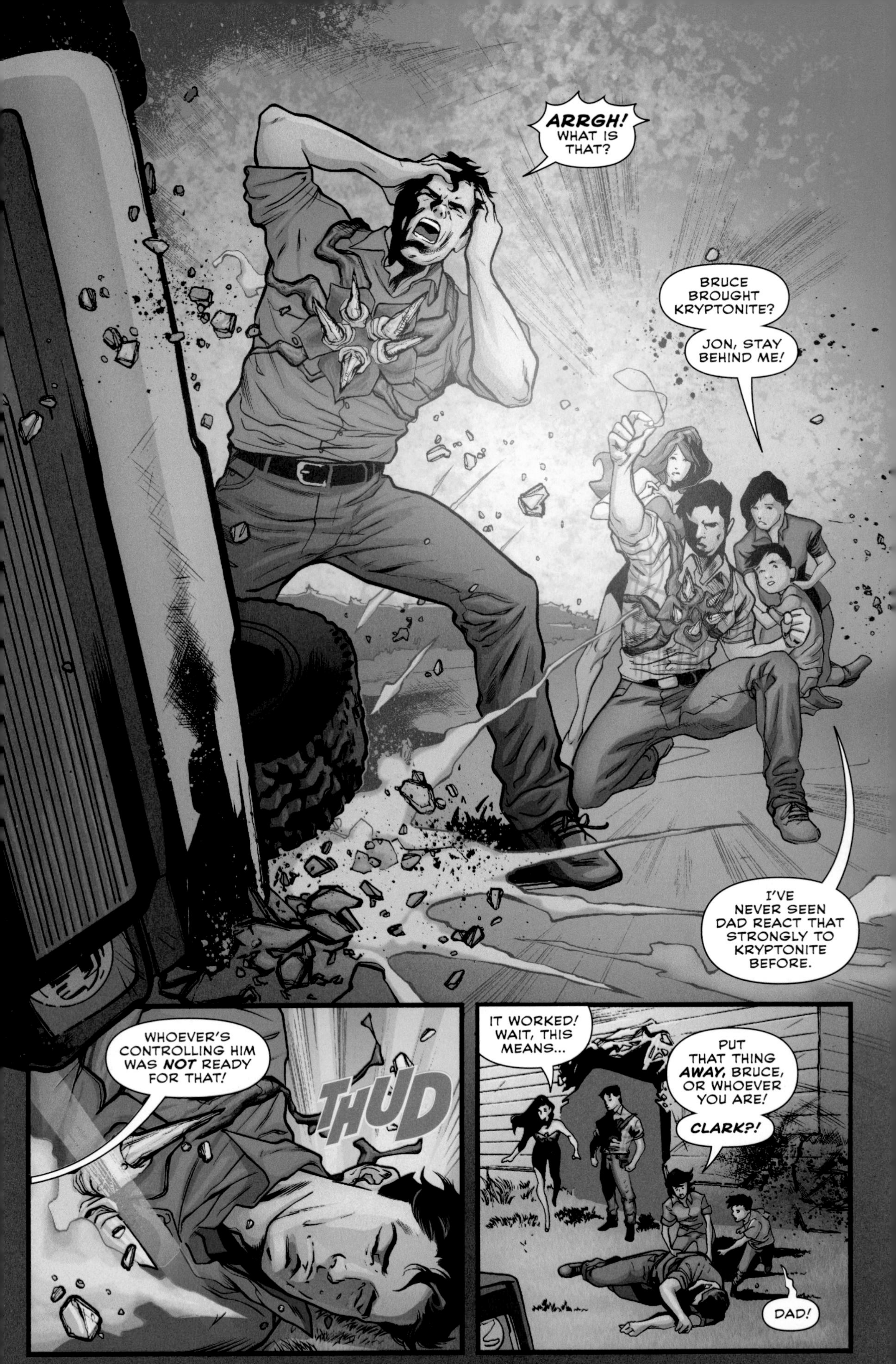
ARRGH! WHAT IS THAT?
BRUCE BROUGHT KRYPTONITE?
JON, STAY BEHIND ME!
I'VE NEVER SEEN DAD REACT THAT STRONGLY TO KRYPTONITE BEFORE.
WHOEVER'S CONTROLLING HIM WAS NOT READY FOR THAT!
THUD
IT WORKED! WAIT, THIS MEANS...
PUT THAT THING AWAY, BRUCE, OR WHOEVER YOU ARE!
CLARK?!
DAD!

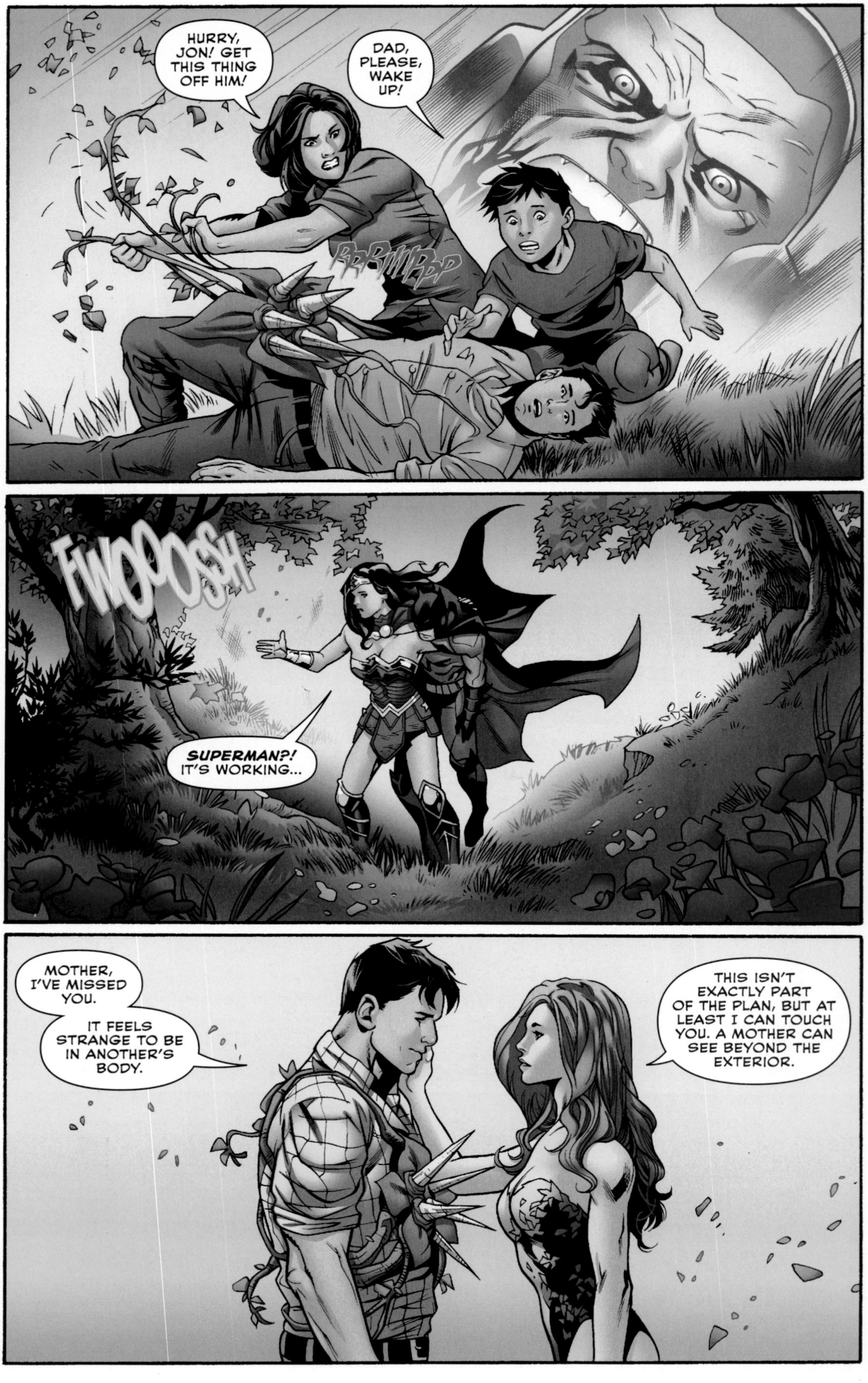
HURRY, JON! GET THIS THING OFF HIM!
DAD, PLEASE, WAKE UP!
FWOOOSH
SUPERMAN?! IT'S WORKING...
MOTHER, I'VE MISSED YOU.
IT FEELS STRANGE TO BE IN ANOTHER'S BODY.
THIS ISN'T EXACTLY PART OF THE PLAN, BUT AT LEAST I CAN TOUCH YOU. A MOTHER CAN SEE BEYOND THE EXTERIOR.

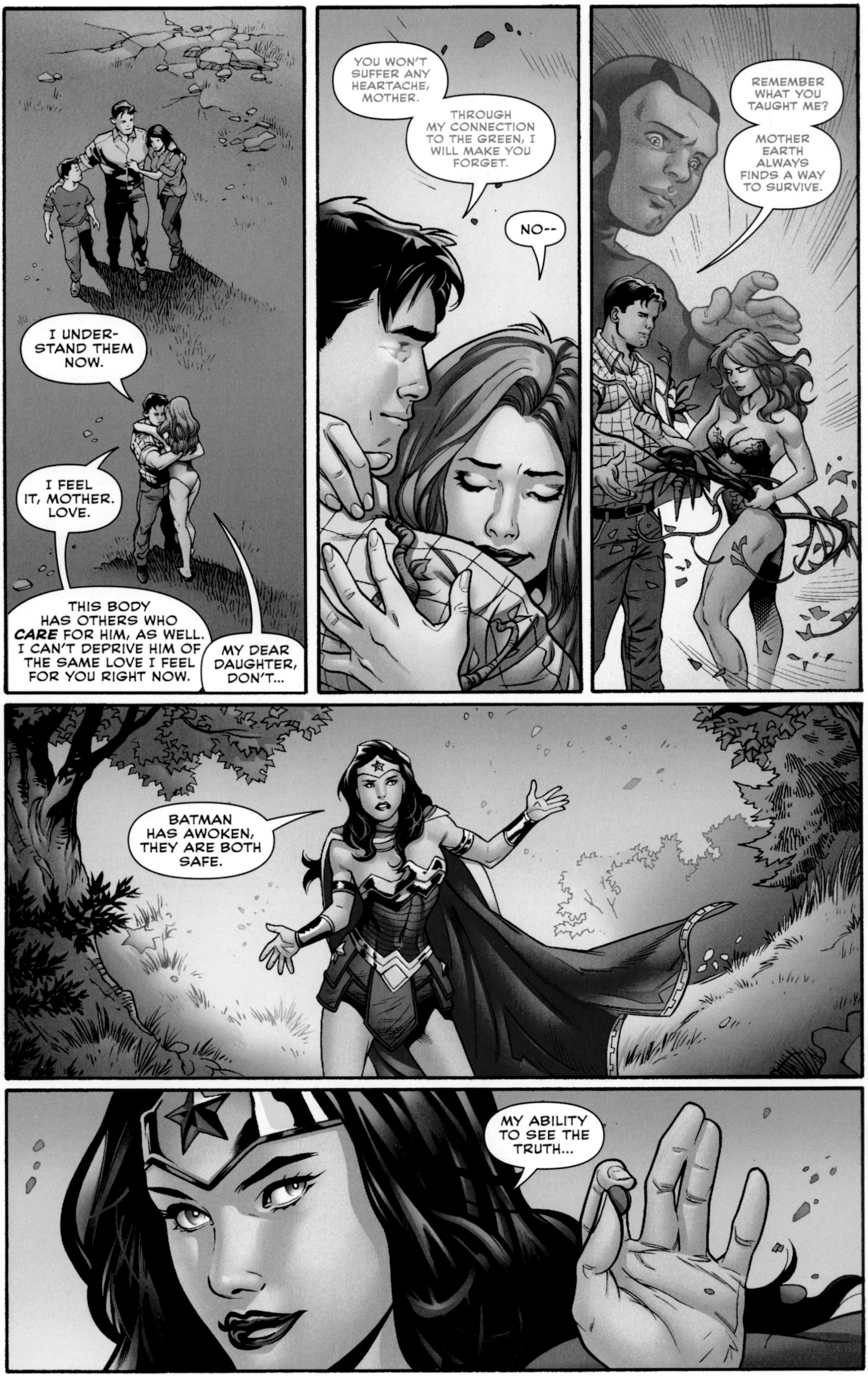
I UNDER-STAND THEM NOW.
I FEEL IT, MOTHER. LOVE.
THIS BODY HAS OTHERS WHO *CARE* FOR HIM, AS WELL. I CAN'T DEPRIVE HIM OF THE SAME LOVE I FEEL FOR YOU RIGHT NOW.
MY DEAR DAUGHTER, DON'T...
YOU WON'T SUFFER ANY HEARTACHE, MOTHER.
THROUGH MY CONNECTION TO THE GREEN, I WILL MAKE YOU FORGET.
NO--
REMEMBER WHAT YOU TAUGHT ME?
MOTHER EARTH ALWAYS FINDS A WAY TO SURVIVE.
BATMAN HAS AWOKEN, THEY ARE BOTH SAFE.
MY ABILITY TO SEE THE TRUTH...

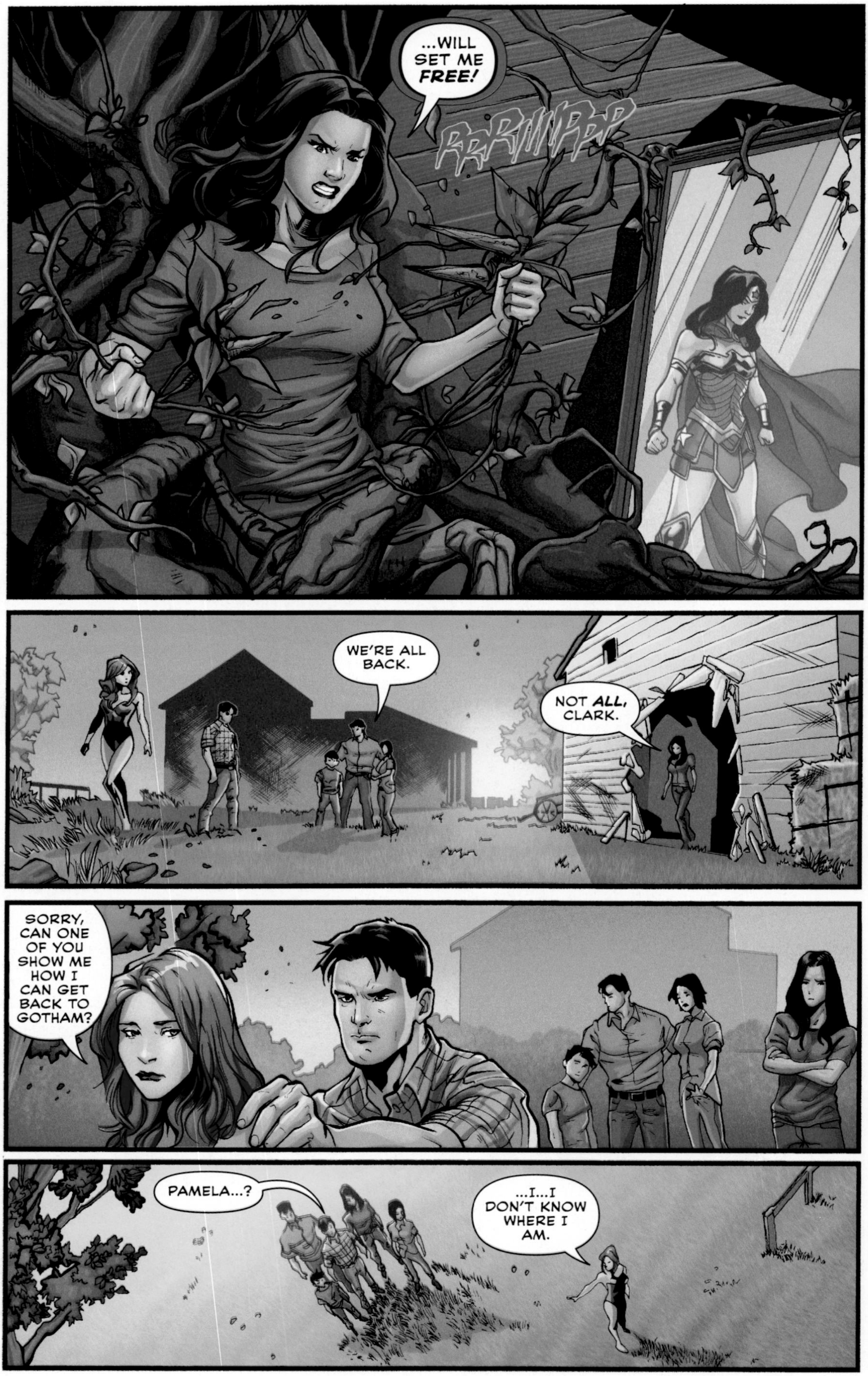
...WILL SET ME FREE!
RRRIIIPPP
WE'RE ALL BACK.
NOT ALL, CLARK.
SORRY, CAN ONE OF YOU SHOW ME HOW I CAN GET BACK TO GOTHAM?
PAMELA...?
...I...I DON'T KNOW WHERE I AM.

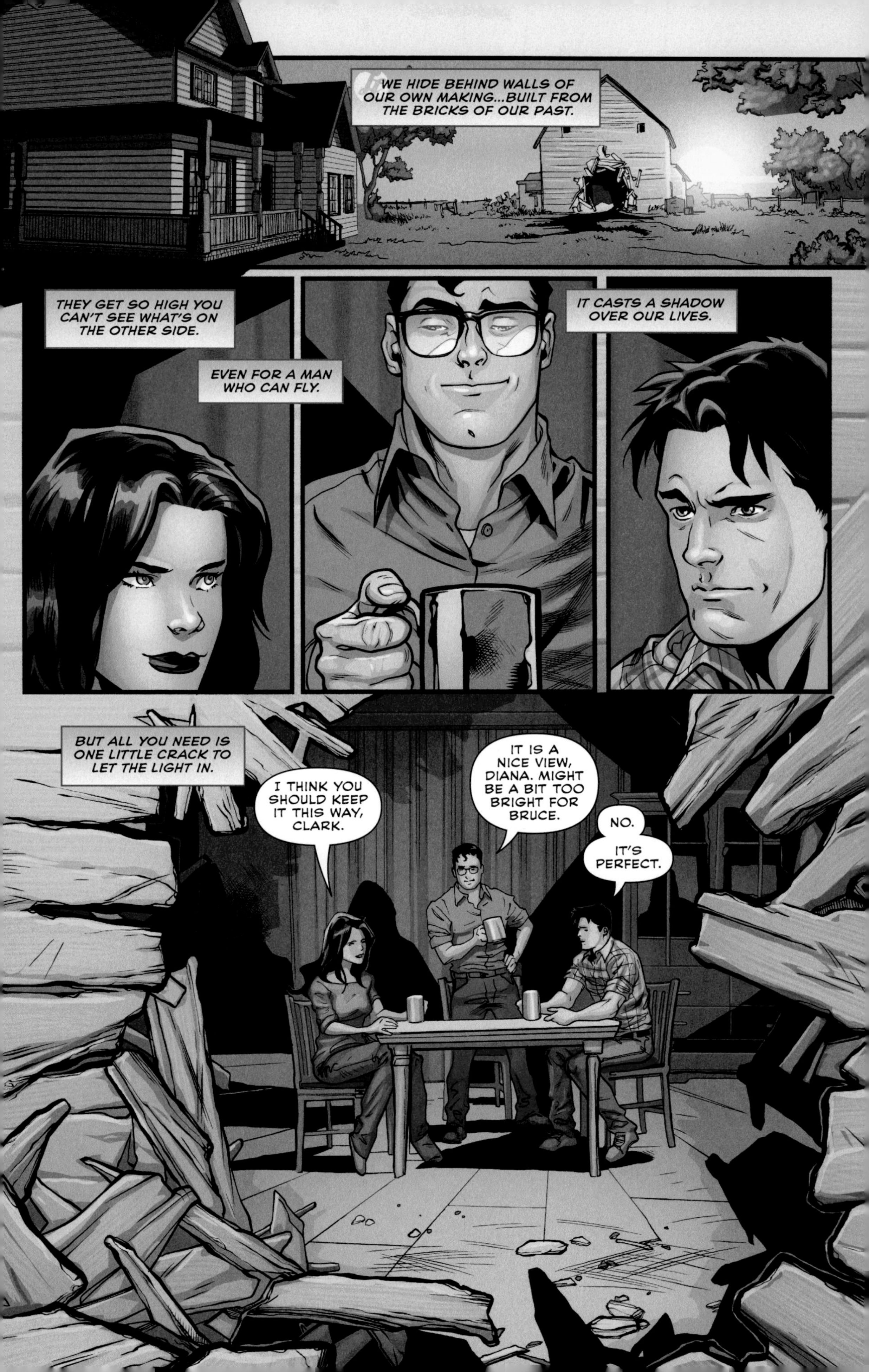
WE HIDE BEHIND WALLS OF OUR OWN MAKING...BUILT FROM THE BRICKS OF OUR PAST.
THEY GET SO HIGH YOU CAN'T SEE WHAT'S ON THE OTHER SIDE.
EVEN FOR A MAN WHO CAN FLY.
IT CASTS A SHADOW OVER OUR LIVES.
BUT ALL YOU NEED IS ONE LITTLE CRACK TO LET THE LIGHT IN.
I THINK YOU SHOULD KEEP IT THIS WAY, CLARK.
IT IS A NICE VIEW, DIANA. MIGHT BE A BIT TOO BRIGHT FOR BRUCE.
NO.
IT'S PERFECT.

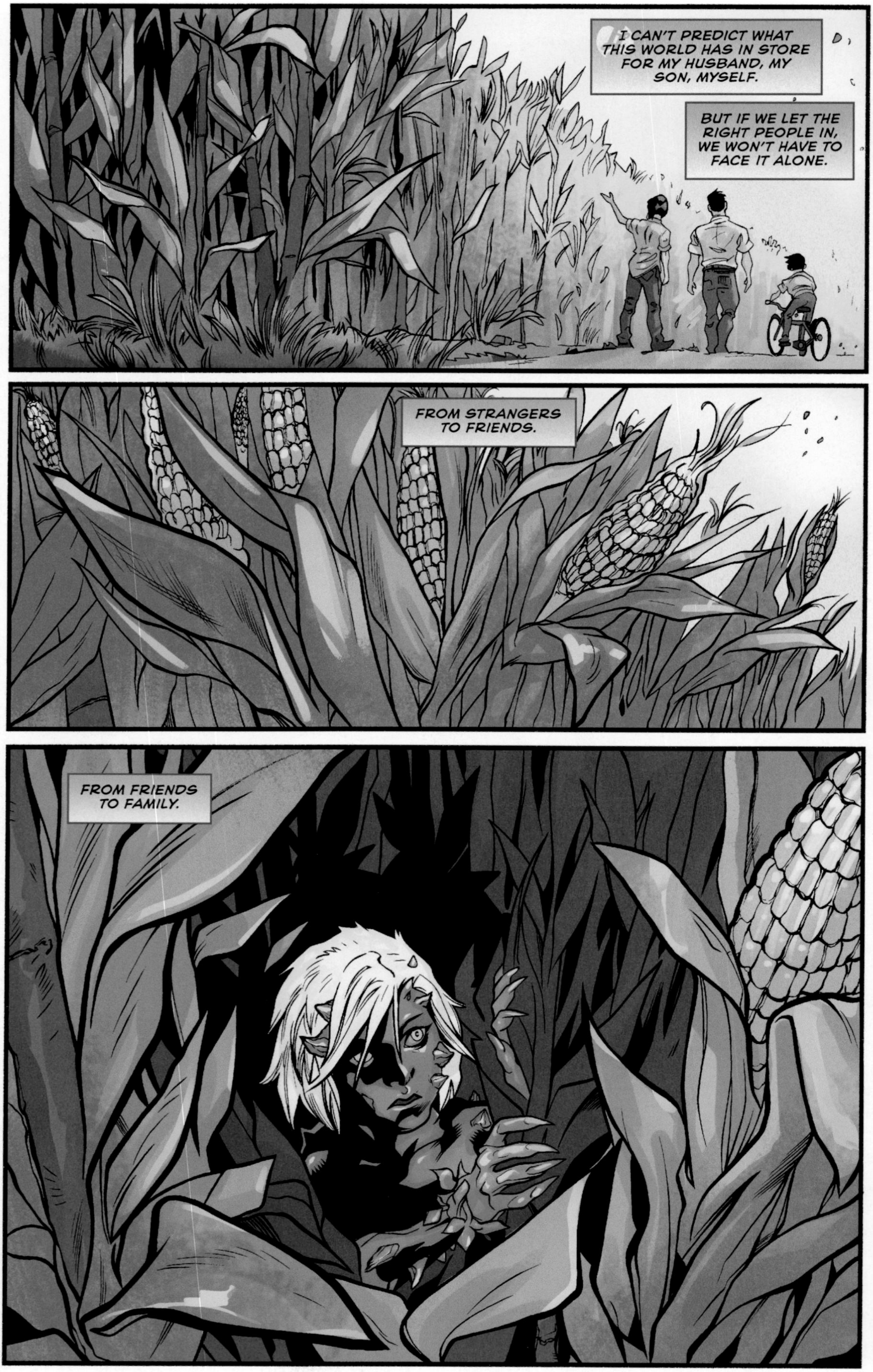
I CAN'T PREDICT WHAT THIS WORLD HAS IN STORE FOR MY HUSBAND, MY SON, MYSELF.
BUT IF WE LET THE RIGHT PEOPLE IN, WE WON'T HAVE TO FACE IT ALONE.
FROM STRANGERS TO FRIENDS.
FROM FRIENDS TO FAMILY.

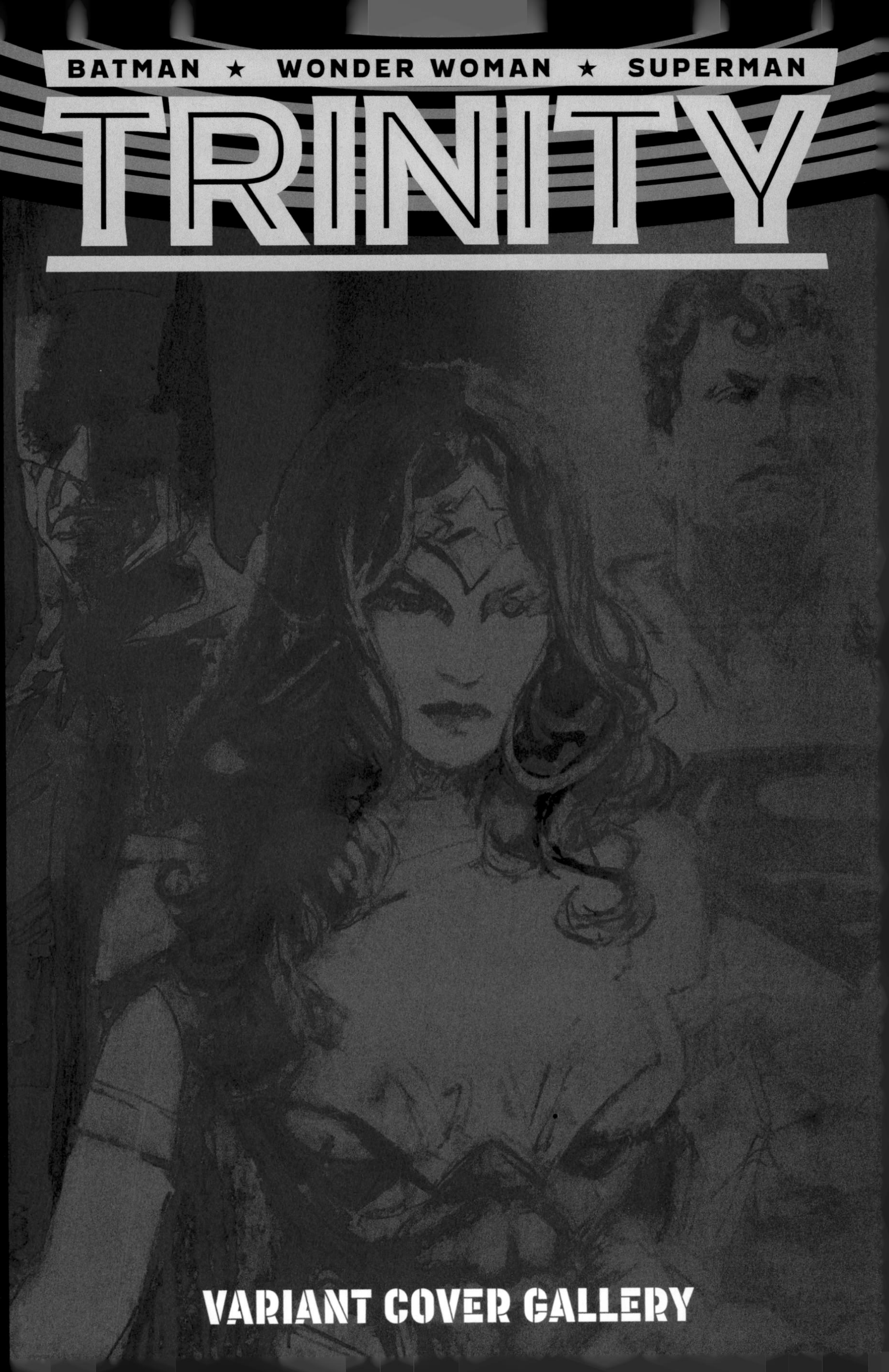
BATMAN ★ WONDER WOMAN ★ SUPERMAN
TRINITY
VARIANT COVER GALLERY

TRINITY #1 Variant Cover by JASON FABOK and BRAD ANDERSON

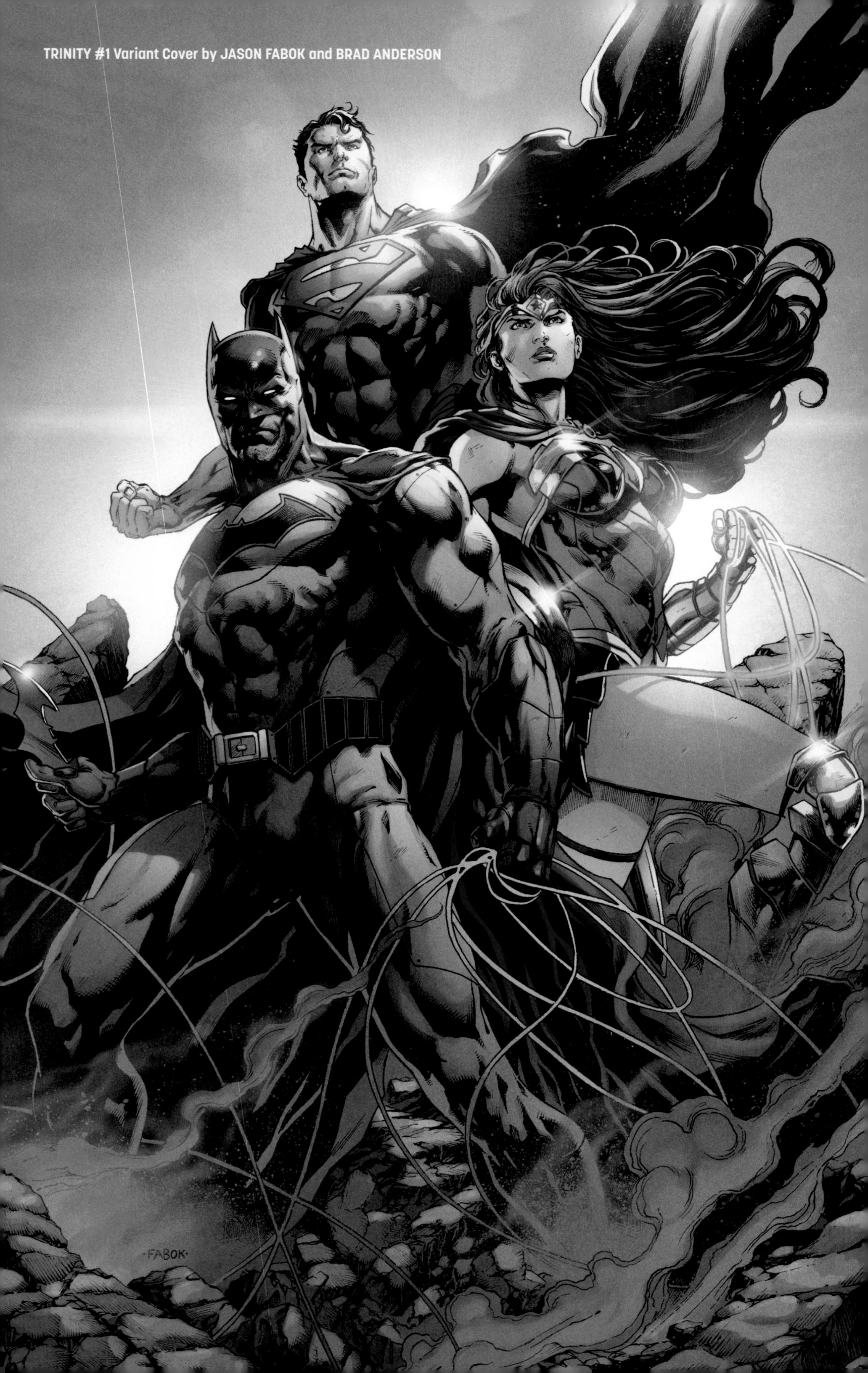
FABOK

TRINITY #2 Variant Cover by FRANK CHO and LAURA MARTIN

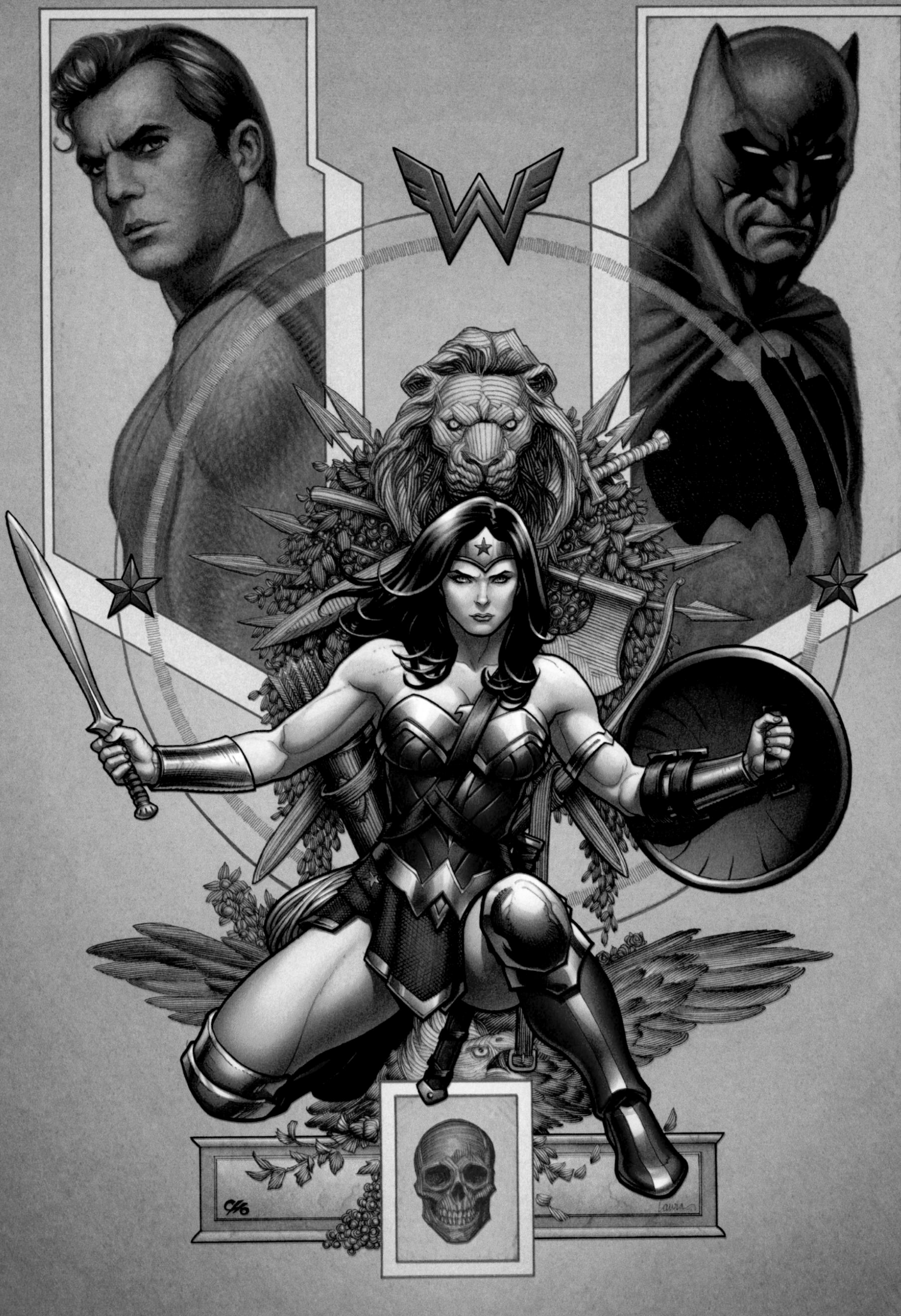

TRINITY #3 Variant Cover by STEVE EPTING

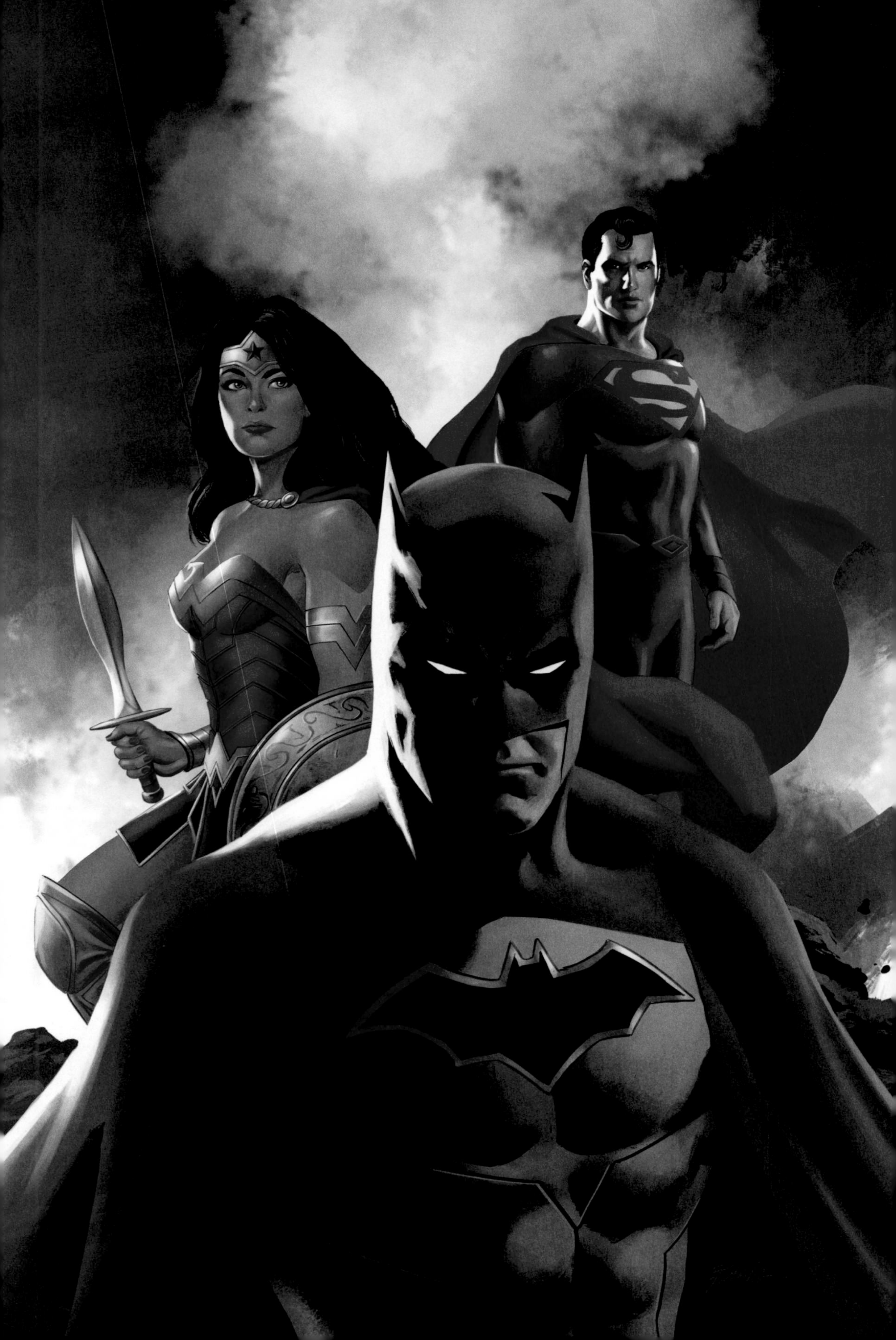

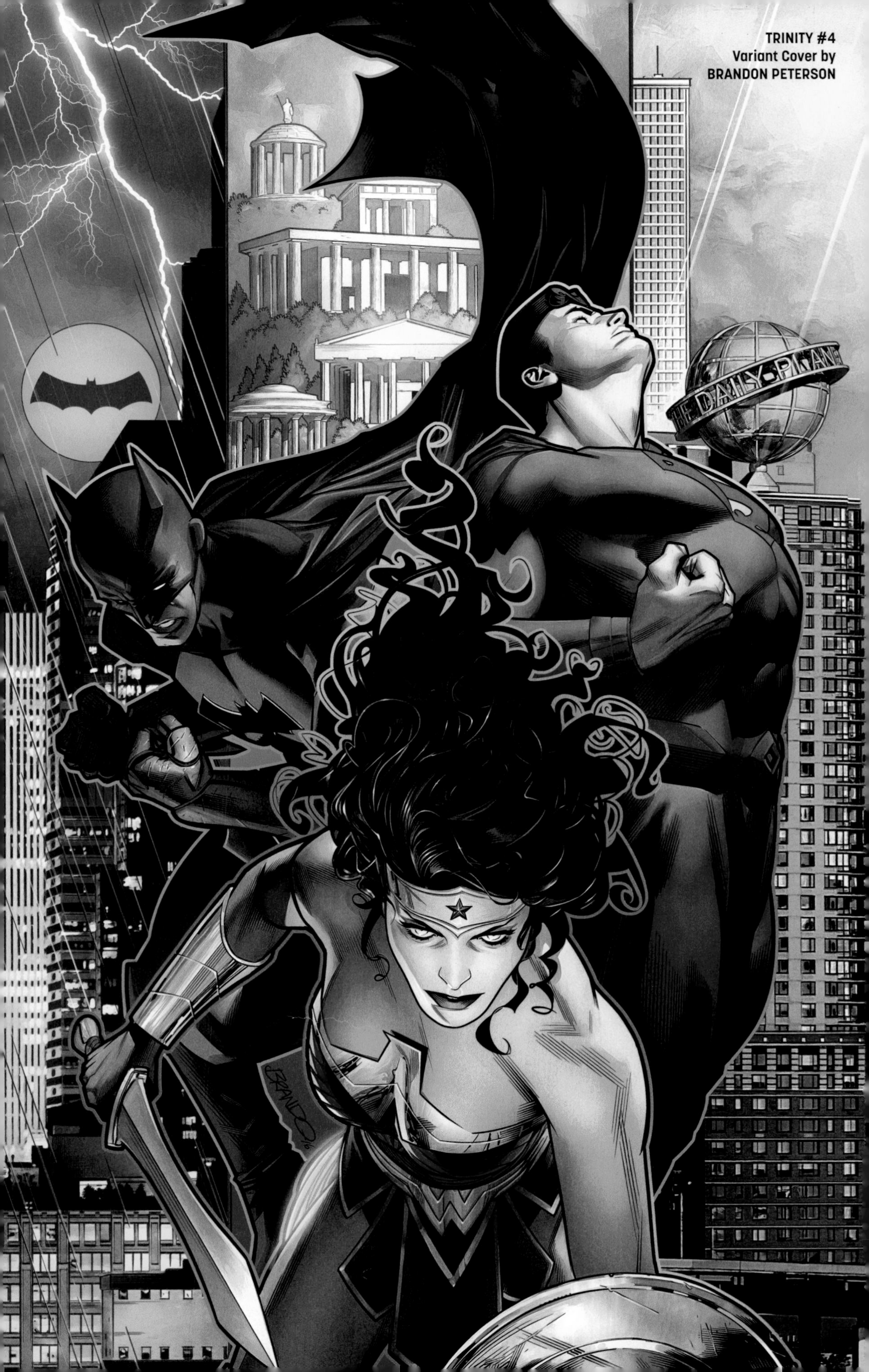

TRINITY #4
Variant Cover by
BRANDON PETERSON

TRINITY #5 Variant Cover by BILL SIENKIEWICZ

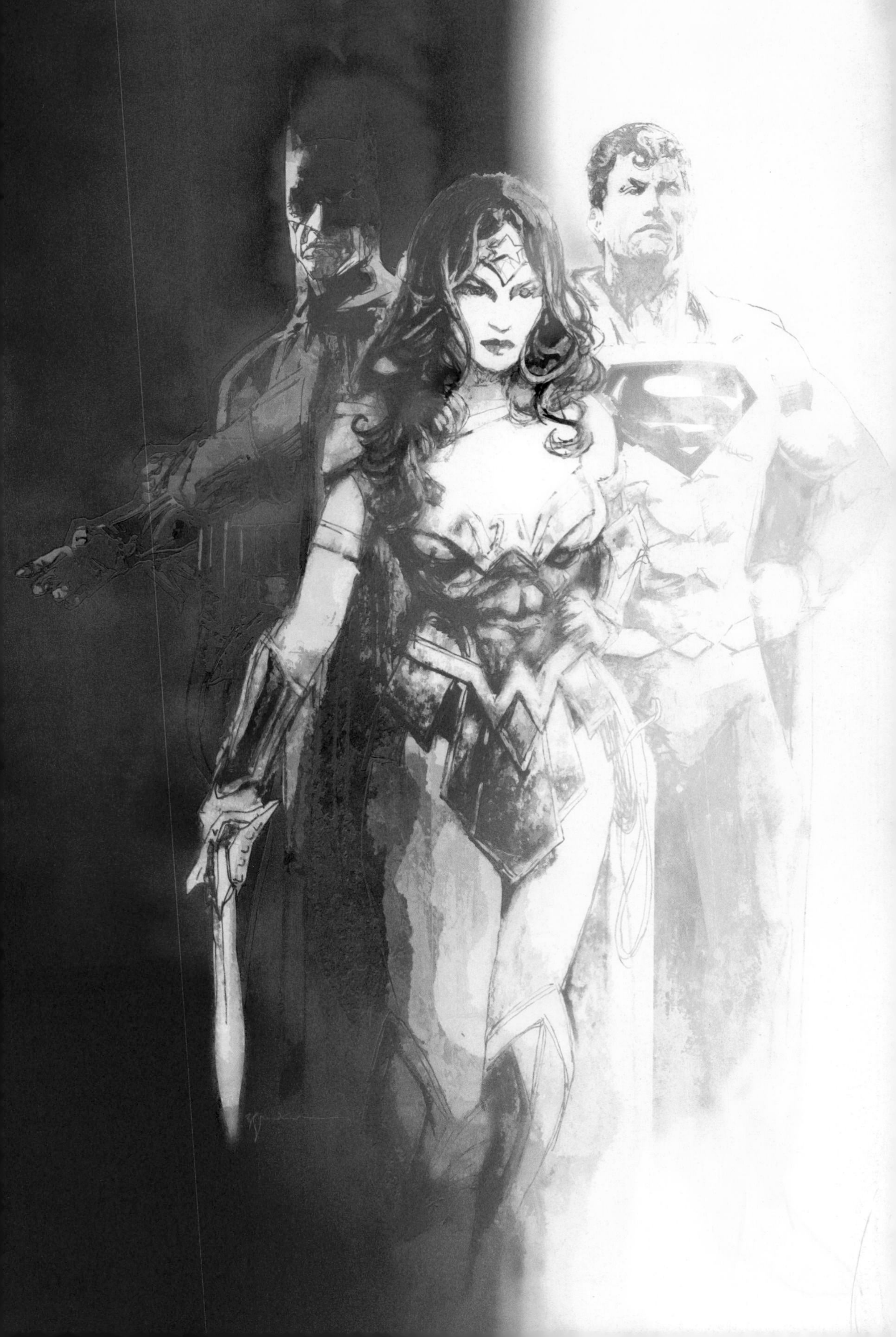

TRINITY #6 Variant Cover by BILL SIENKIEWICZ

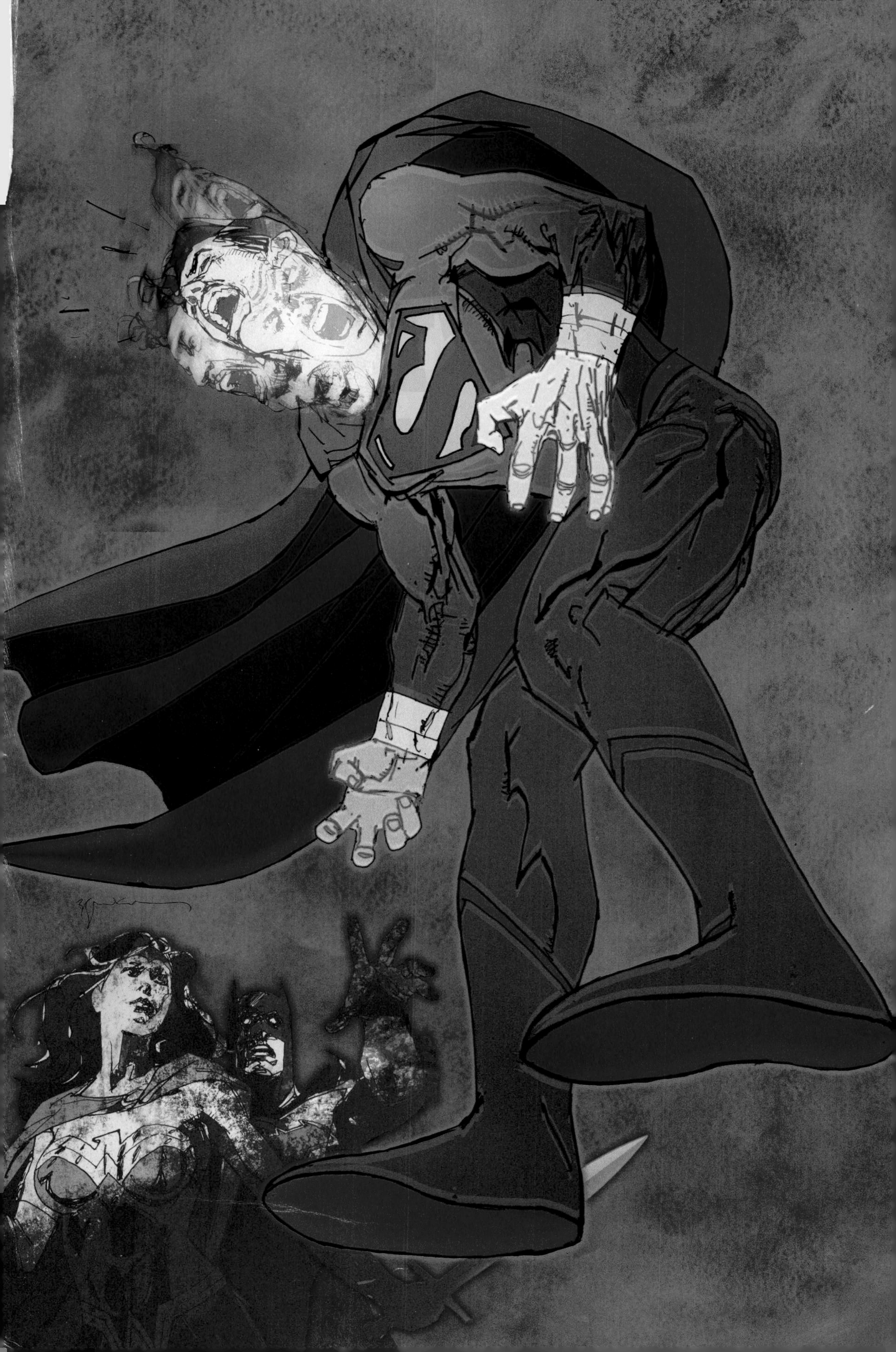

WHITE MERCY DESIGNS

by Francis Manapul

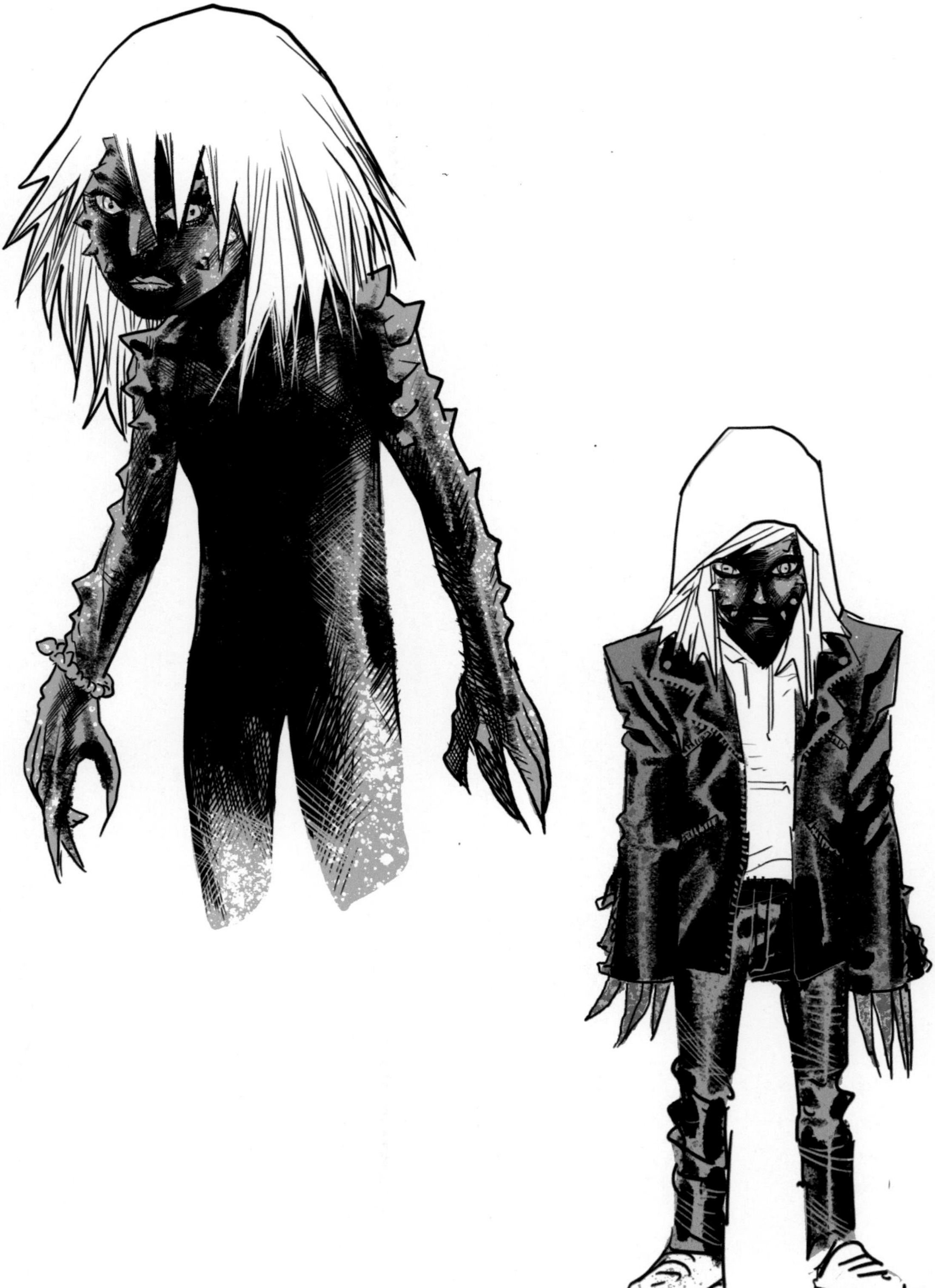